STAR WARS

SANA STARROS

FAMILY MATTERS

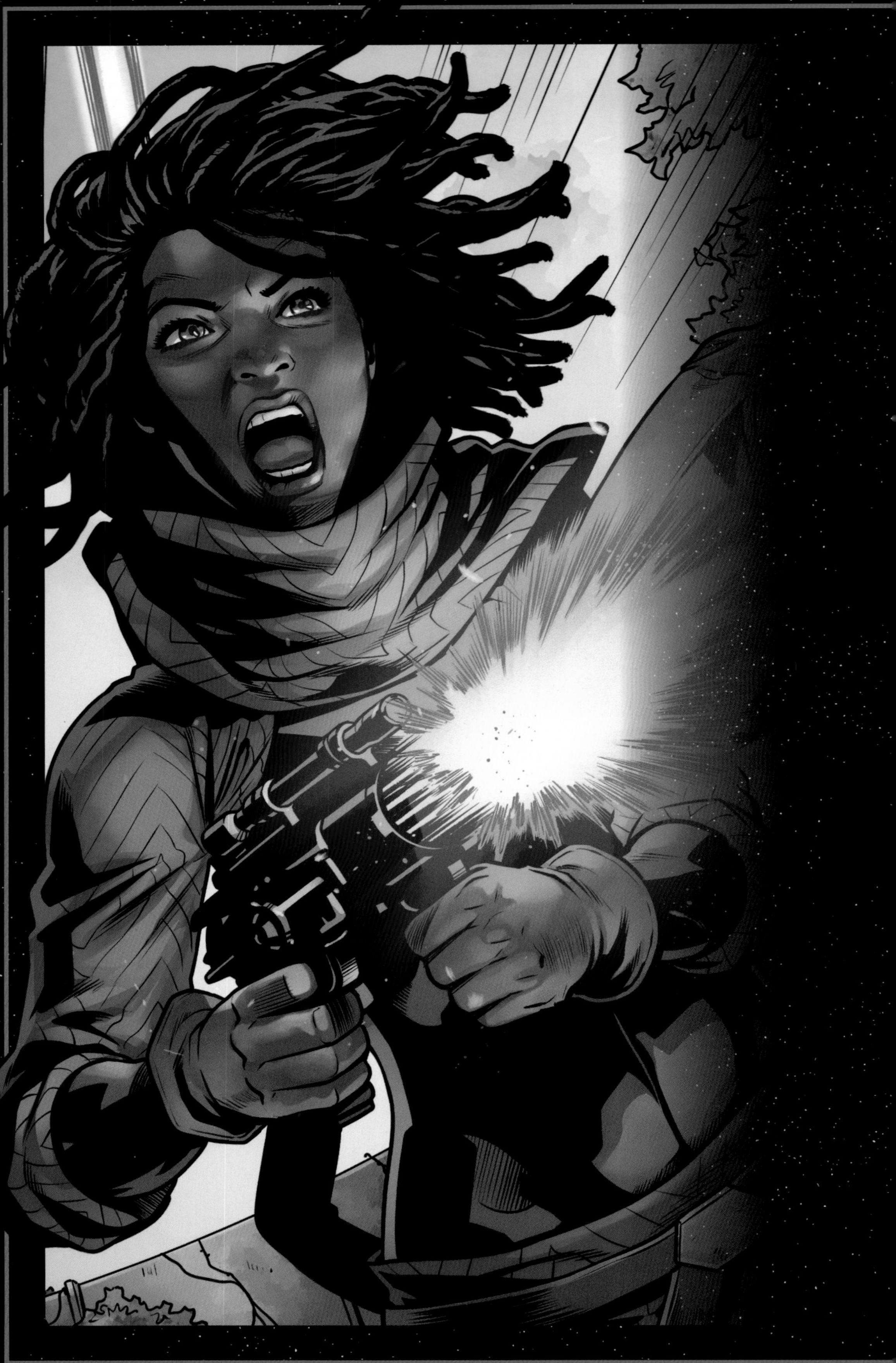

STAR WARS

SANA STARROS

FAMILY MATTERS

Writer
JUSTINA IRELAND

Artist
PERE PÉREZ

Color Artists
JAY DAVIS RAMOS (#1),
PROTOBUNKER's DONO SÁNCHEZ-ALMARA (#2-5) &
PROTOBUNKER's FER SIFUENTES-SUJO (#5)

Letterer
VC's TRAVIS LANHAM

Cover Art
KEN LASHLEY & JUAN FERNANDEZ

Recap Design
CARLOS LAO

Assistant Editor
MIKEY J. BASSO

Associate Editor
DANNY KHAZEM

Editor
MARK PANICCIA

Collection Editor **JENNIFER GRÜNWALD**
Assistant Editor **DANIEL KIRCHHOFFER**
Assistant Managing Editor **MAIA LOY**
Associate Manager, Talent Relations **LISA MONTALBANO**
VP Production & Special Projects **JEFF YOUNGQUIST**
Book Designer **ADAM DEL RE**
Lead Designer **JAY BOWEN**
SVP Print, Sales & Marketing **DAVID GABRIEL**
Editor in Chief **C.B. CEBULSKI**

For Lucasfilm:
Senior Editor **ROBERT SIMPSON**
Creative Director **MICHAEL SIGLAIN**
Art Director **TROY ALDERS**
Lucasfilm Story Group **MATT MARTIN**
PABLO HIDALGO
EMILY SHKOUKANI
Creative Art Manager **PHIL SZOSTAK**

STAR WARS: SANA STARROS — FAMILY MATTERS. Contains material originally published in magazine form as STAR WARS: SANA STARROS (2023) #1-5. First printing 2023. ISBN 978-1-302-93307-4. Published by MARVEL WORLDWIDE, INC., a subsidiary of MARVEL ENTERTAINMENT, LLC. OFFICE OF PUBLICATION: 1290 Avenue of the Americas, New York, NY 10104. **Printed in the U.S.A.** KEVIN FEIGE, Chief Creative Officer; DAN BUCKLEY, President, Marvel Entertainment; DAVID BOGART, Associate Publisher & SVP of Talent Affairs; TOM BREVOORT, VP, Executive Editor; NICK LOWE, Executive Editor, VP of Content, Digital Publishing; DAVID GABRIEL, VP of Print & Digital Publishing; SVEN LARSEN, VP of Licensed Publishing; MARK ANNUNZIATO, VP of Planning & Forecasting; JEFF YOUNGQUIST, VP of Production & Special Projects; ALEX MORALES, Director of Publishing Operations; DAN EDINGTON, Director of Editorial Operations; RICKEY PURDIN, Director of Talent Relations; JENNIFER GRÜNWALD, Director of Production & Special Projects; SUSAN CRESPI, Production Manager; STAN LEE, Chairman Emeritus. For information regarding advertising in Marvel Comics or on Marvel.com, please contact Vit DeBellis, Custom Solutions & Integrated Advertising Manager, at vdebellis@marvel.com. For Marvel subscription inquiries, please call 888-511-5480. **Manufactured between 6/23/2023 and 8/1/2023 by SEAWAY PRINTING, GREEN BAY, WI, USA.**

10 9 8 7 6 5 4 3 2 1

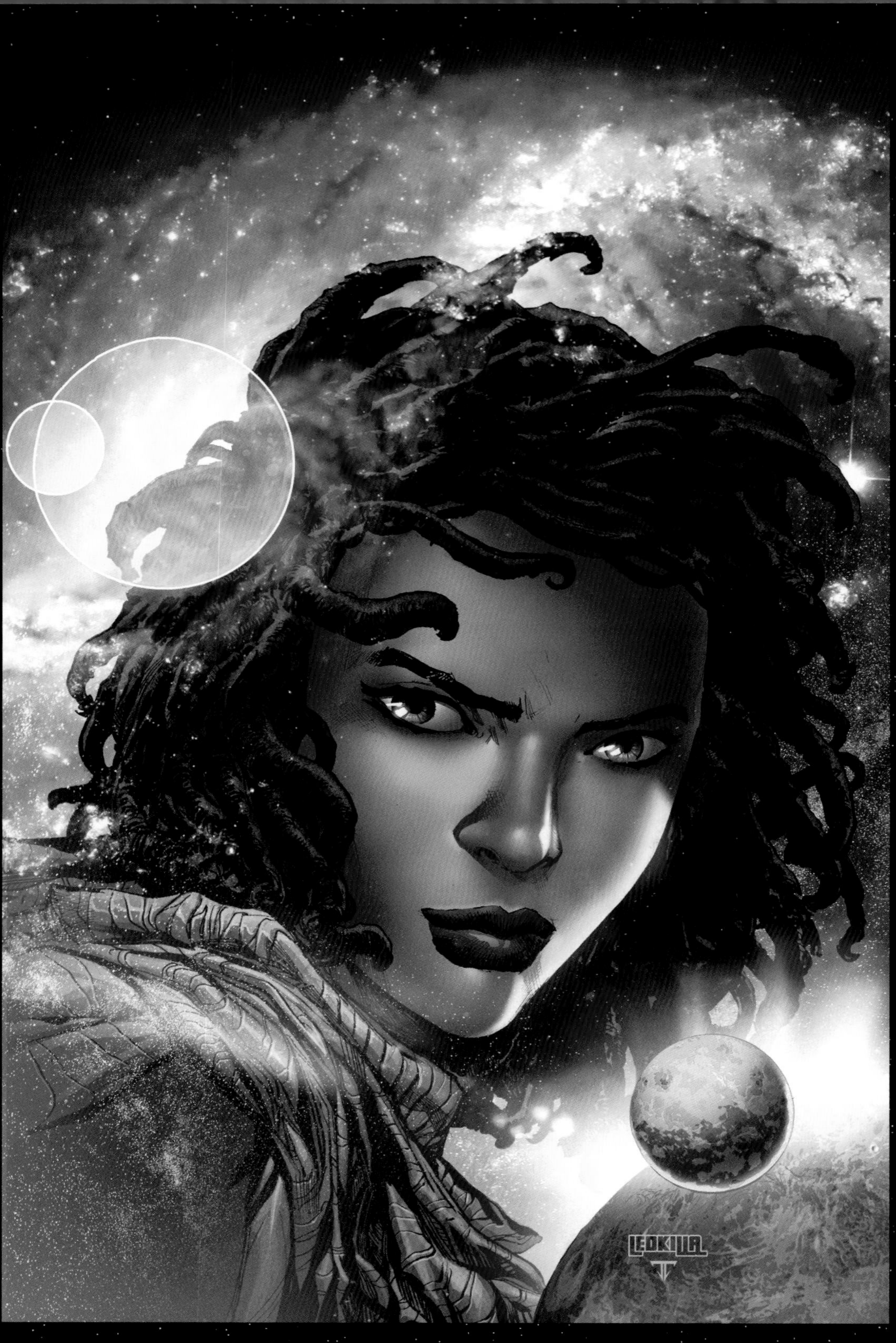

1 — BACK TO BASICS

Sana Starros has made her way across the galaxy, pulling heists with Han Solo, getting mixed up with
Doctor Aphra and everything in between. After a bad breakup, Sana decides to chart a new path....

STAR WARS
SANA STARROS

FAMILY MATTERS
PART TWO: ALL IN THE FAMILY

Upon returning to the Starros family homestead, Sana is greeted by her Grammy Thea Starros and cousin
Aryssha, who is pregnant with the first children of the next generation of the Starros family! There's only
one complication: The father is Imperial Officer Cerasus Ehllo who is NOT fond of the Starros family and who
ordered an attack on the family's home to retrieve Aryssha and have the children born into Imperial care.

But now Sana, Grammy Thea and Aryssha's mother, Mevera, are hot on the tail of the Imperials, seeking to
retrieve both Aryssha and a lost family heirloom....

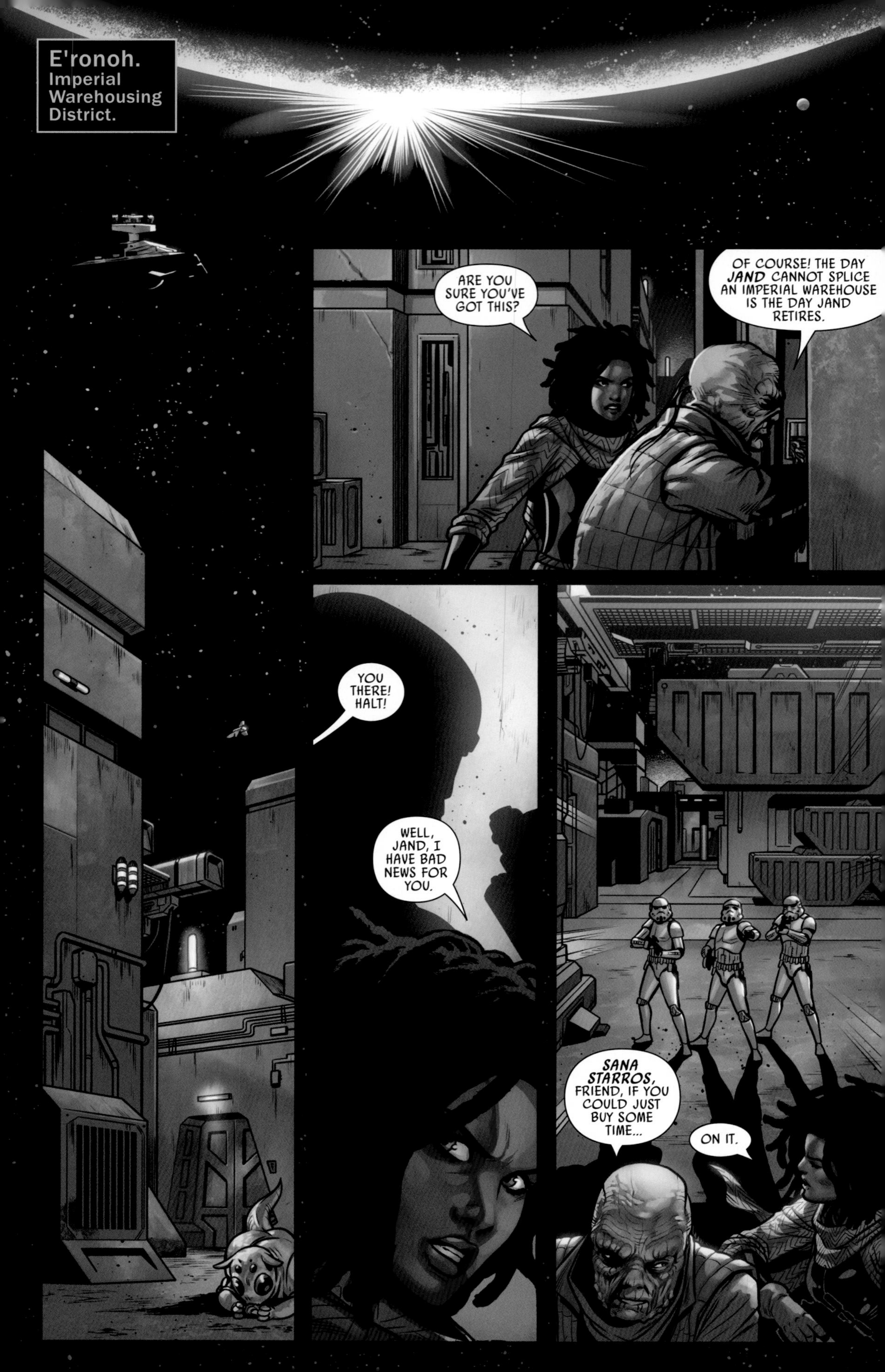
E'ronoh. Imperial Warehousing District.
ARE YOU SURE YOU'VE GOT THIS?
OF COURSE! THE DAY JAND CANNOT SPLICE AN IMPERIAL WAREHOUSE IS THE DAY JAND RETIRES.
YOU THERE! HALT!
WELL, JAND, I HAVE BAD NEWS FOR YOU.
SANA STARROS, FRIEND, IF YOU COULD JUST BUY SOME TIME...
ON IT.

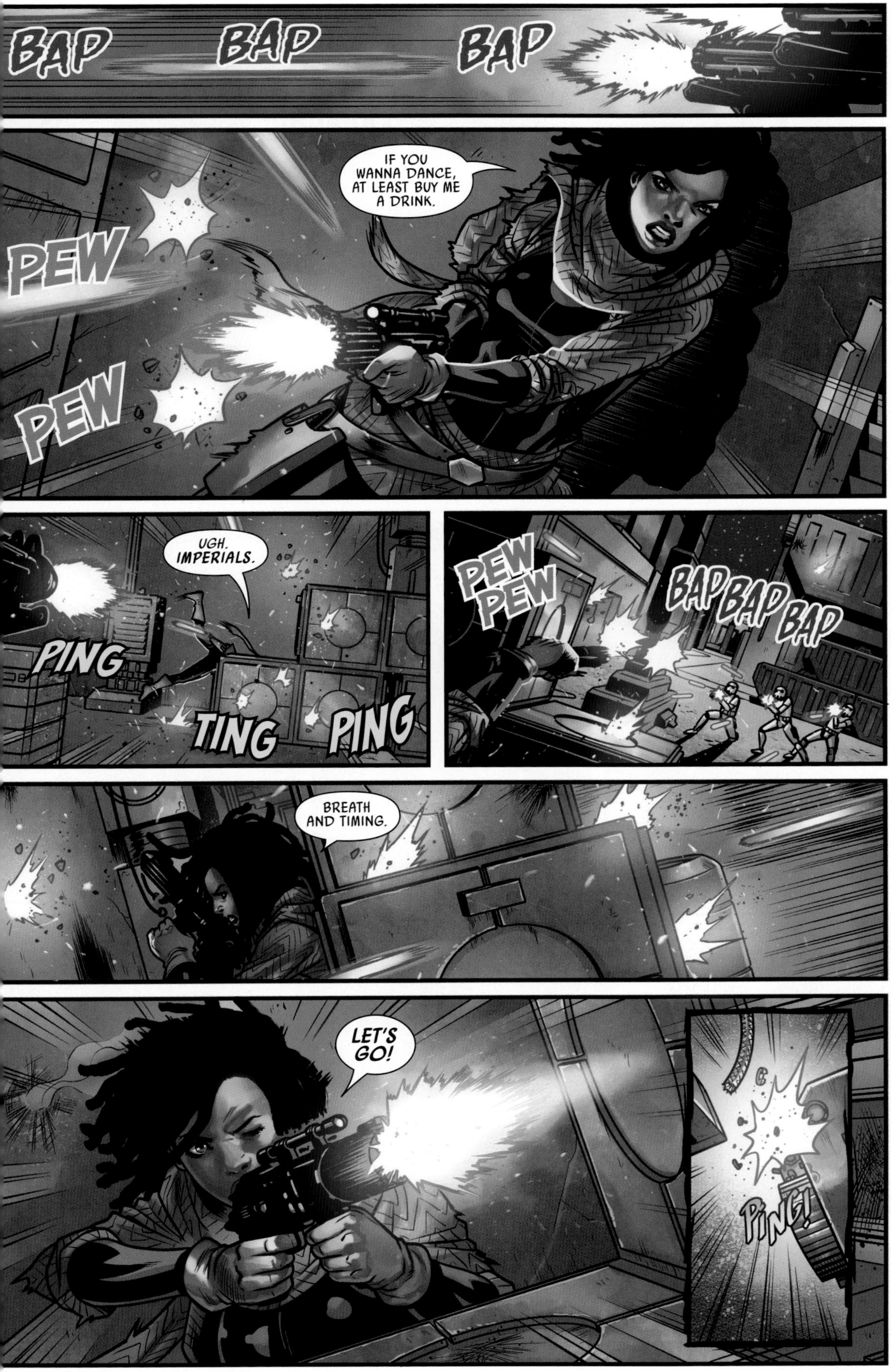
BAP
BAP
BAP
IF YOU WANNA DANCE, AT LEAST BUY ME A DRINK.
PEW
PEW
UGH. IMPERIALS.
PING
TING
PING
PEW
PEW
BAP BAP BAP
BREATH AND TIMING.
LET'S GO!
PING!

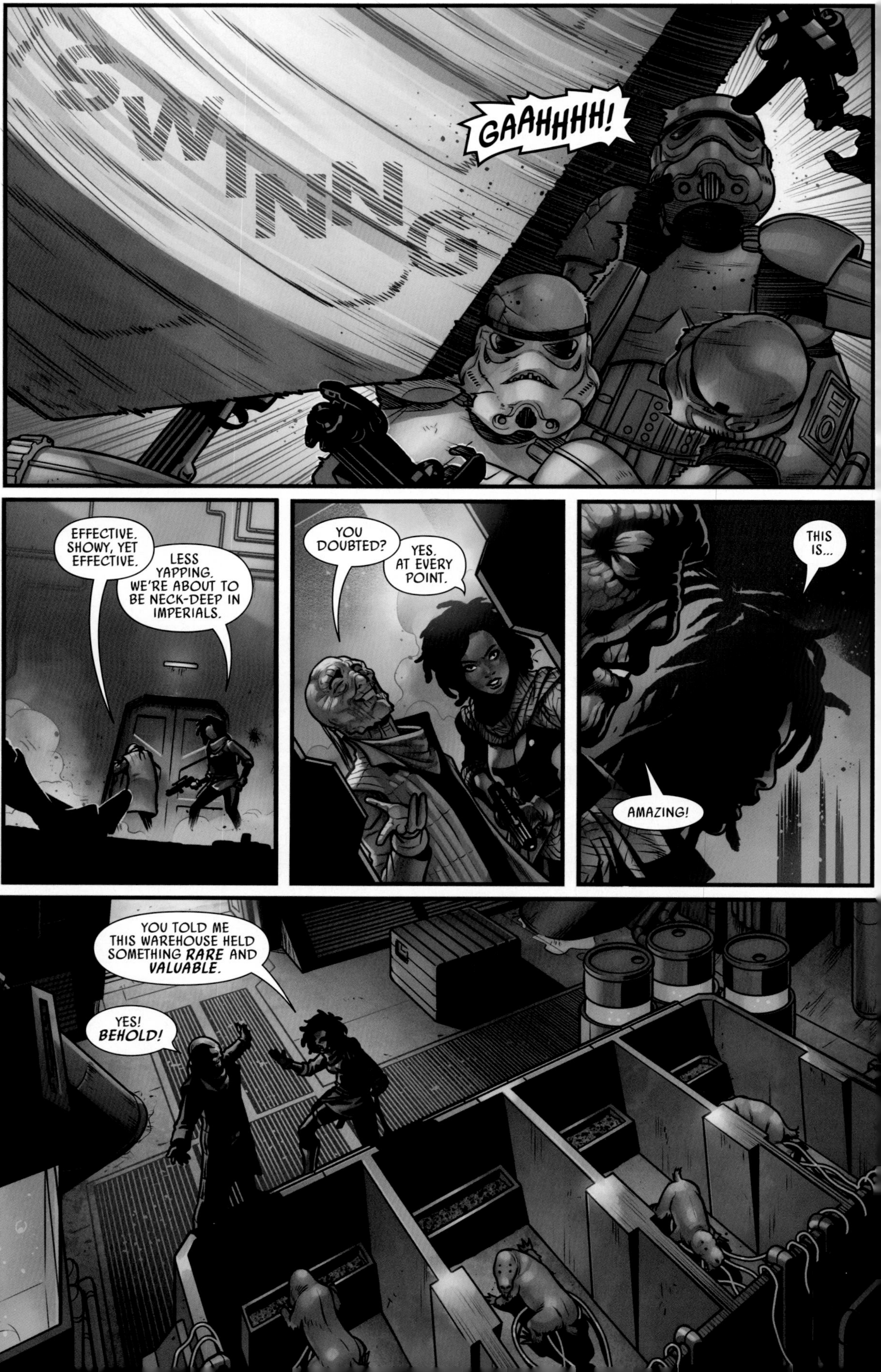
SWINNG
GAAHHHH!
EFFECTIVE. SHOWY, YET EFFECTIVE.
LESS YAPPING. WE'RE ABOUT TO BE NECK-DEEP IN IMPERIALS.
YOU DOUBTED?
YES. AT EVERY POINT.
THIS IS...
AMAZING!
YOU TOLD ME THIS WAREHOUSE HELD SOMETHING RARE AND VALUABLE.
YES! BEHOLD!

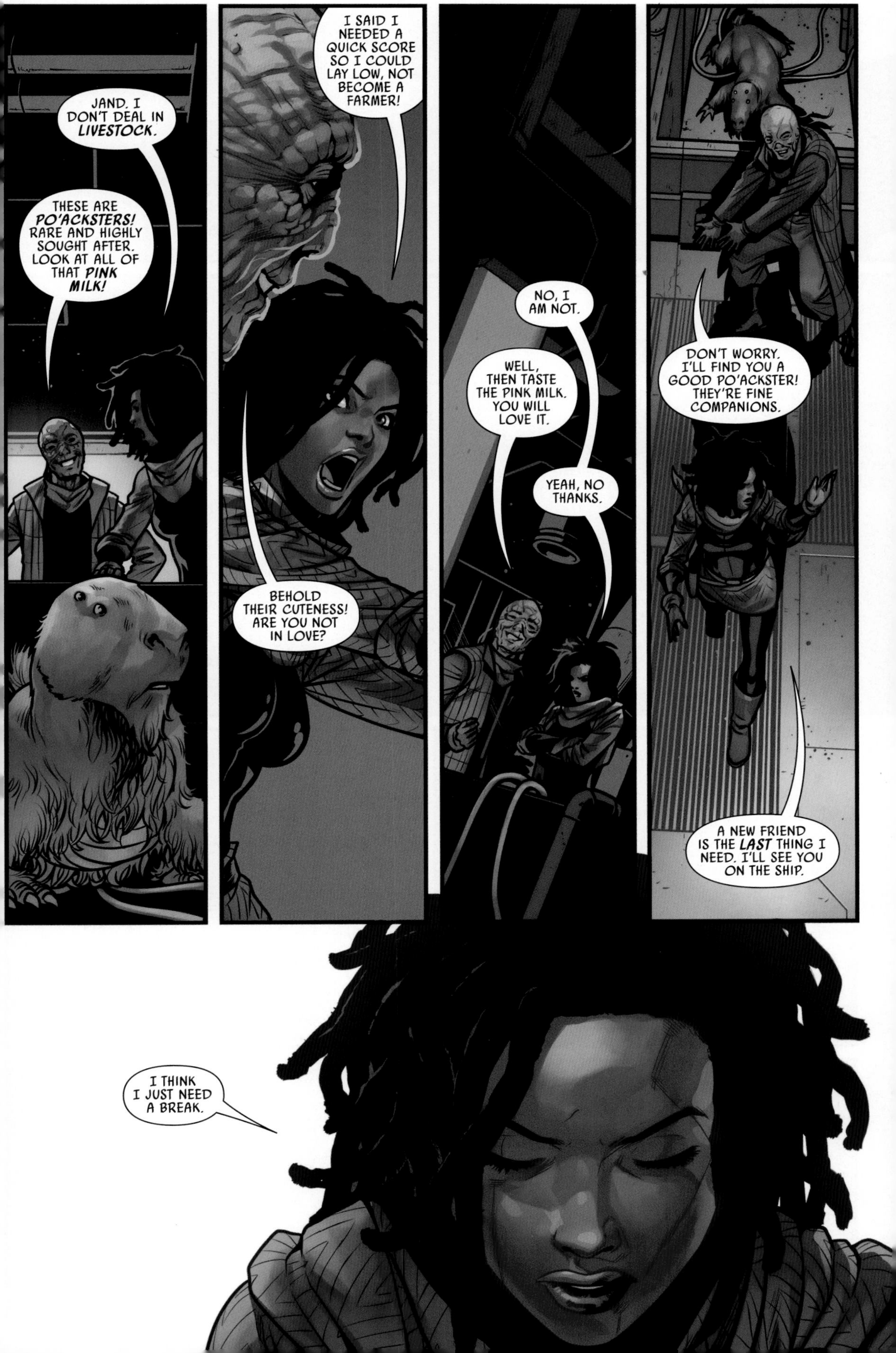
JAND. I DON'T DEAL IN LIVESTOCK.
THESE ARE PO'ACKSTERS! RARE AND HIGHLY SOUGHT AFTER. LOOK AT ALL OF THAT PINK MILK!
I SAID I NEEDED A QUICK SCORE SO I COULD LAY LOW, NOT BECOME A FARMER!
BEHOLD THEIR CUTENESS! ARE YOU NOT IN LOVE?
NO, I AM NOT.
WELL, THEN TASTE THE PINK MILK. YOU WILL LOVE IT.
YEAH, NO THANKS.
DON'T WORRY. I'LL FIND YOU A GOOD PO'ACKSTER! THEY'RE FINE COMPANIONS.
A NEW FRIEND IS THE LAST THING I NEED. I'LL SEE YOU ON THE SHIP.
I THINK I JUST NEED A BREAK.

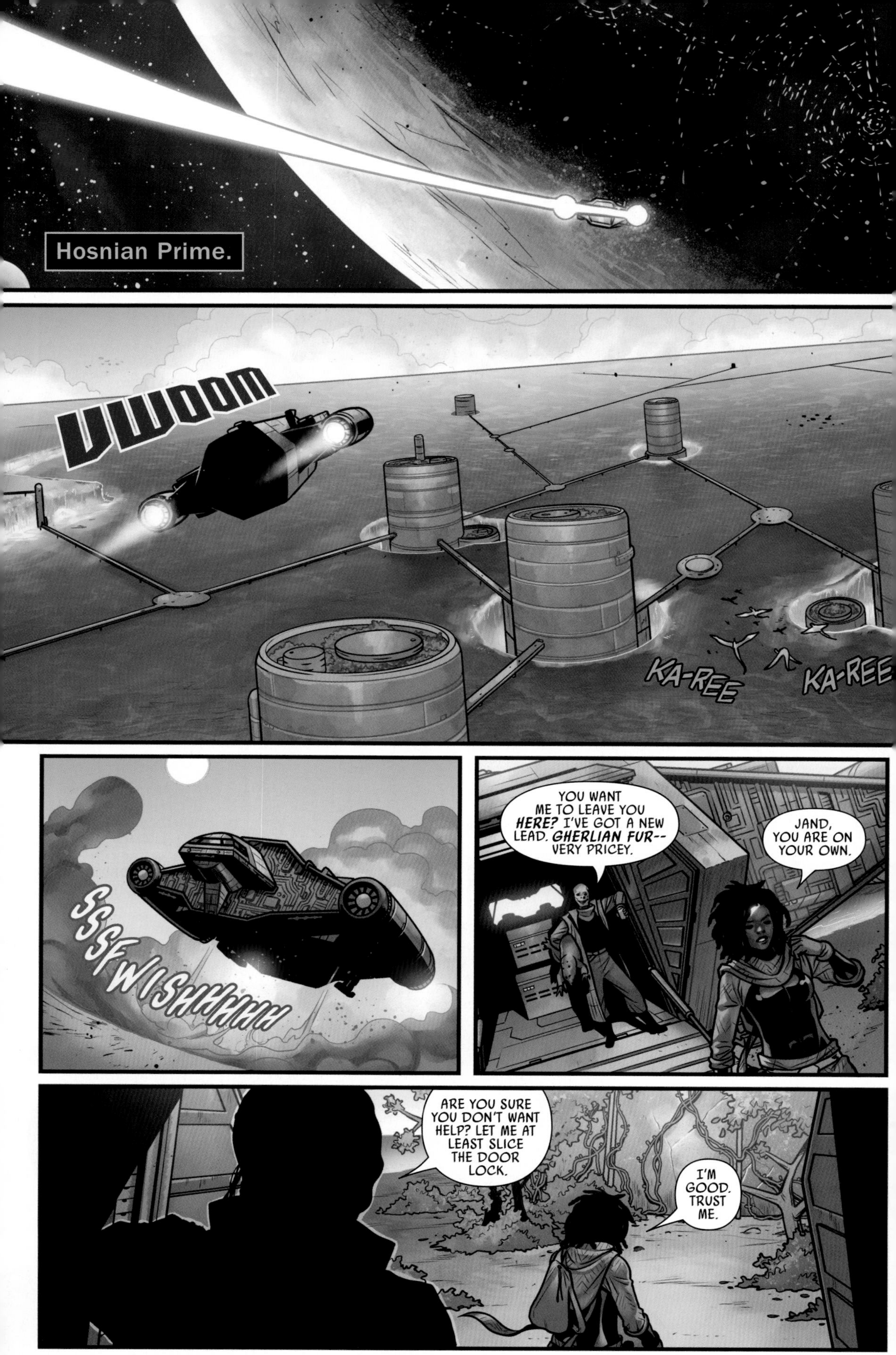
Hosnian Prime.
VWOOM
KA-REE
KA-REE
SSSFWISHHHHH
YOU WANT ME TO LEAVE YOU *HERE?* I'VE GOT A NEW LEAD. *GHERLIAN FUR--* VERY PRICEY.
JAND, YOU ARE ON YOUR OWN.
ARE YOU SURE YOU DON'T WANT HELP? LET ME AT LEAST SLICE THE DOOR LOCK.
I'M GOOD. TRUST ME.

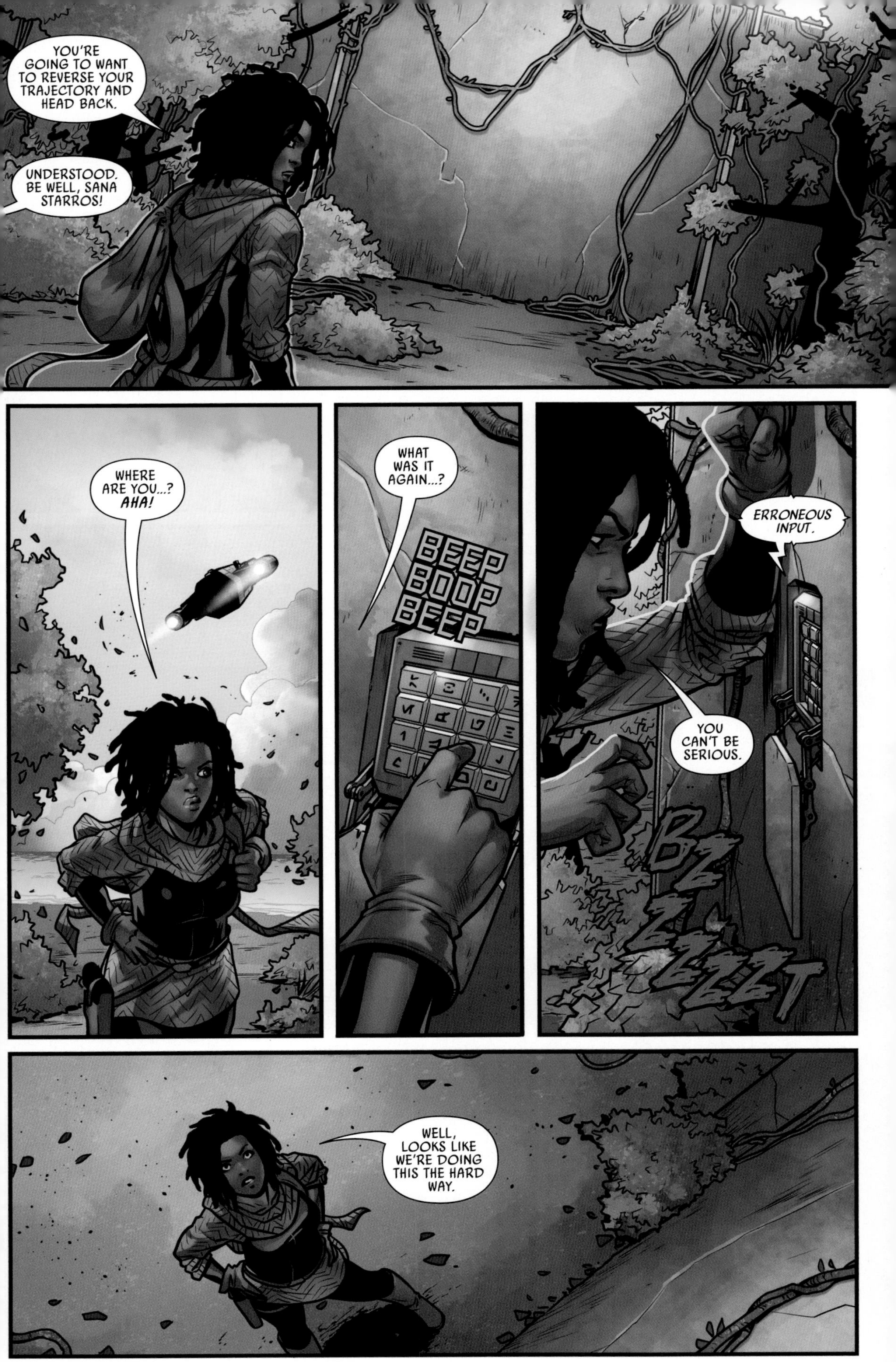

YOU'RE GOING TO WANT TO REVERSE YOUR TRAJECTORY AND HEAD BACK.
UNDERSTOOD. BE WELL, SANA STARROS!
WHERE ARE YOU...? AHA!
WHAT WAS IT AGAIN...?
BEEP BOOP BEEP
ERRONEOUS INPUT.
YOU CAN'T BE SERIOUS.
BZZZZZZT
WELL, LOOKS LIKE WE'RE DOING THIS THE HARD WAY.

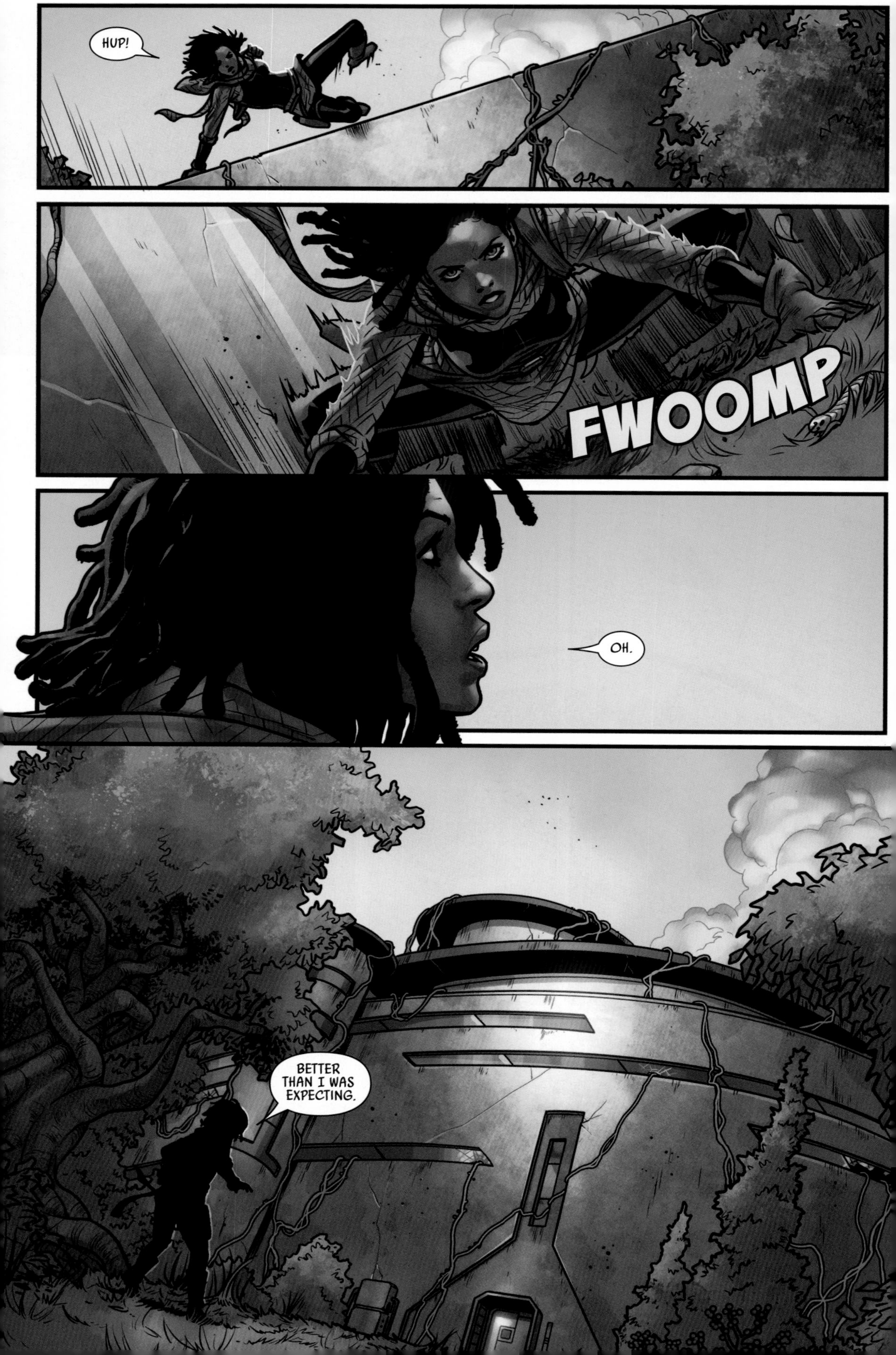
HUP!
FWOOMP
OH.
BETTER THAN I WAS EXPECTING.

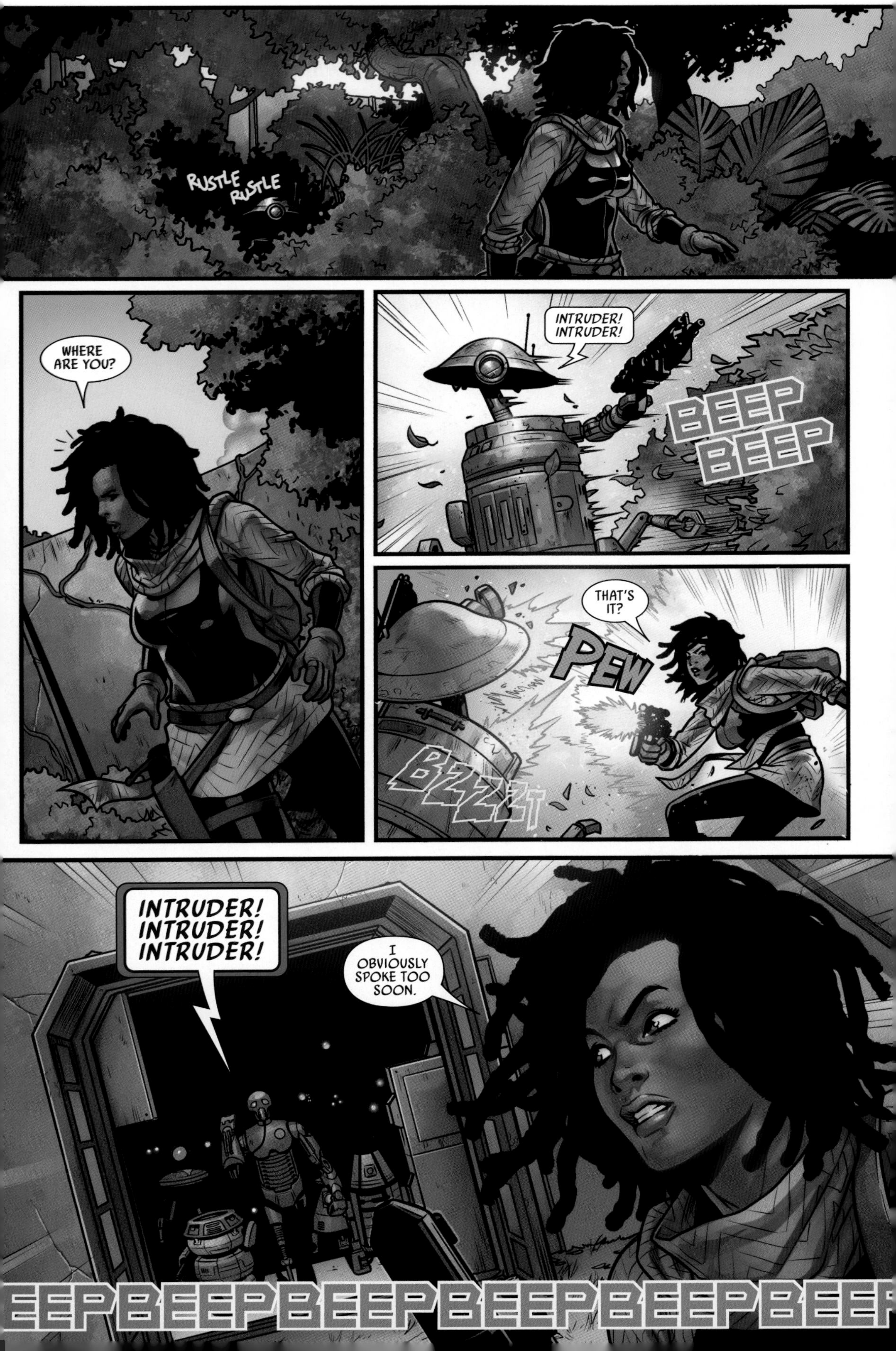
RUSTLE RUSTLE
WHERE ARE YOU?
INTRUDER! INTRUDER!
BEEP BEEP
THAT'S IT?
PEW
BZZZT
INTRUDER! INTRUDER! INTRUDER!
I OBVIOUSLY SPOKE TOO SOON.
EEPBEEPBEEPBEEPBEEPBEEPBEEP

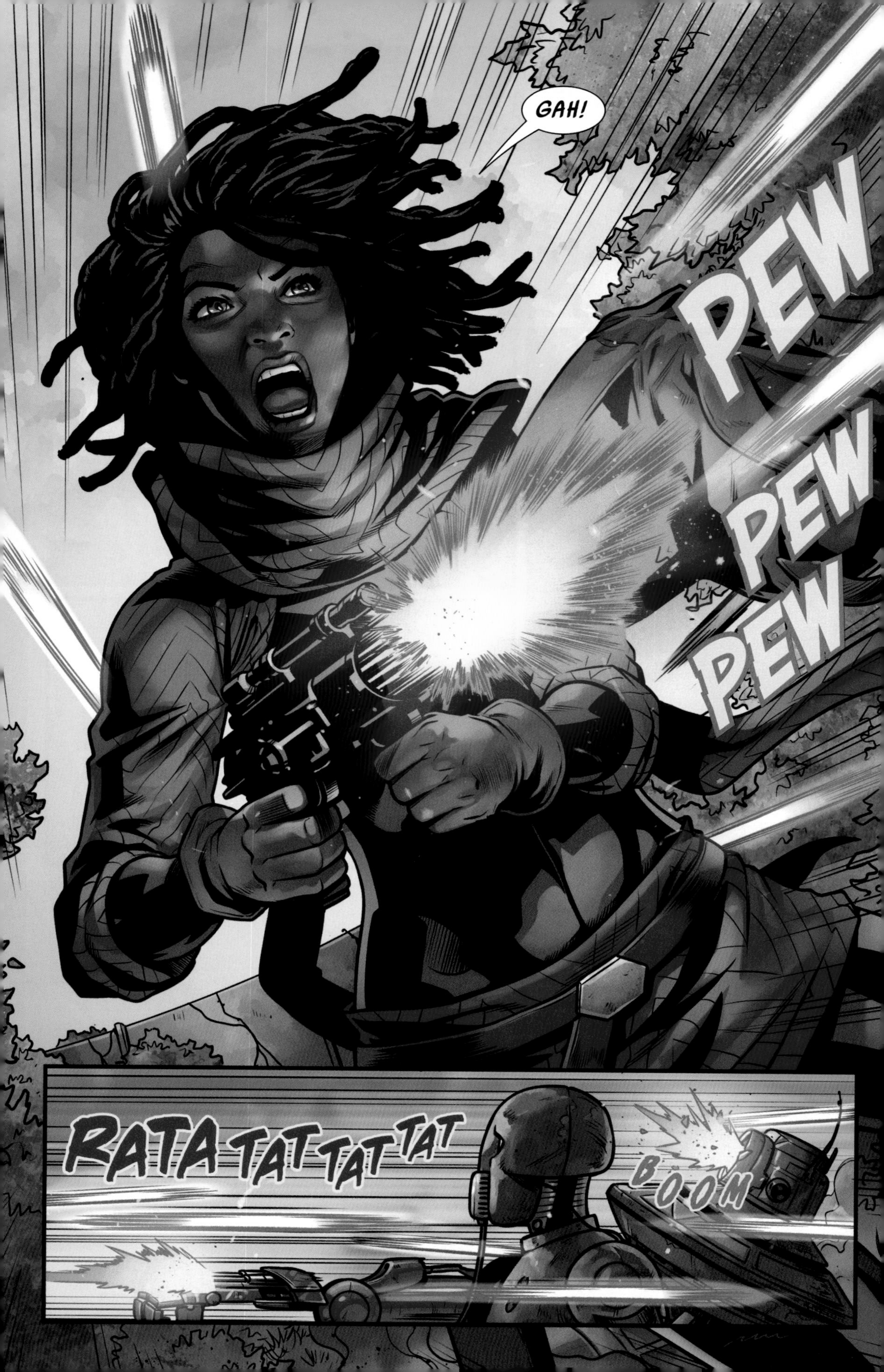
GAH!
PEW
PEW
PEW
RATA TAT TAT TAT
BOOM

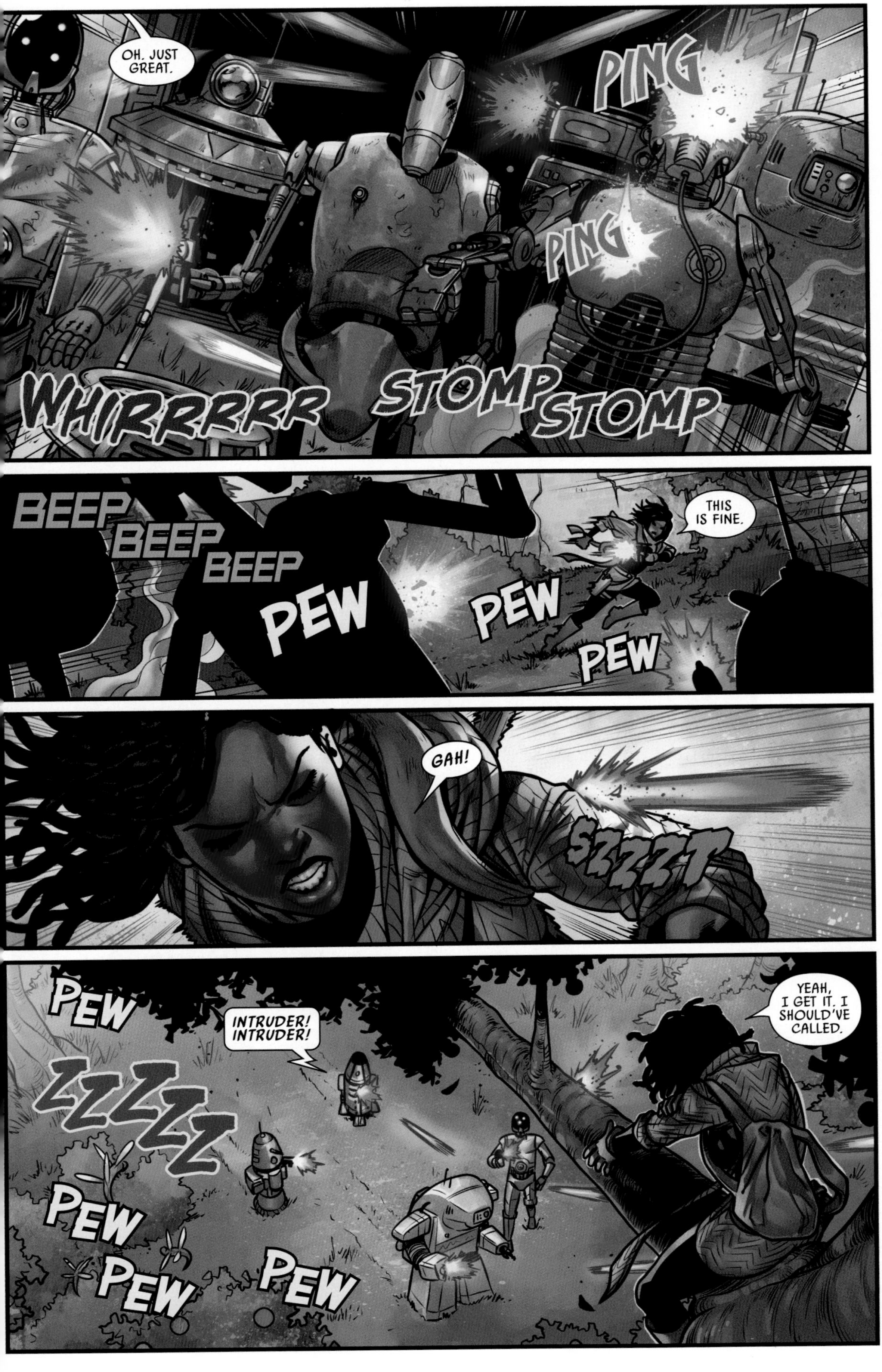
OH. JUST GREAT.
PING
PING
WHIRRRRRR
STOMP
STOMP
BEEP
BEEP
BEEP
PEW
PEW
PEW
THIS IS FINE.
GAH!
SZZZT
PEW
INTRUDER! INTRUDER!
YEAH, I GET IT. I SHOULD'VE CALLED.
ZZZZZ
PEW
PEW
PEW

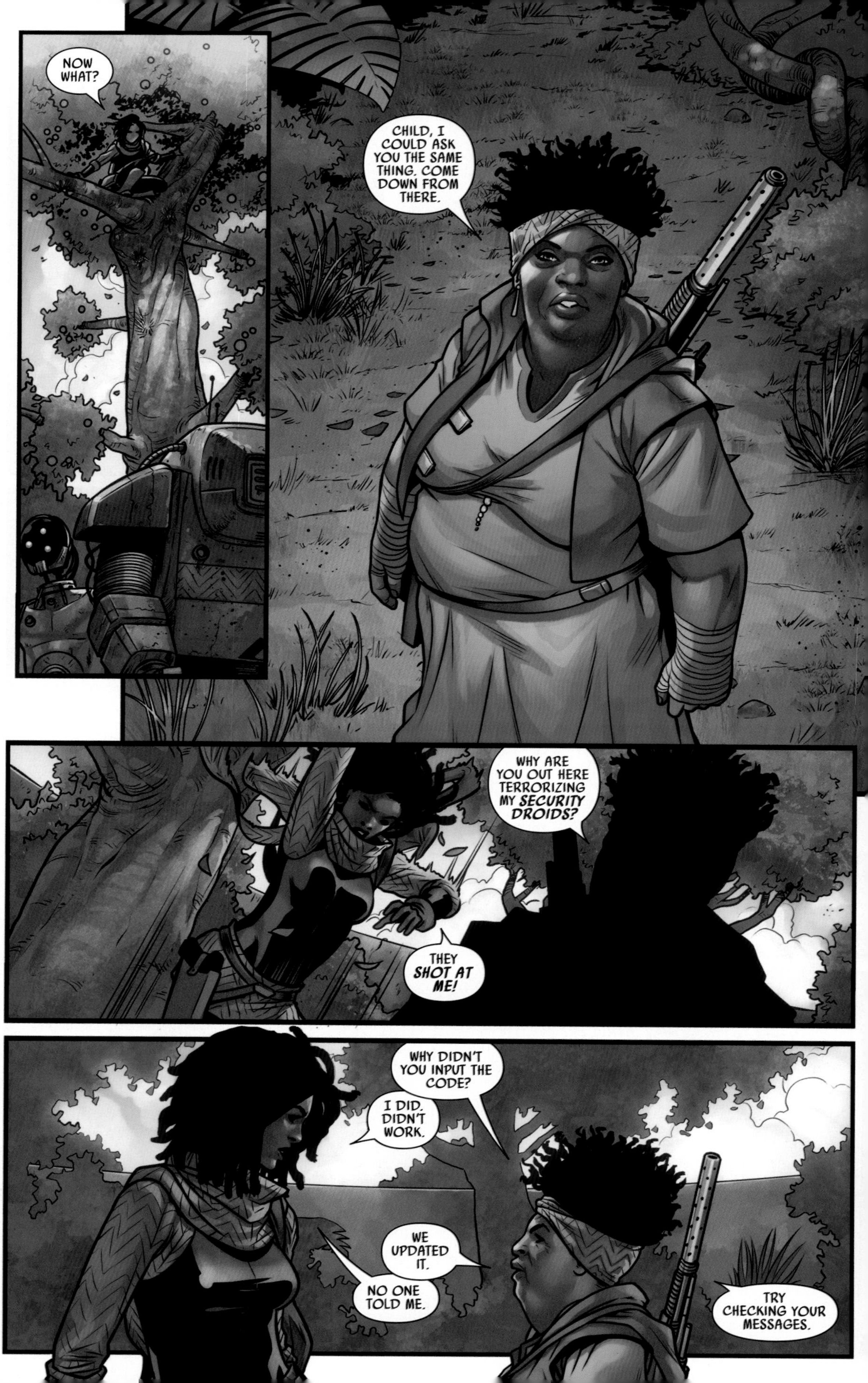
NOW WHAT?
CHILD, I COULD ASK YOU THE SAME THING. COME DOWN FROM THERE.
WHY ARE YOU OUT HERE TERRORIZING MY SECURITY DROIDS?
THEY SHOT AT ME!
WHY DIDN'T YOU INPUT THE CODE?
I DID. DIDN'T WORK.
WE UPDATED IT.
NO ONE TOLD ME.
TRY CHECKING YOUR MESSAGES.

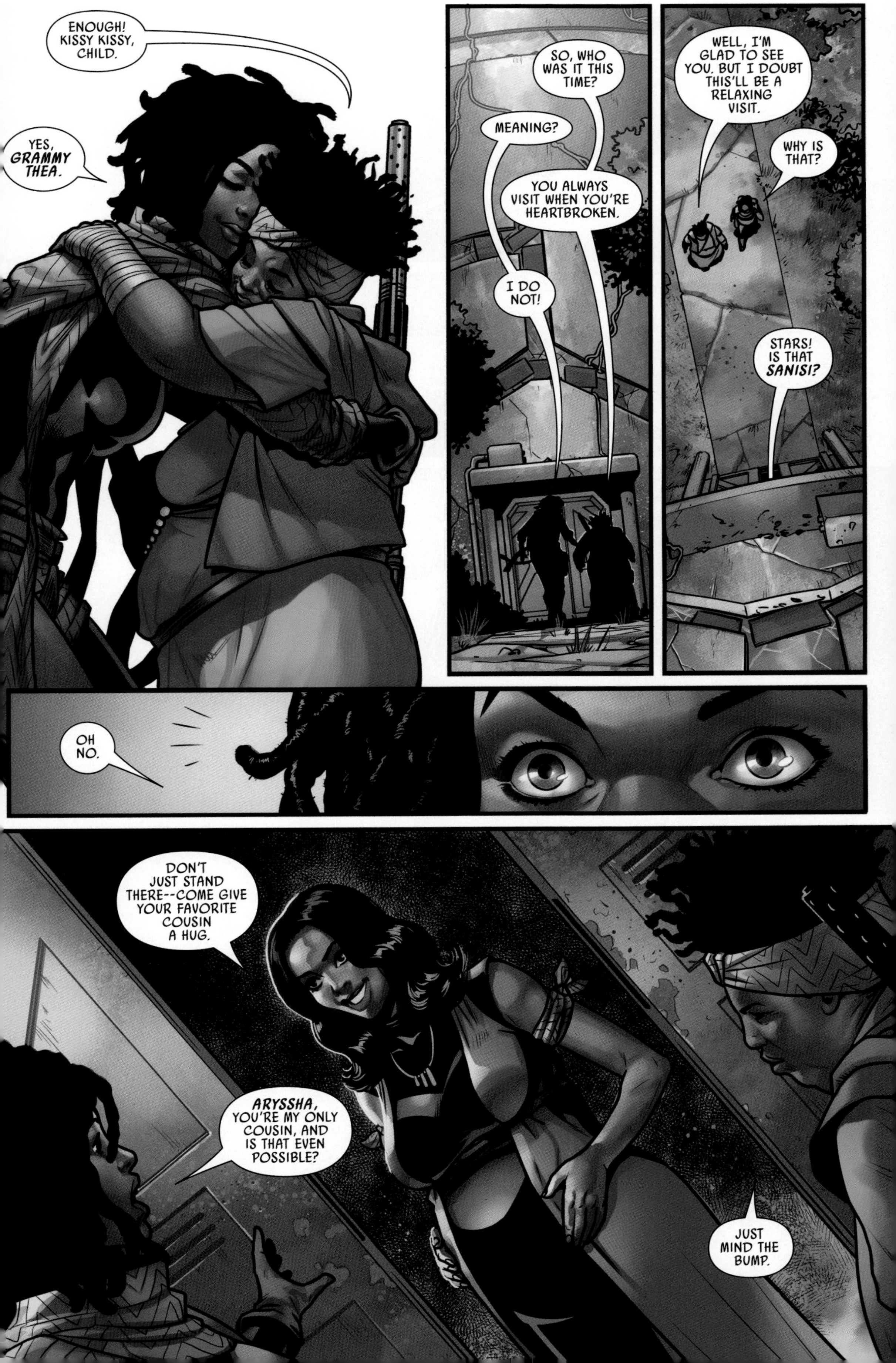

ENOUGH! KISSY KISSY, CHILD.
YES, GRAMMY THEA.
SO, WHO WAS IT THIS TIME?
MEANING?
YOU ALWAYS VISIT WHEN YOU'RE HEARTBROKEN.
I DO NOT!
WELL, I'M GLAD TO SEE YOU. BUT I DOUBT THIS'LL BE A RELAXING VISIT.
WHY IS THAT?
STARS! IS THAT SANISI?
OH NO.
DON'T JUST STAND THERE--COME GIVE YOUR FAVORITE COUSIN A HUG.
ARYSSHA, YOU'RE MY ONLY COUSIN, AND IS THAT EVEN POSSIBLE?
JUST MIND THE BUMP.

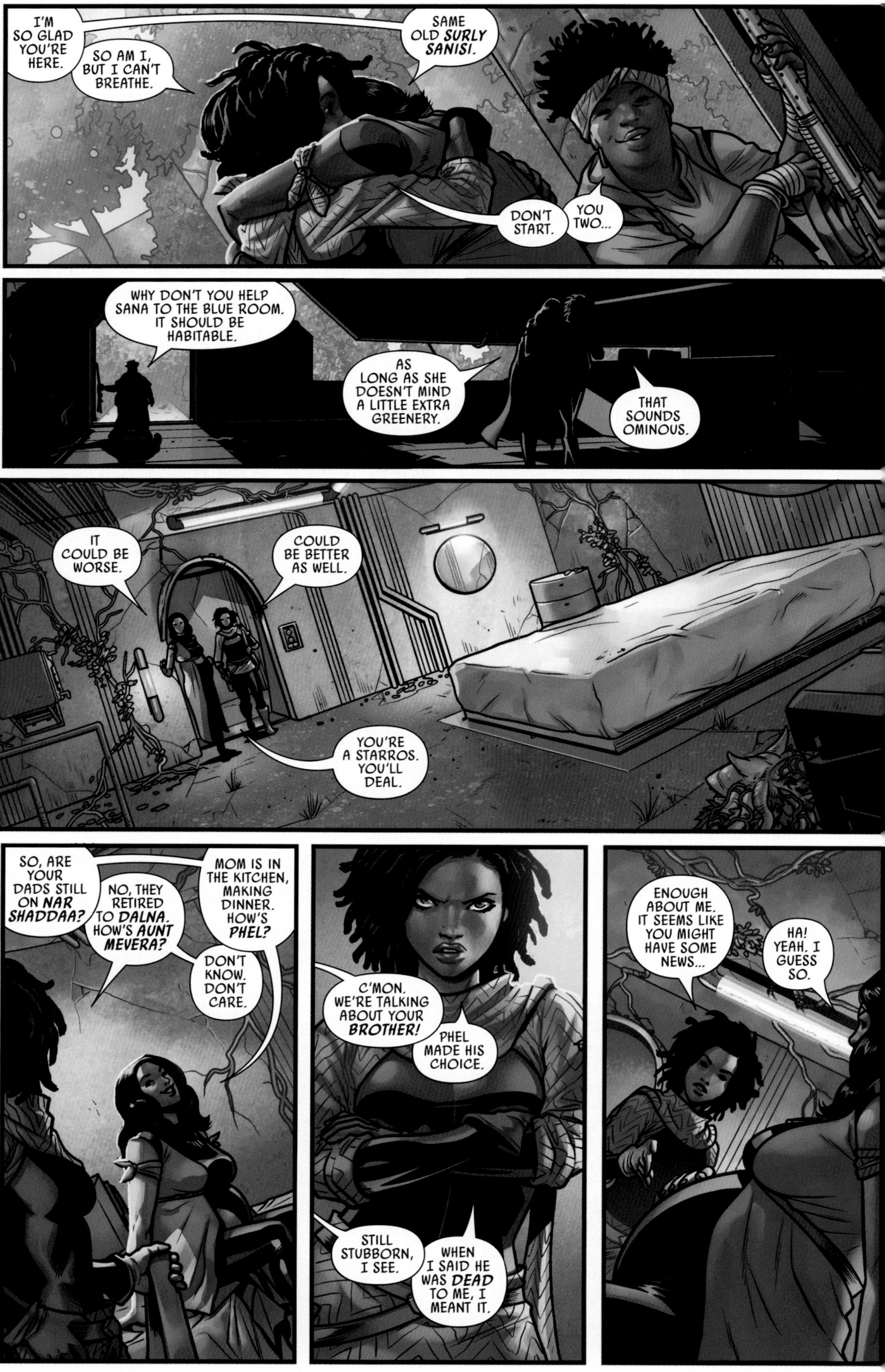

I'M SO GLAD YOU'RE HERE.
SAME OLD SURLY SANISI.
SO AM I, BUT I CAN'T BREATHE.
DON'T START.
YOU TWO...
WHY DON'T YOU HELP SANA TO THE BLUE ROOM. IT SHOULD BE HABITABLE.
AS LONG AS SHE DOESN'T MIND A LITTLE EXTRA GREENERY.
THAT SOUNDS OMINOUS.
IT COULD BE WORSE.
COULD BE BETTER AS WELL.
YOU'RE A STARROS. YOU'LL DEAL.
SO, ARE YOUR DADS STILL ON NAR SHADDAA?
NO, THEY RETIRED TO DALNA. HOW'S AUNT MEVERA?
MOM IS IN THE KITCHEN, MAKING DINNER. HOW'S PHEL?
DON'T KNOW. DON'T CARE.
C'MON. WE'RE TALKING ABOUT YOUR BROTHER!
PHEL MADE HIS CHOICE.
STILL STUBBORN, I SEE.
WHEN I SAID HE WAS DEAD TO ME, I MEANT IT.
ENOUGH ABOUT ME. IT SEEMS LIKE YOU MIGHT HAVE SOME NEWS...
HA! YEAH. I GUESS SO.

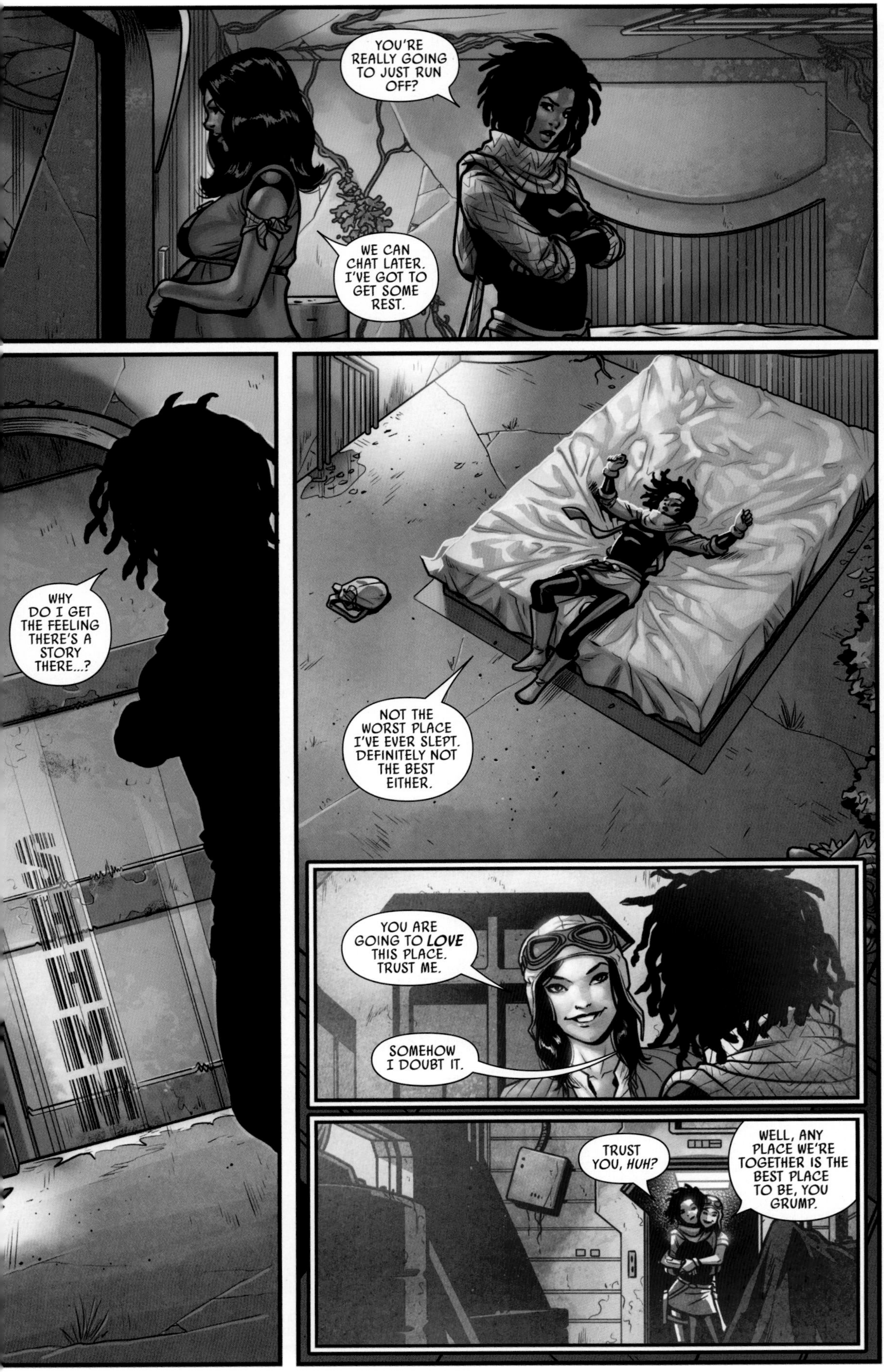
YOU'RE REALLY GOING TO JUST RUN OFF?
WE CAN CHAT LATER. I'VE GOT TO GET SOME REST.
WHY DO I GET THE FEELING THERE'S A STORY THERE...?
NOT THE WORST PLACE I'VE EVER SLEPT. DEFINITELY NOT THE BEST EITHER.
YOU ARE GOING TO LOVE THIS PLACE. TRUST ME.
SOMEHOW I DOUBT IT.
TRUST YOU, HUH?
WELL, ANY PLACE WE'RE TOGETHER IS THE BEST PLACE TO BE, YOU GRUMP.

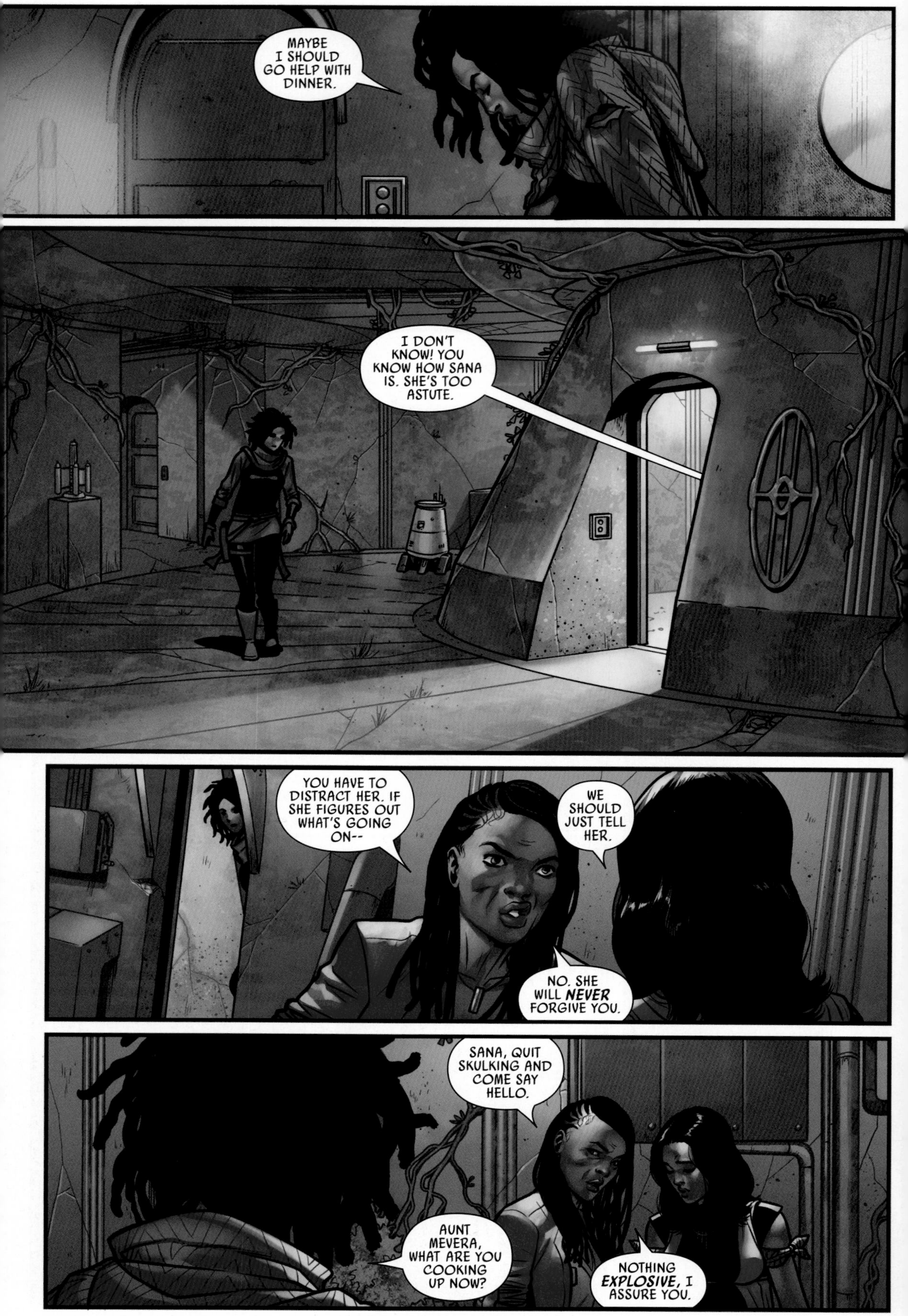
MAYBE I SHOULD GO HELP WITH DINNER.
I DON'T KNOW! YOU KNOW HOW SANA IS. SHE'S TOO ASTUTE.
YOU HAVE TO DISTRACT HER. IF SHE FIGURES OUT WHAT'S GOING ON--
WE SHOULD JUST TELL HER.
NO. SHE WILL **NEVER** FORGIVE YOU.
SANA, QUIT SKULKING AND COME SAY HELLO.
AUNT MEVERA, WHAT ARE YOU COOKING UP NOW?
NOTHING ***EXPLOSIVE,*** I ASSURE YOU.

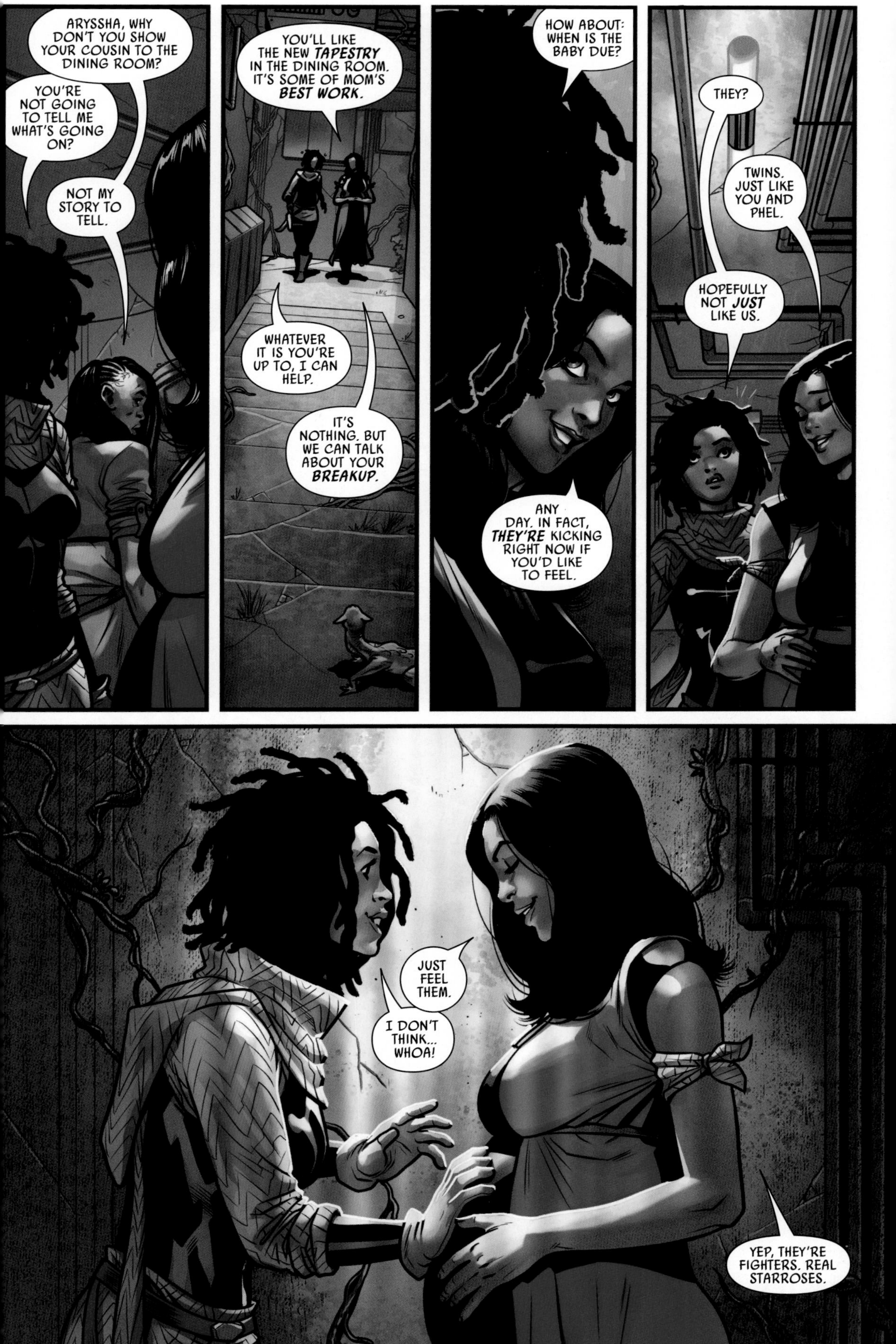
ARYSSHA, WHY DON'T YOU SHOW YOUR COUSIN TO THE DINING ROOM?
YOU'RE NOT GOING TO TELL ME WHAT'S GOING ON?
NOT MY STORY TO TELL.
YOU'LL LIKE THE NEW TAPESTRY IN THE DINING ROOM. IT'S SOME OF MOM'S BEST WORK.
WHATEVER IT IS YOU'RE UP TO, I CAN HELP.
IT'S NOTHING. BUT WE CAN TALK ABOUT YOUR BREAKUP.
HOW ABOUT: WHEN IS THE BABY DUE?
ANY DAY. IN FACT, THEY'RE KICKING RIGHT NOW IF YOU'D LIKE TO FEEL.
THEY?
TWINS. JUST LIKE YOU AND PHEL.
HOPEFULLY NOT JUST LIKE US.
JUST FEEL THEM.
I DON'T THINK... WHOA!
YEP, THEY'RE FIGHTERS. REAL STARROSES.

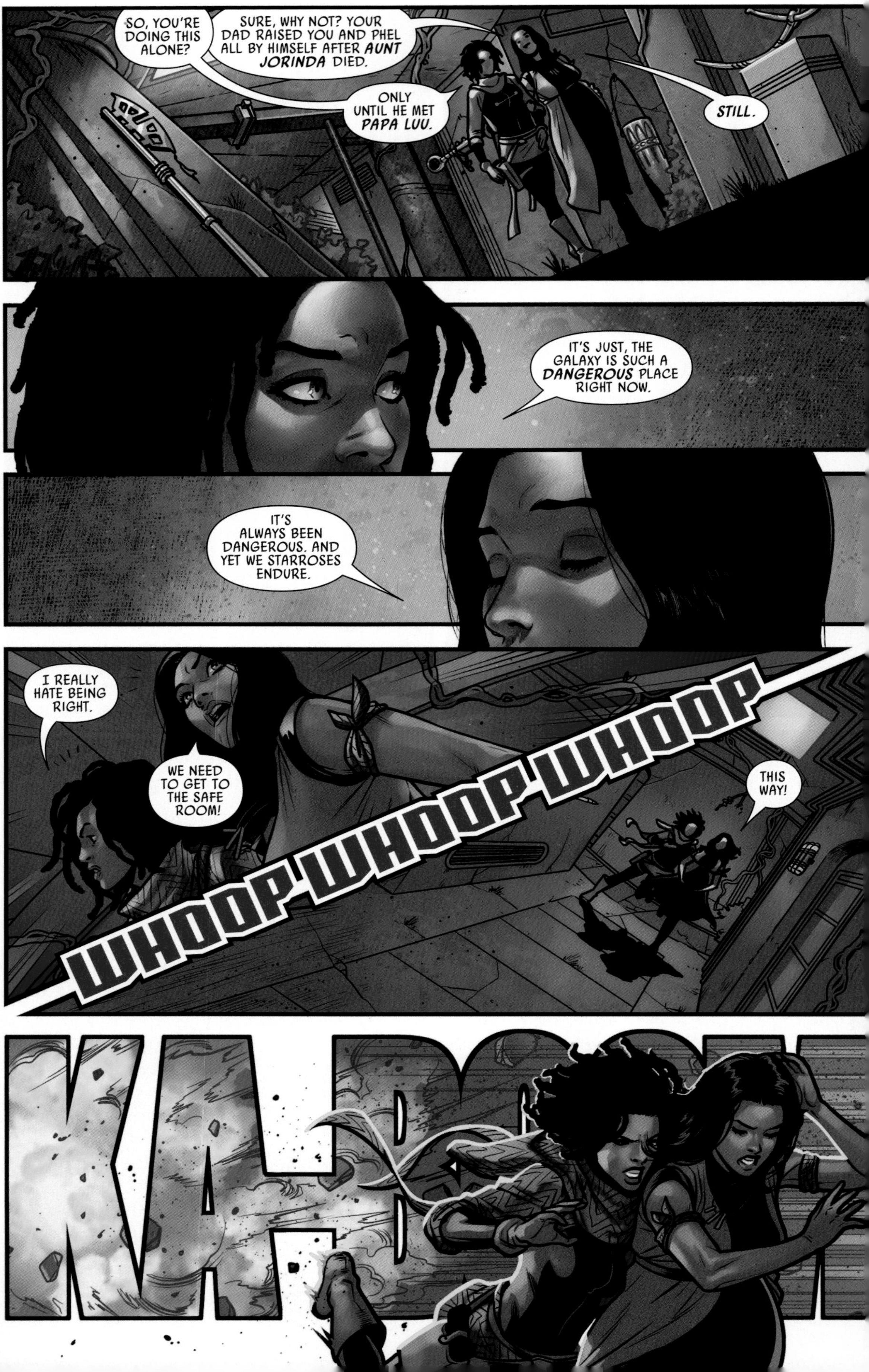
SO, YOU'RE DOING THIS ALONE?
SURE, WHY NOT? YOUR DAD RAISED YOU AND PHEL ALL BY HIMSELF AFTER AUNT JORINDA DIED.
ONLY UNTIL HE MET PAPA LUU.
STILL.
IT'S JUST, THE GALAXY IS SUCH A DANGEROUS PLACE RIGHT NOW.
IT'S ALWAYS BEEN DANGEROUS. AND YET WE STARROSES ENDURE.
I REALLY HATE BEING RIGHT.
WE NEED TO GET TO THE SAFE ROOM!
WHOOP WHOOP WHOOP WHOOP
THIS WAY!

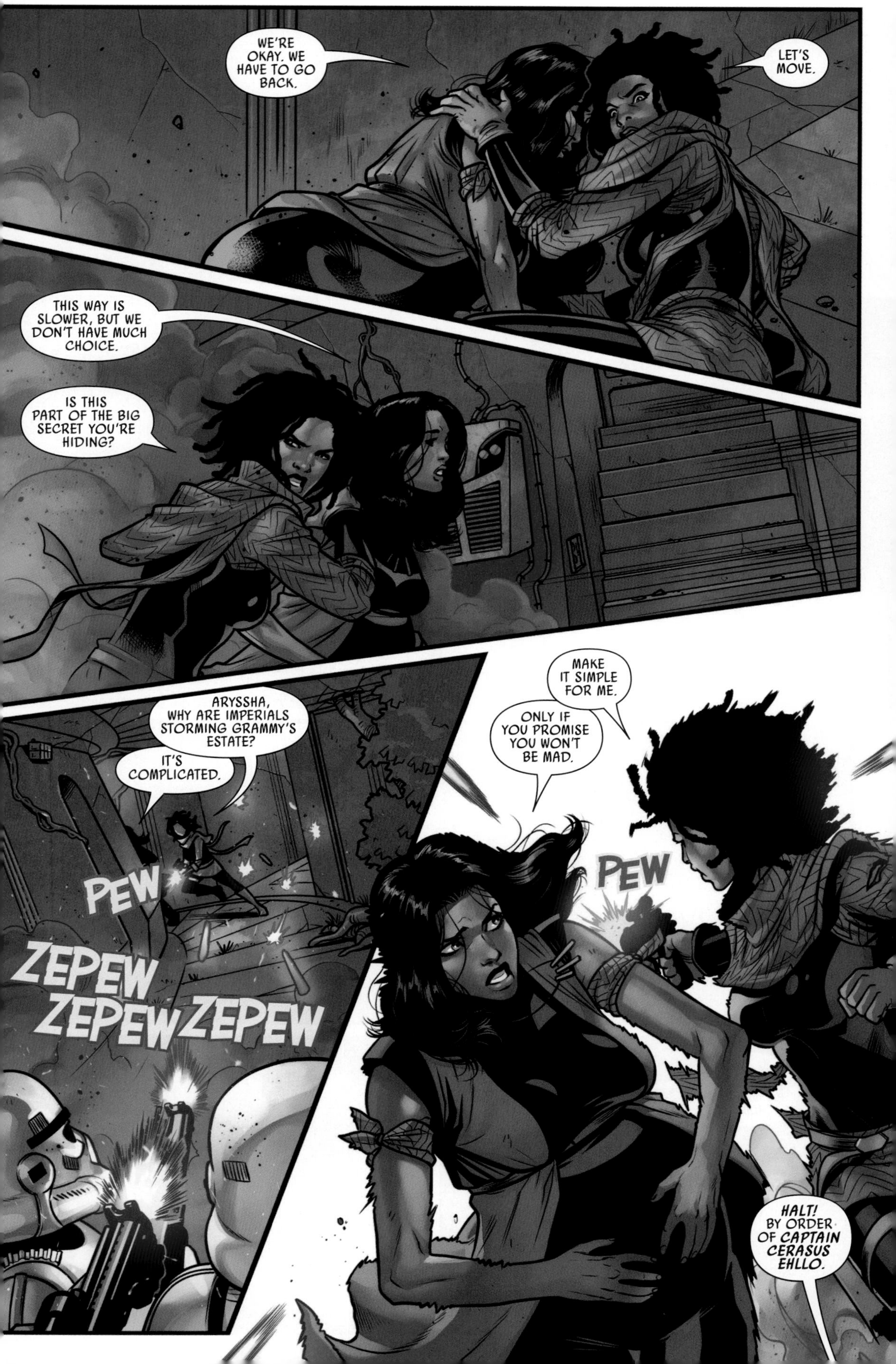
WE'RE OKAY. WE HAVE TO GO BACK.
LET'S MOVE.
THIS WAY IS SLOWER, BUT WE DON'T HAVE MUCH CHOICE.
IS THIS PART OF THE BIG SECRET YOU'RE HIDING?
ARYSSHA, WHY ARE IMPERIALS STORMING GRAMMY'S ESTATE?
IT'S COMPLICATED.
PEW
ZEPEW ZEPEW ZEPEW
MAKE IT SIMPLE FOR ME.
ONLY IF YOU PROMISE YOU WON'T BE MAD.
PEW
HALT! BY ORDER OF CAPTAIN CERASUS EHLLO.

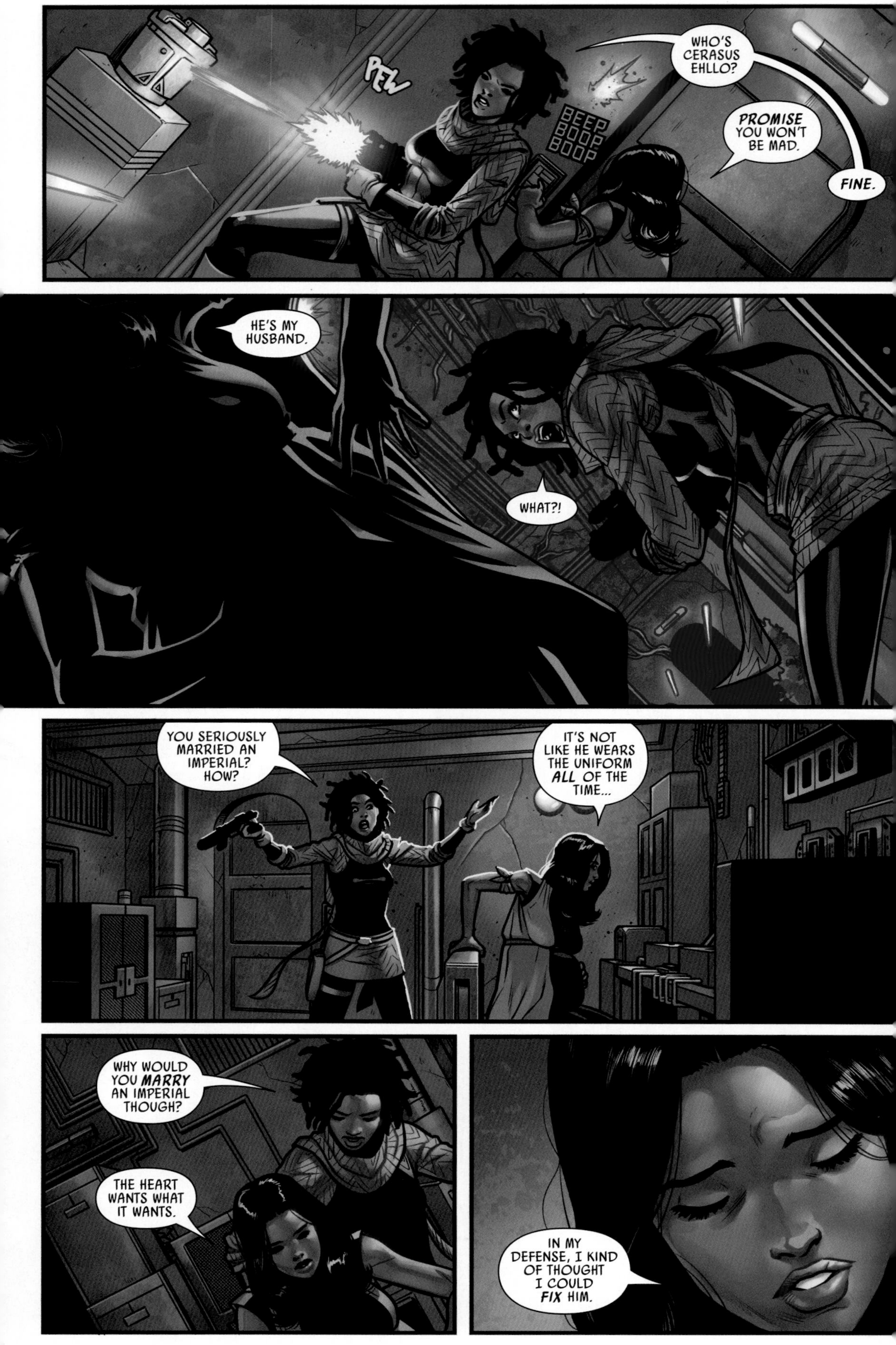
PEW
BEEP BOOP BOOP
WHO'S CERASUS EHLLO?
PROMISE YOU WON'T BE MAD.
FINE.
HE'S MY HUSBAND.
WHAT?!
YOU SERIOUSLY MARRIED AN IMPERIAL? HOW?
IT'S NOT LIKE HE WEARS THE UNIFORM ALL OF THE TIME...
WHY WOULD YOU MARRY AN IMPERIAL THOUGH?
THE HEART WANTS WHAT IT WANTS.
IN MY DEFENSE, I KIND OF THOUGHT I COULD FIX HIM.

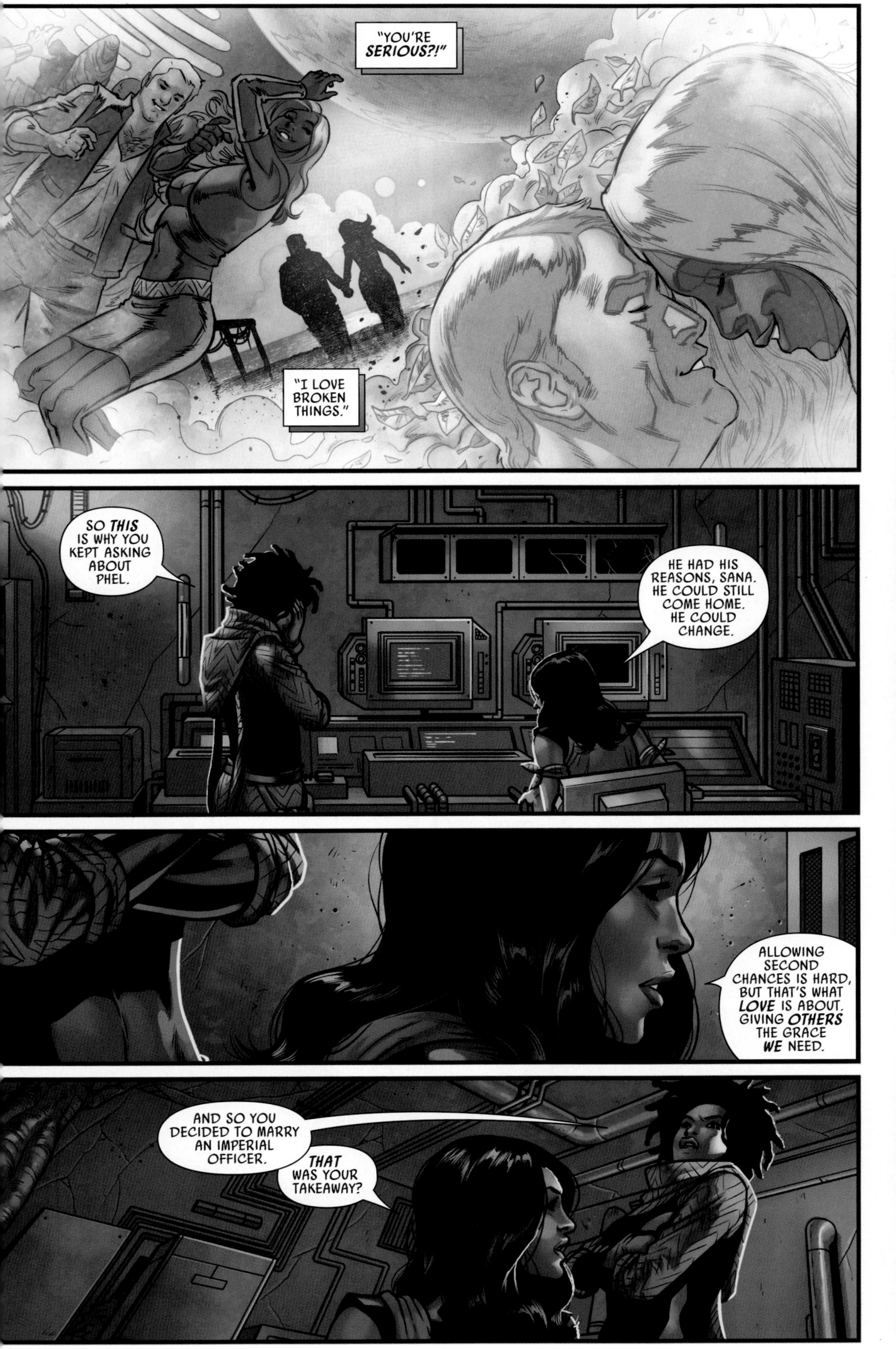
"YOU'RE SERIOUS?!"
"I LOVE BROKEN THINGS."
SO THIS IS WHY YOU KEPT ASKING ABOUT PHEL.
HE HAD HIS REASONS, SANA. HE COULD STILL COME HOME. HE COULD CHANGE.
ALLOWING SECOND CHANCES IS HARD, BUT THAT'S WHAT LOVE IS ABOUT. GIVING OTHERS THE GRACE WE NEED.
AND SO YOU DECIDED TO MARRY AN IMPERIAL OFFICER.
THAT WAS YOUR TAKEAWAY?

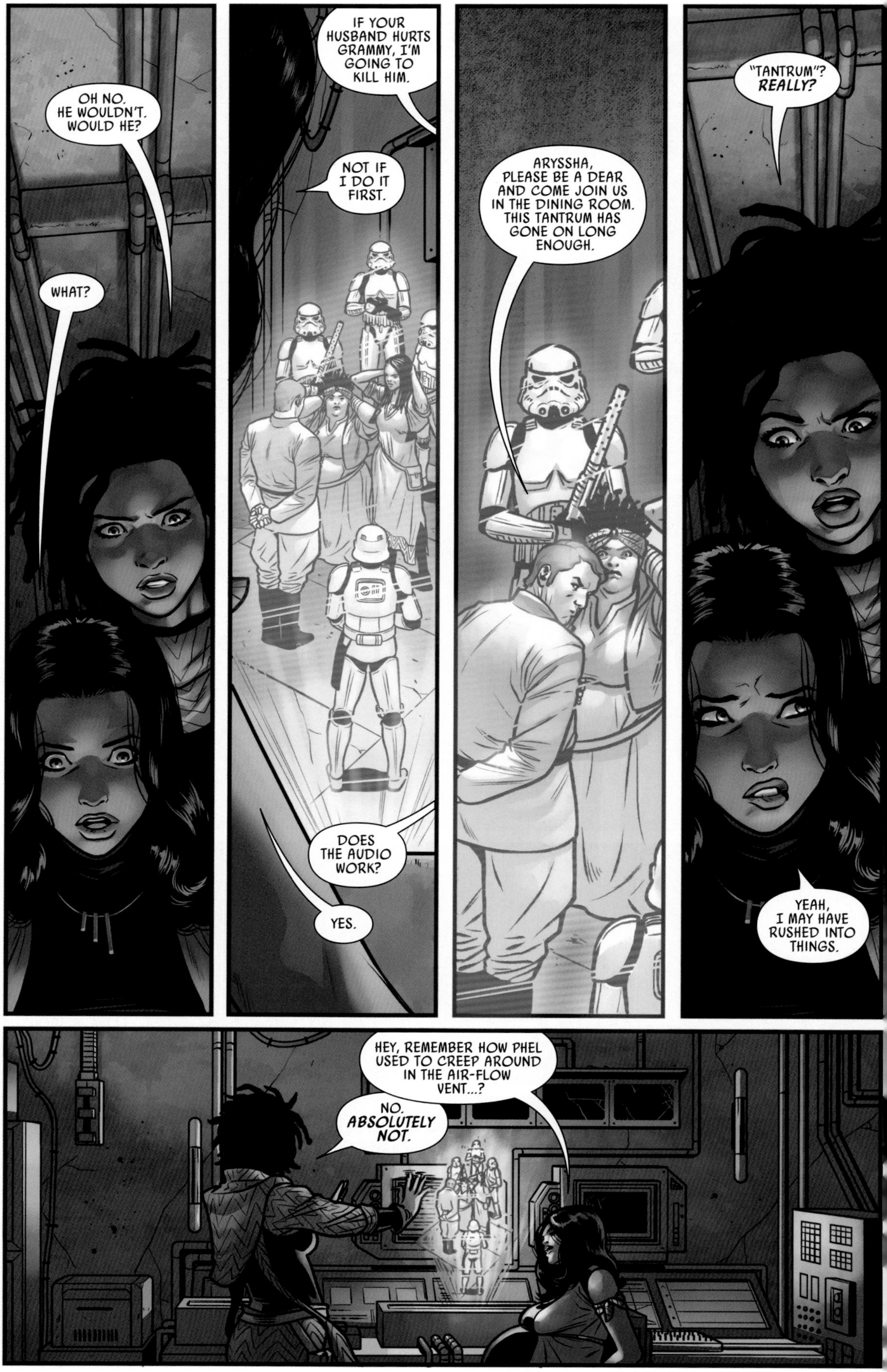

OH NO. HE WOULDN'T. WOULD HE?
WHAT?
IF YOUR HUSBAND HURTS GRAMMY, I'M GOING TO KILL HIM.
NOT IF I DO IT FIRST.
DOES THE AUDIO WORK?
YES.
ARYSSHA, PLEASE BE A DEAR AND COME JOIN US IN THE DINING ROOM. THIS TANTRUM HAS GONE ON LONG ENOUGH.
"TANTRUM"? *REALLY?*
YEAH, I MAY HAVE RUSHED INTO THINGS.
HEY, REMEMBER HOW PHEL USED TO CREEP AROUND IN THE AIR-FLOW VENT...?
NO. ***ABSOLUTELY NOT.***

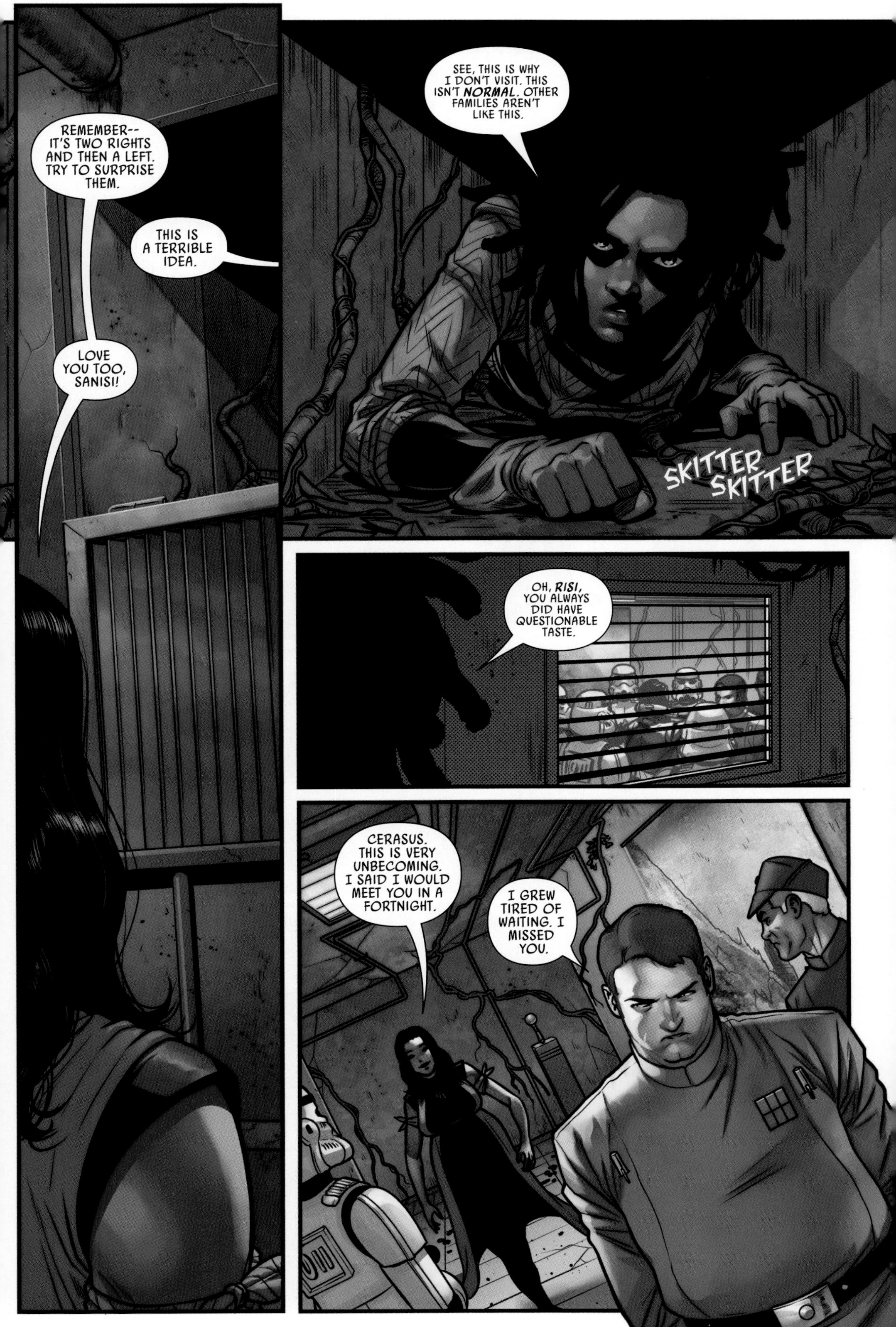
SEE, THIS IS WHY I DON'T VISIT. THIS ISN'T NORMAL. OTHER FAMILIES AREN'T LIKE THIS.
REMEMBER-- IT'S TWO RIGHTS AND THEN A LEFT. TRY TO SURPRISE THEM.
THIS IS A TERRIBLE IDEA.
LOVE YOU TOO, SANISI!
SKITTER SKITTER
OH, RISI, YOU ALWAYS DID HAVE QUESTIONABLE TASTE.
CERASUS. THIS IS VERY UNBECOMING. I SAID I WOULD MEET YOU IN A FORTNIGHT.
I GREW TIRED OF WAITING. I MISSED YOU.

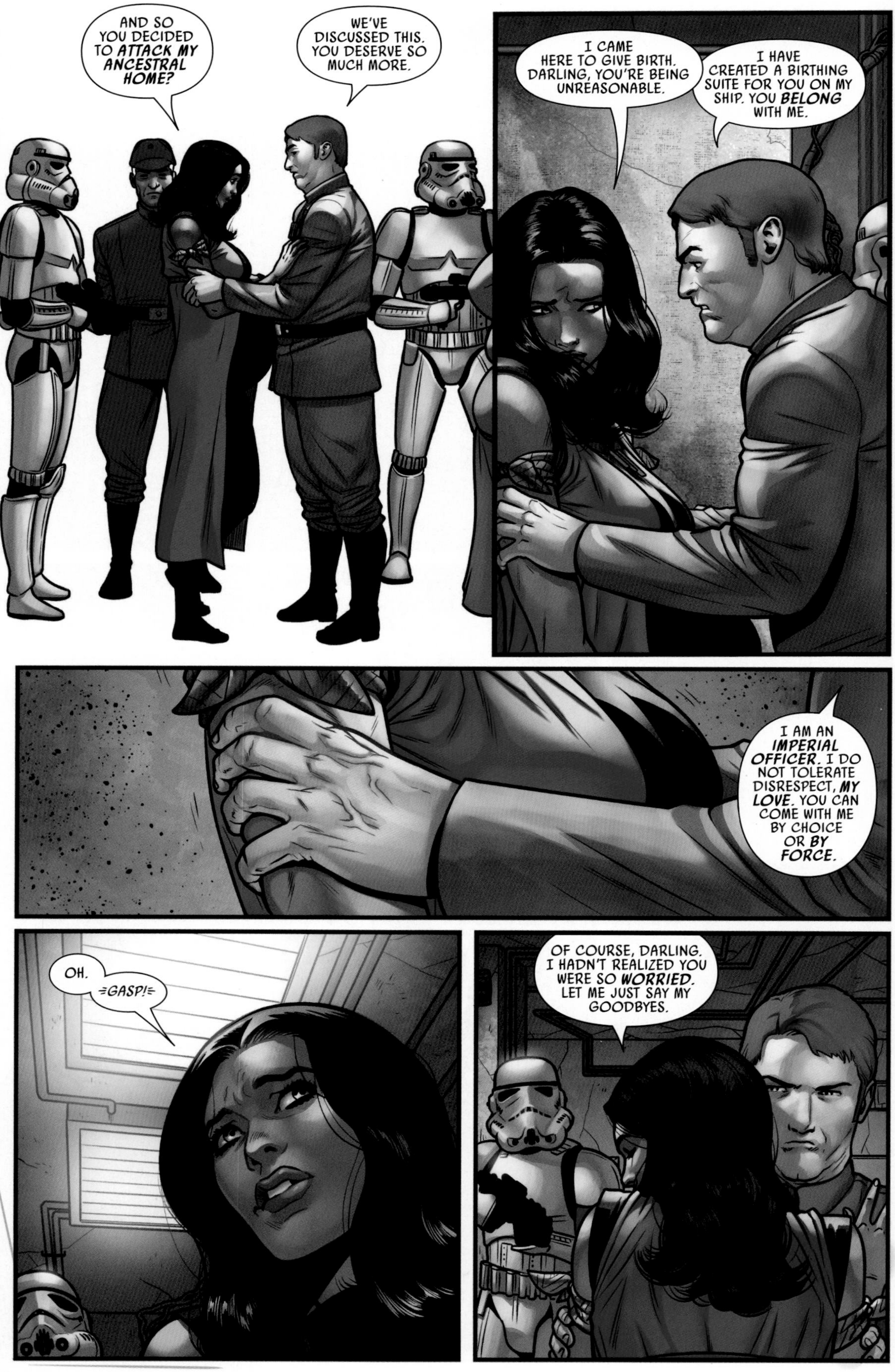
AND SO YOU DECIDED TO ATTACK MY ANCESTRAL HOME?
WE'VE DISCUSSED THIS. YOU DESERVE SO MUCH MORE.
I CAME HERE TO GIVE BIRTH. DARLING, YOU'RE BEING UNREASONABLE.
I HAVE CREATED A BIRTHING SUITE FOR YOU ON MY SHIP. YOU BELONG WITH ME.
I AM AN IMPERIAL OFFICER. I DO NOT TOLERATE DISRESPECT, MY LOVE. YOU CAN COME WITH ME BY CHOICE OR BY FORCE.
OH.
=GASP!=
OF COURSE, DARLING. I HADN'T REALIZED YOU WERE SO WORRIED. LET ME JUST SAY MY GOODBYES.

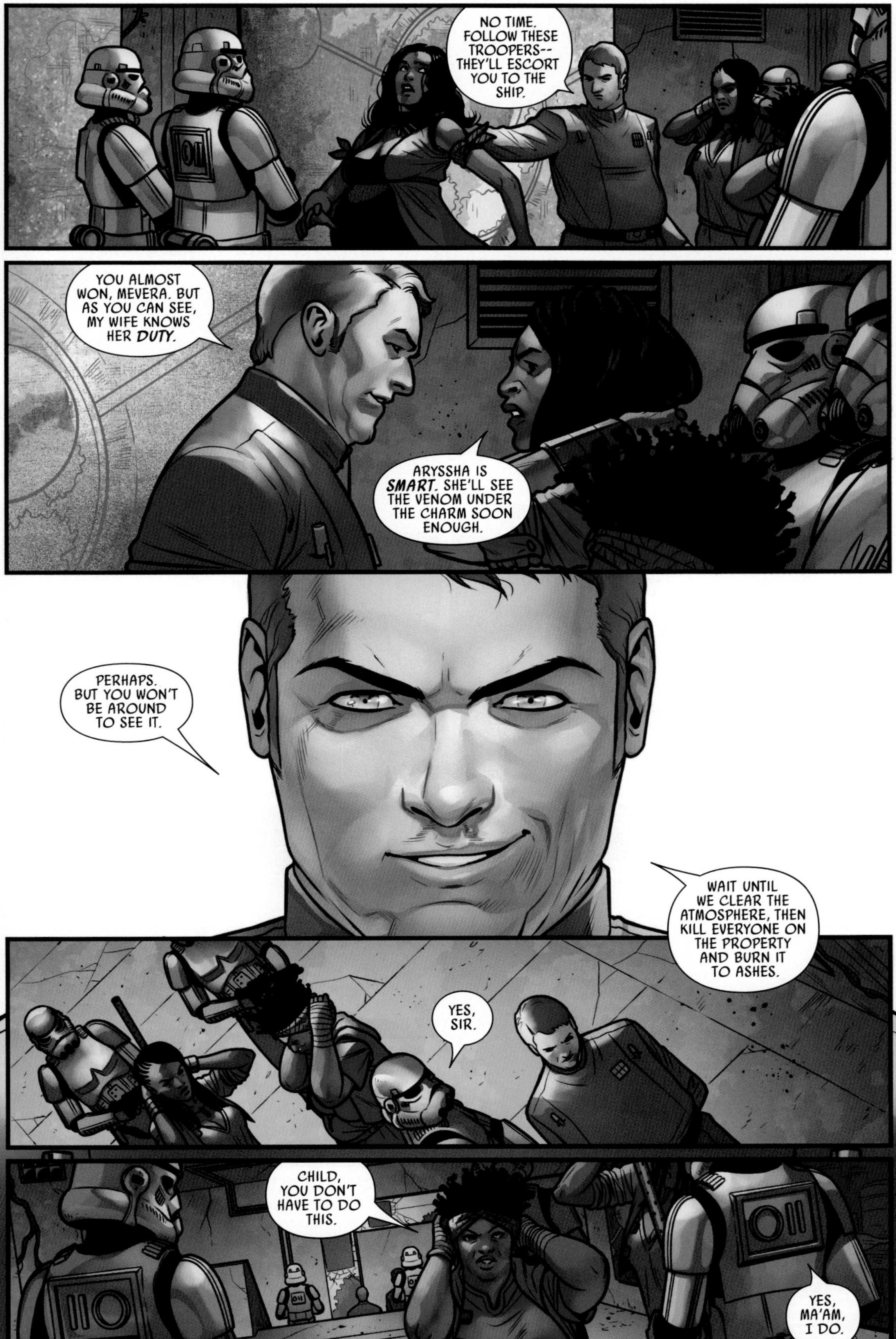
NO TIME. FOLLOW THESE TROOPERS-- THEY'LL ESCORT YOU TO THE SHIP.
YOU ALMOST WON, MEVERA. BUT AS YOU CAN SEE, MY WIFE KNOWS HER DUTY.
ARYSSHA IS SMART. SHE'LL SEE THE VENOM UNDER THE CHARM SOON ENOUGH.
PERHAPS. BUT YOU WON'T BE AROUND TO SEE IT.
WAIT UNTIL WE CLEAR THE ATMOSPHERE, THEN KILL EVERYONE ON THE PROPERTY AND BURN IT TO ASHES.
YES, SIR.
CHILD, YOU DON'T HAVE TO DO THIS.
YES, MA'AM, I DO.

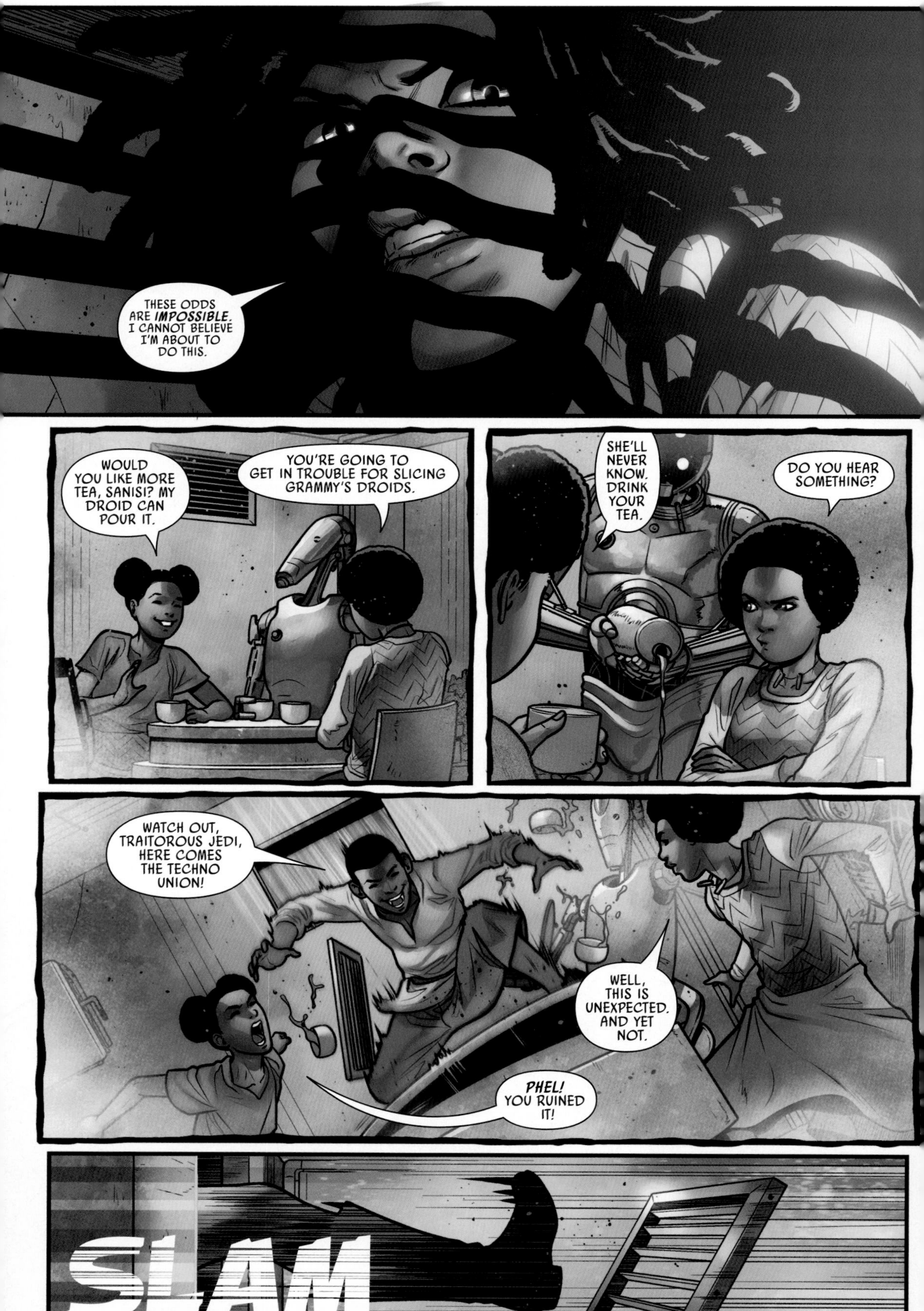
THESE ODDS ARE IMPOSSIBLE. I CANNOT BELIEVE I'M ABOUT TO DO THIS.
WOULD YOU LIKE MORE TEA, SANISI? MY DROID CAN POUR IT.
YOU'RE GOING TO GET IN TROUBLE FOR SLICING GRAMMY'S DROIDS.
SHE'LL NEVER KNOW. DRINK YOUR TEA.
DO YOU HEAR SOMETHING?
WATCH OUT, TRAITOROUS JEDI, HERE COMES THE TECHNO UNION!
WELL, THIS IS UNEXPECTED. AND YET NOT.
PHEL! YOU RUINED IT!
SLAM

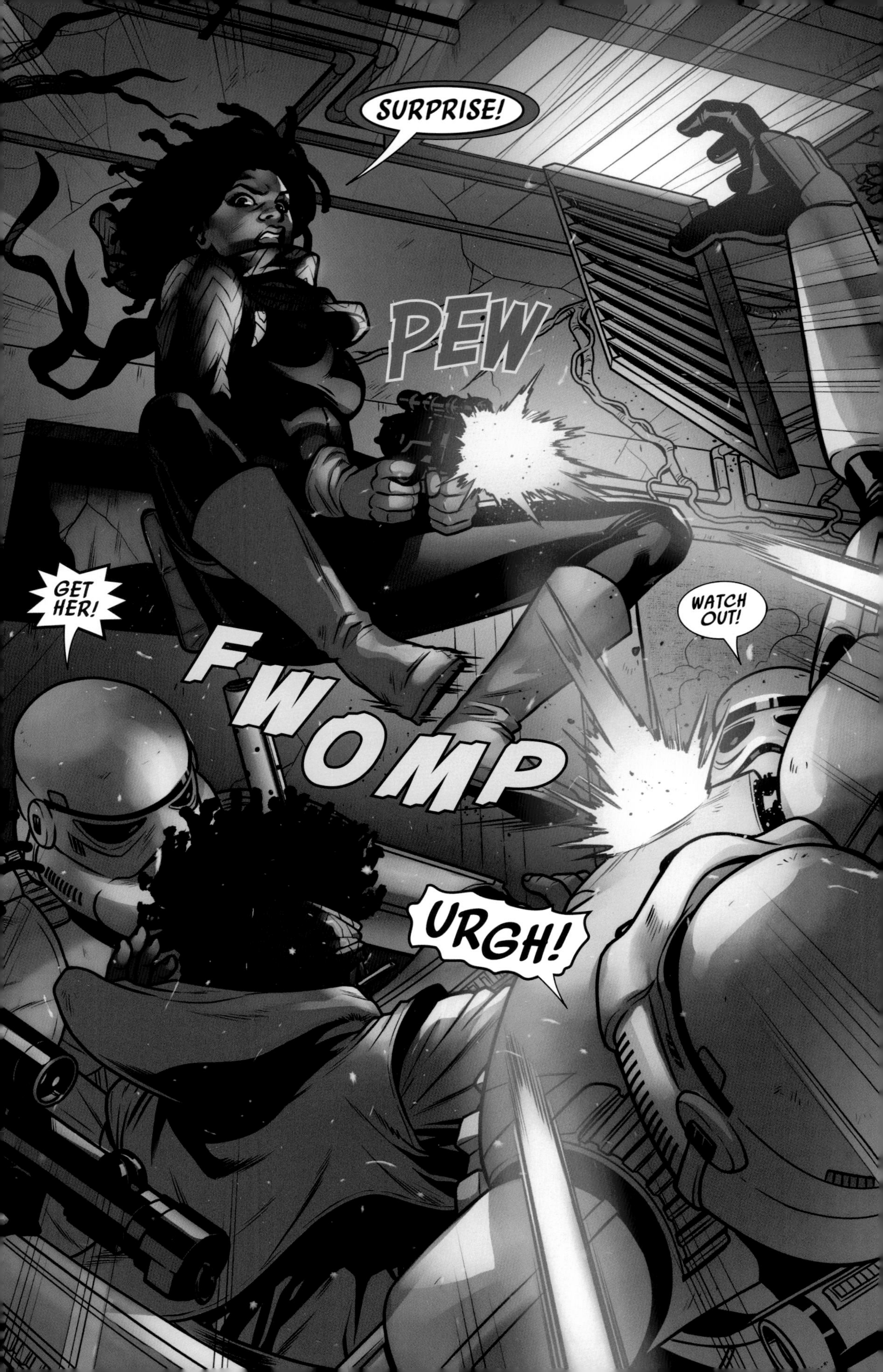
SURPRISE!
PEW
GET HER!
WATCH OUT!
FWOMP
URGH!

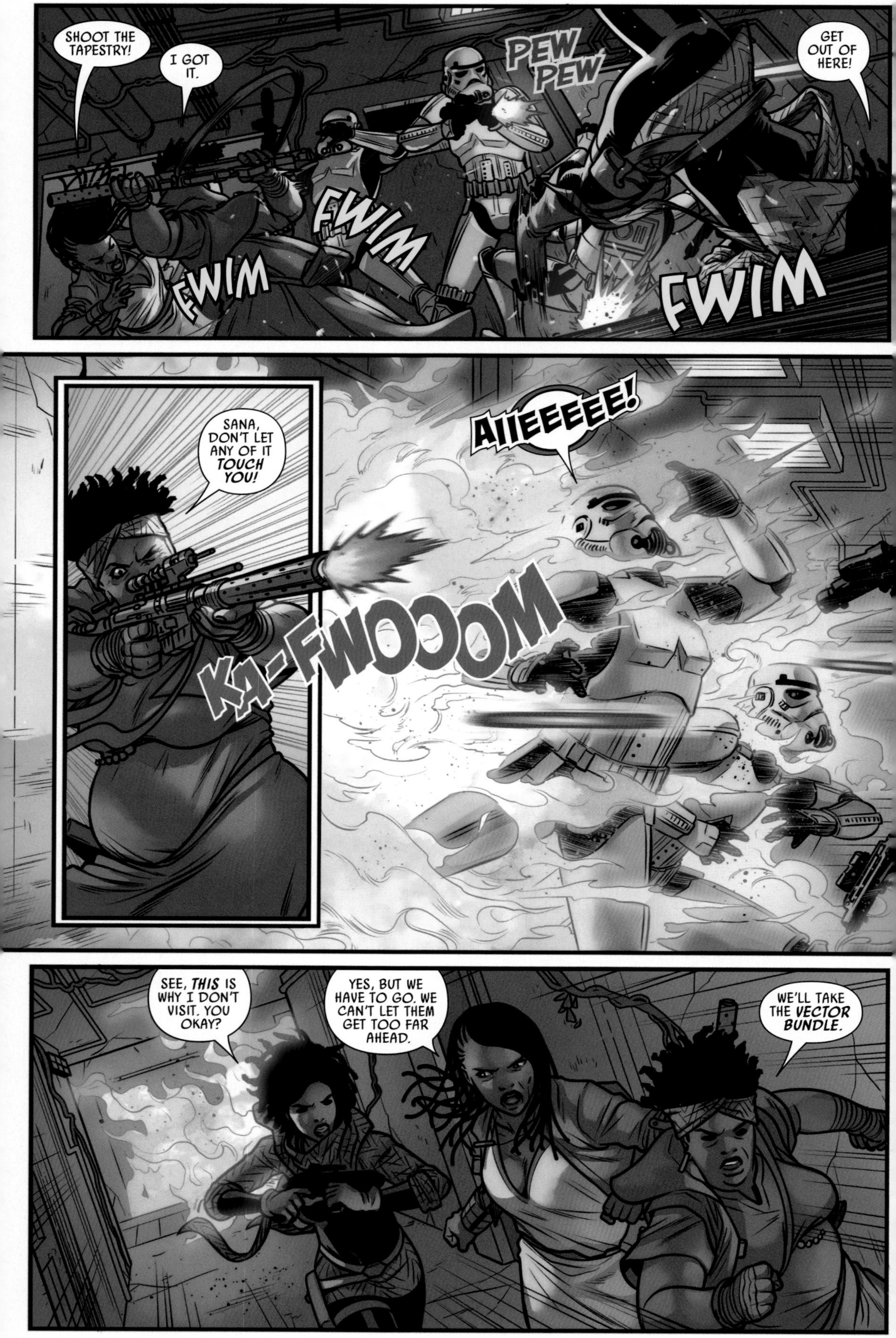
SHOOT THE TAPESTRY!
I GOT IT.
PEW PEW
GET OUT OF HERE!
FWIM
FWIM
FWIM
SANA, DON'T LET ANY OF IT TOUCH YOU!
AIIEEEEE!
KA-FWOOOM
SEE, THIS IS WHY I DON'T VISIT. YOU OKAY?
YES, BUT WE HAVE TO GO. WE CAN'T LET THEM GET TOO FAR AHEAD.
WE'LL TAKE THE VECTOR BUNDLE.

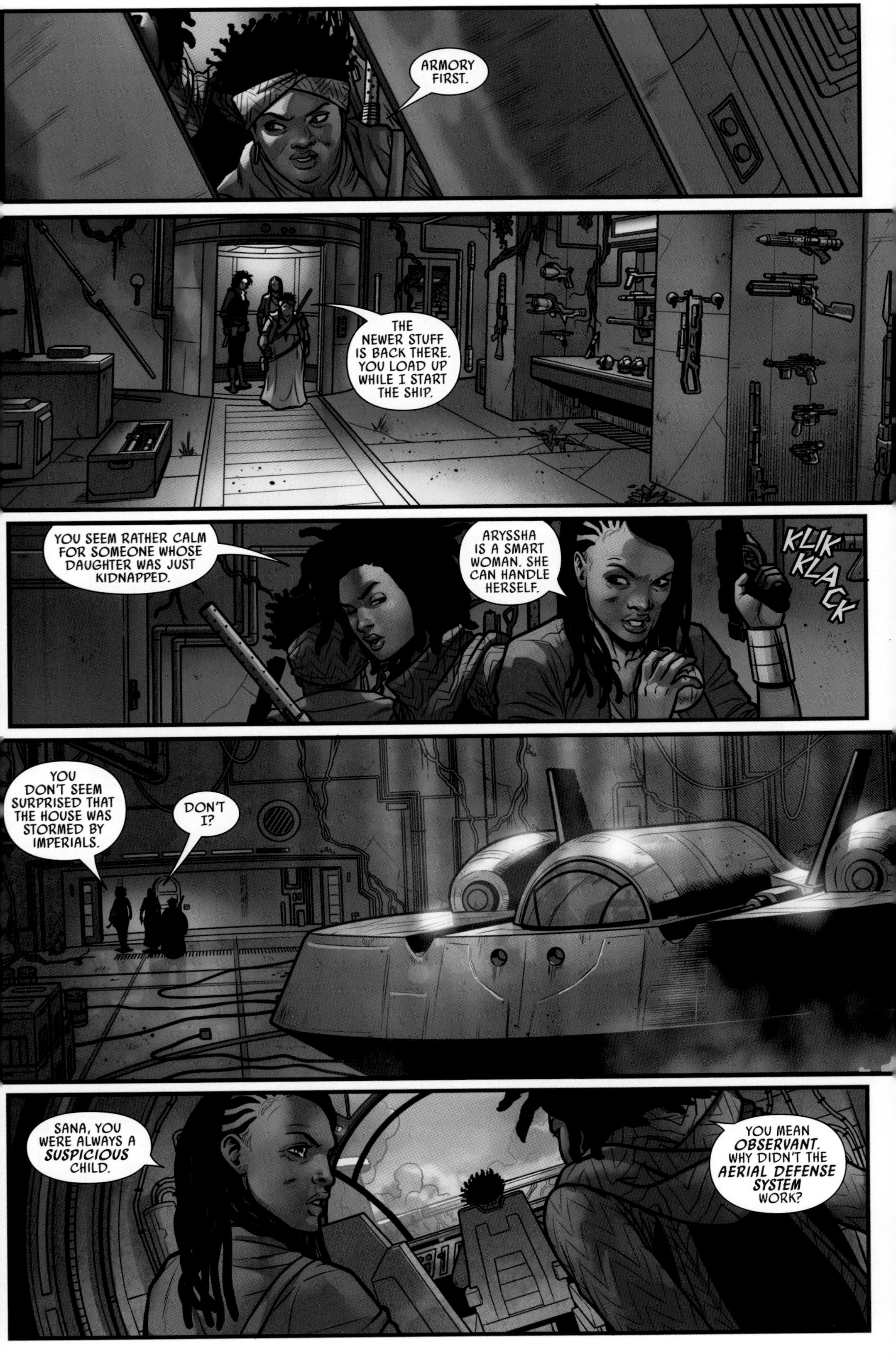
ARMORY FIRST.
THE NEWER STUFF IS BACK THERE. YOU LOAD UP WHILE I START THE SHIP.
YOU SEEM RATHER CALM FOR SOMEONE WHOSE DAUGHTER WAS JUST KIDNAPPED.
ARYSSHA IS A SMART WOMAN. SHE CAN HANDLE HERSELF.
KLIK KLACK
YOU DON'T SEEM SURPRISED THAT THE HOUSE WAS STORMED BY IMPERIALS.
DON'T I?
SANA, YOU WERE ALWAYS A SUSPICIOUS CHILD.
YOU MEAN OBSERVANT. WHY DIDN'T THE AERIAL DEFENSE SYSTEM WORK?

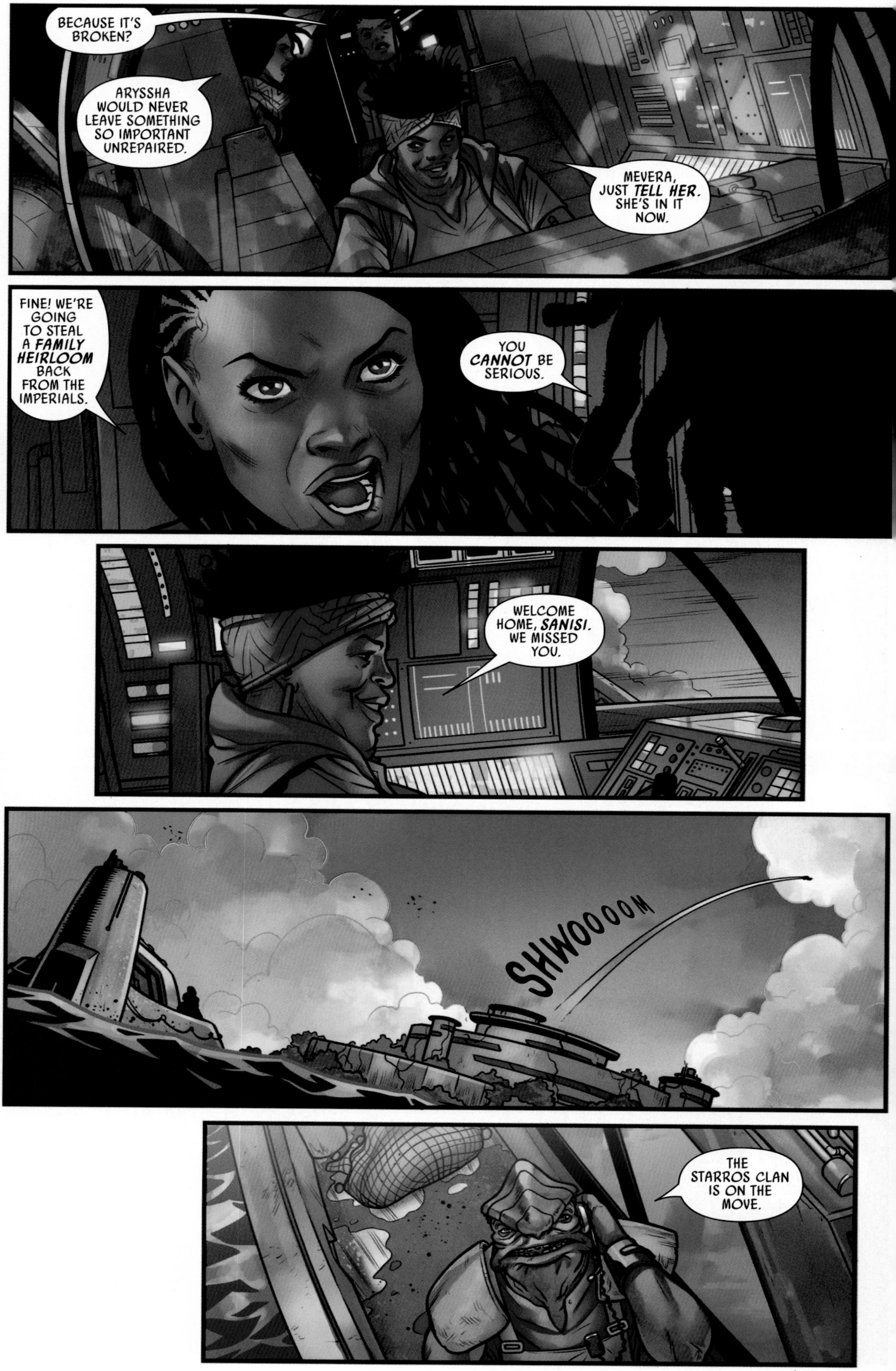
BECAUSE IT'S BROKEN?
ARYSSHA WOULD NEVER LEAVE SOMETHING SO IMPORTANT UNREPAIRED.
MEVERA, JUST TELL HER. SHE'S IN IT NOW.
FINE! WE'RE GOING TO STEAL A FAMILY HEIRLOOM BACK FROM THE IMPERIALS.
YOU CANNOT BE SERIOUS.
WELCOME HOME, SANISI. WE MISSED YOU.
SHWOOOOOM
THE STARROS CLAN IS ON THE MOVE.

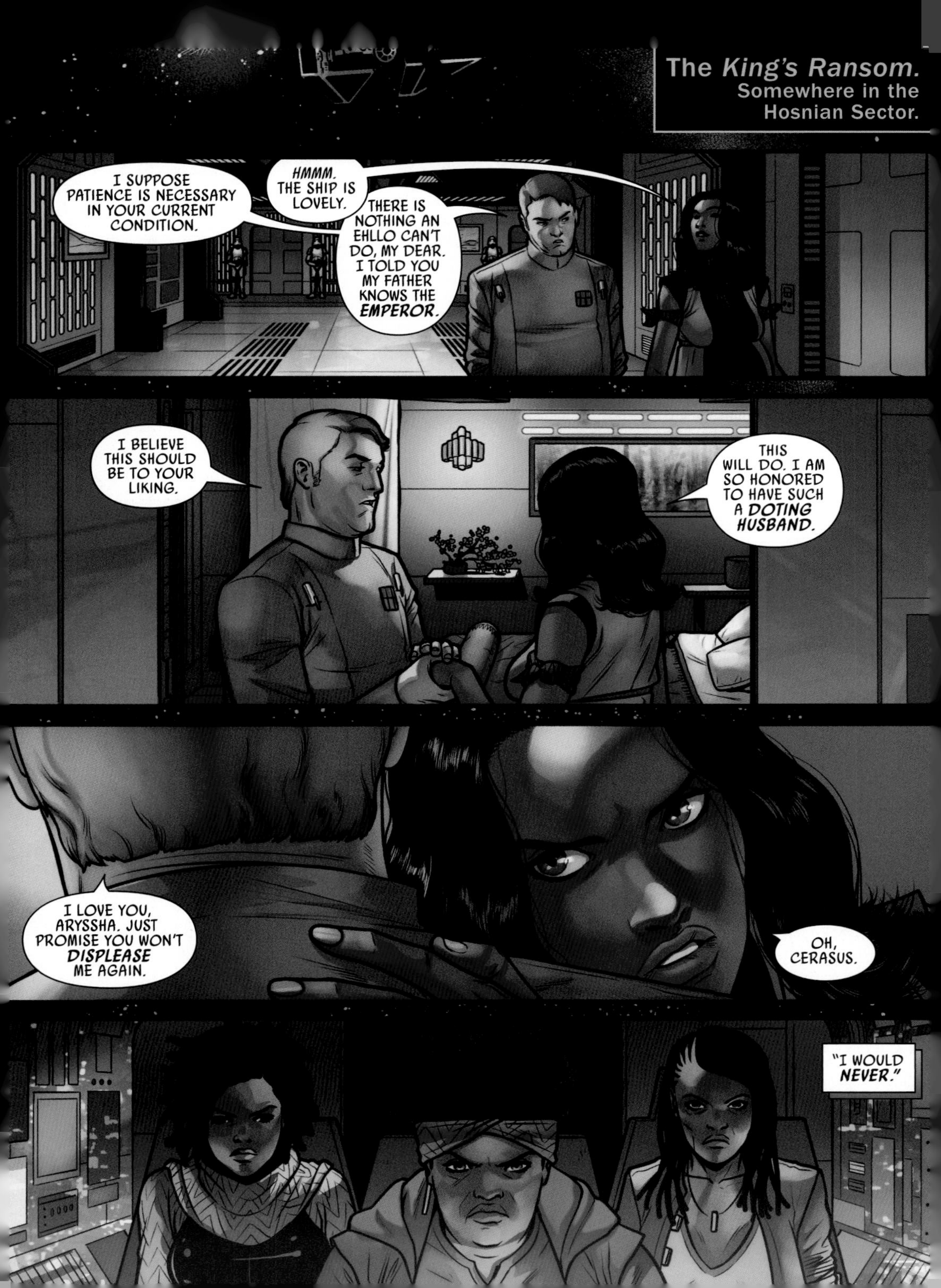
The *King's Ransom.*
Somewhere in the Hosnian Sector.
I SUPPOSE PATIENCE IS NECESSARY IN YOUR CURRENT CONDITION.
HMMM. THE SHIP IS LOVELY.
THERE IS NOTHING AN EHLLO CAN'T DO, MY DEAR. I TOLD YOU MY FATHER KNOWS THE ***EMPEROR.***
I BELIEVE THIS SHOULD BE TO YOUR LIKING.
THIS WILL DO. I AM SO HONORED TO HAVE SUCH A ***DOTING HUSBAND.***
I LOVE YOU, ARYSSHA. JUST PROMISE YOU WON'T ***DISPLEASE*** ME AGAIN.
OH, CERASUS.
"I WOULD ***NEVER.***"

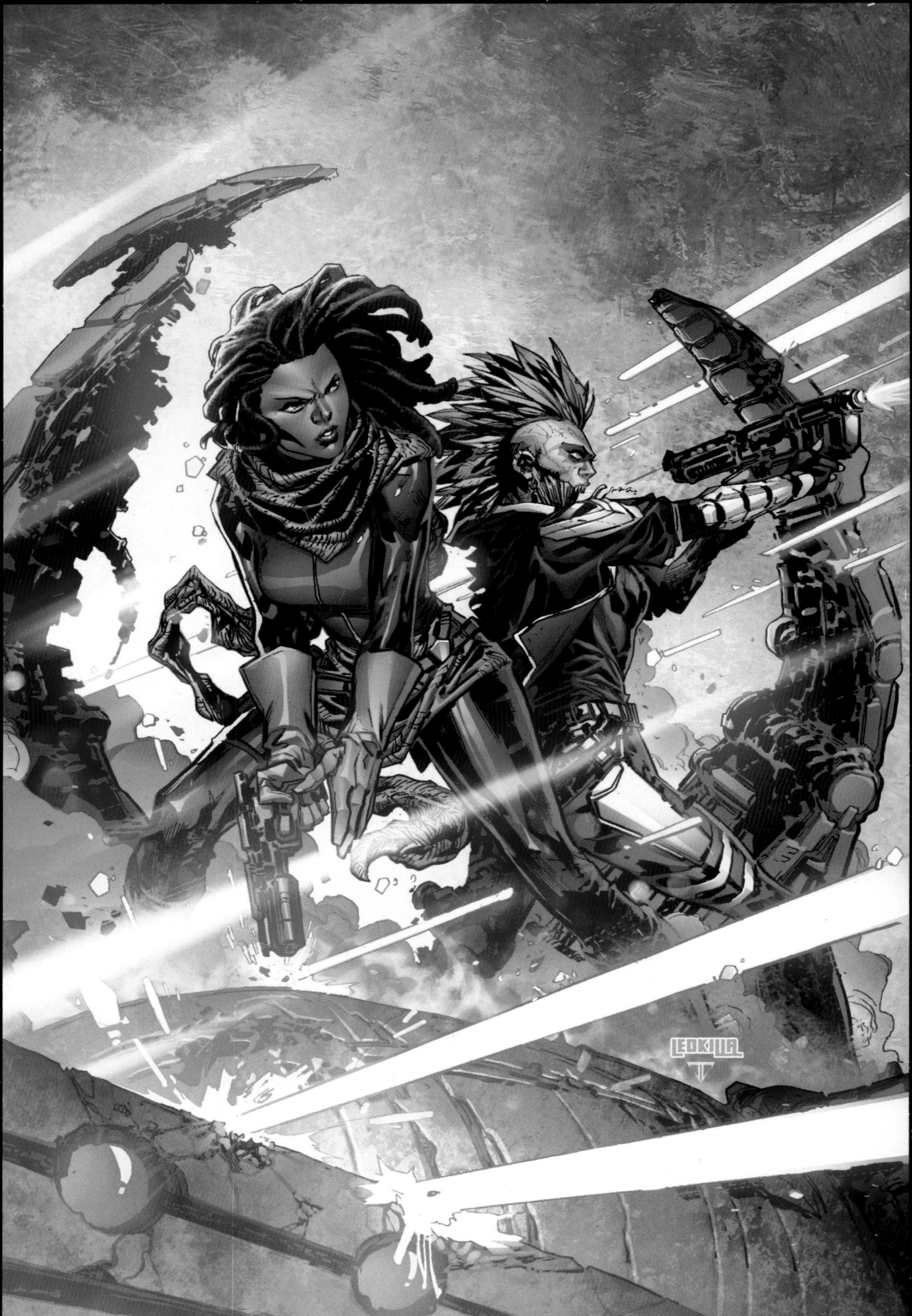
LEOKILLA

2 — ALL IN THE FAMILY

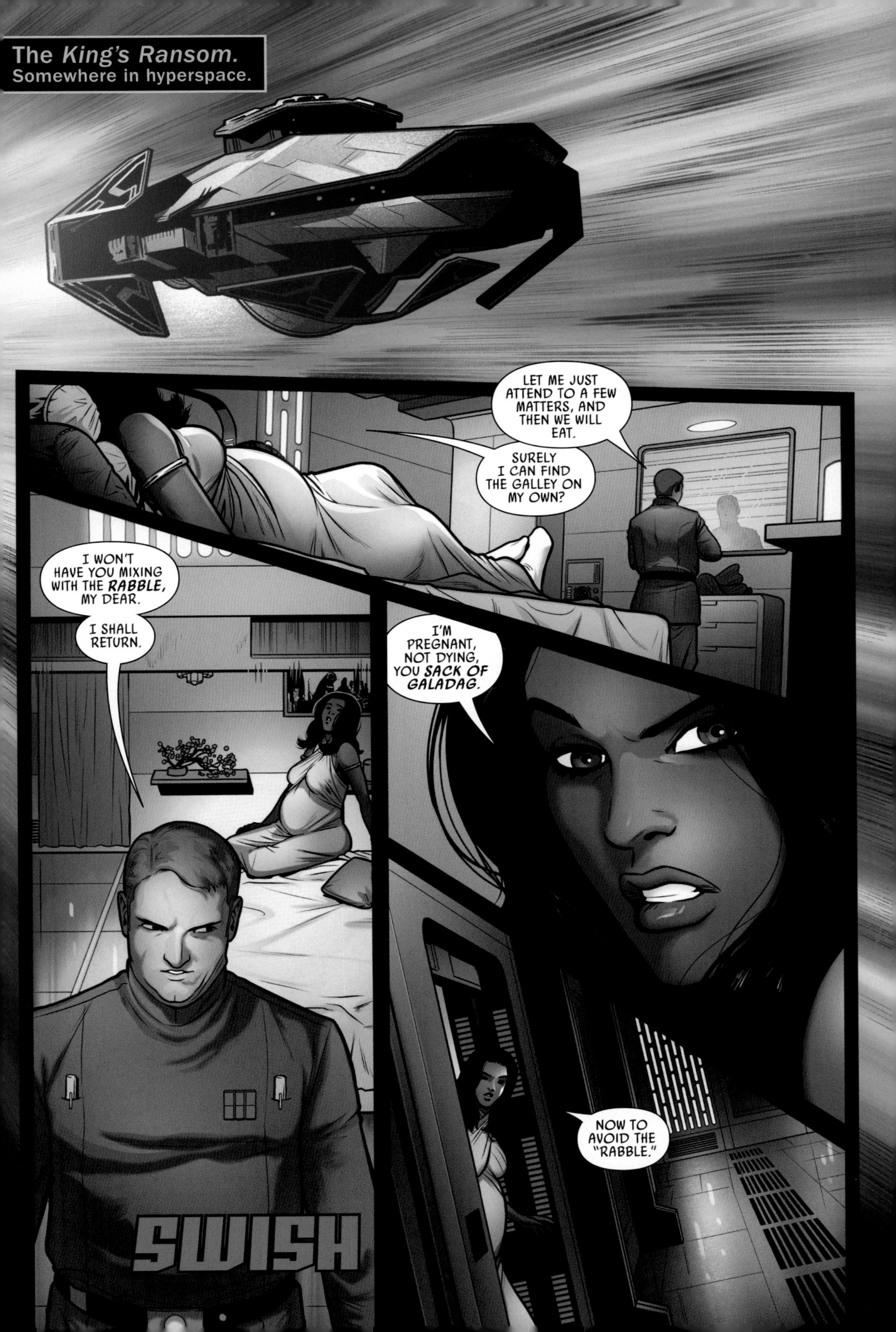
The *King's Ransom.*
Somewhere in hyperspace.
LET ME JUST ATTEND TO A FEW MATTERS, AND THEN WE WILL EAT.
SURELY I CAN FIND THE GALLEY ON MY OWN?
I WON'T HAVE YOU MIXING WITH THE *RABBLE,* MY DEAR.
I SHALL RETURN.
I'M PREGNANT, NOT DYING, YOU *SACK OF GALADAG.*
SWISH
NOW TO AVOID THE "RABBLE."

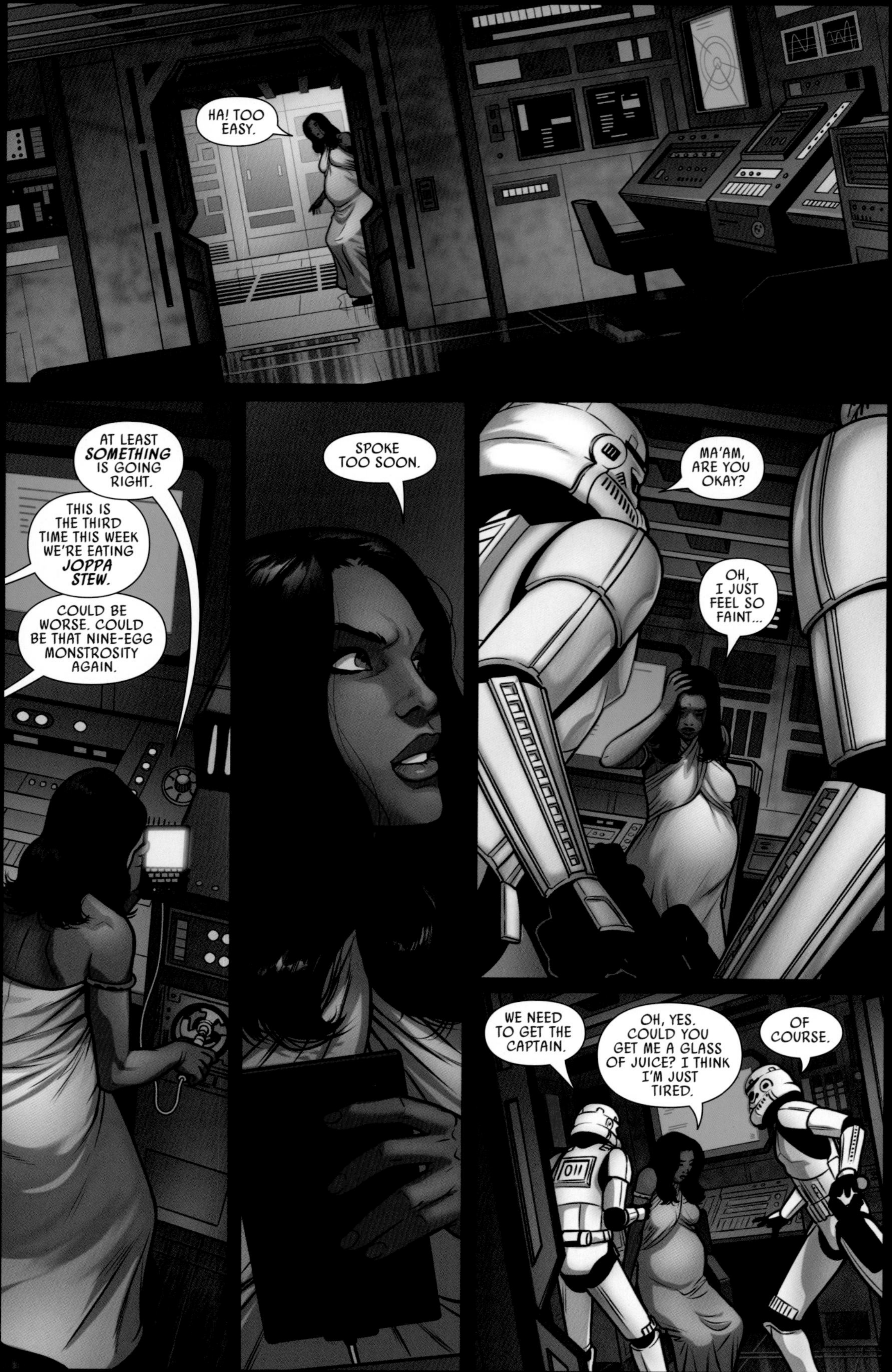
HA! TOO EASY.
AT LEAST SOMETHING IS GOING RIGHT.
THIS IS THE THIRD TIME THIS WEEK WE'RE EATING JOPPA STEW.
COULD BE WORSE. COULD BE THAT NINE-EGG MONSTROSITY AGAIN.
SPOKE TOO SOON.
MA'AM, ARE YOU OKAY?
OH, I JUST FEEL SO FAINT...
WE NEED TO GET THE CAPTAIN.
OH, YES. COULD YOU GET ME A GLASS OF JUICE? I THINK I'M JUST TIRED.
OF COURSE.

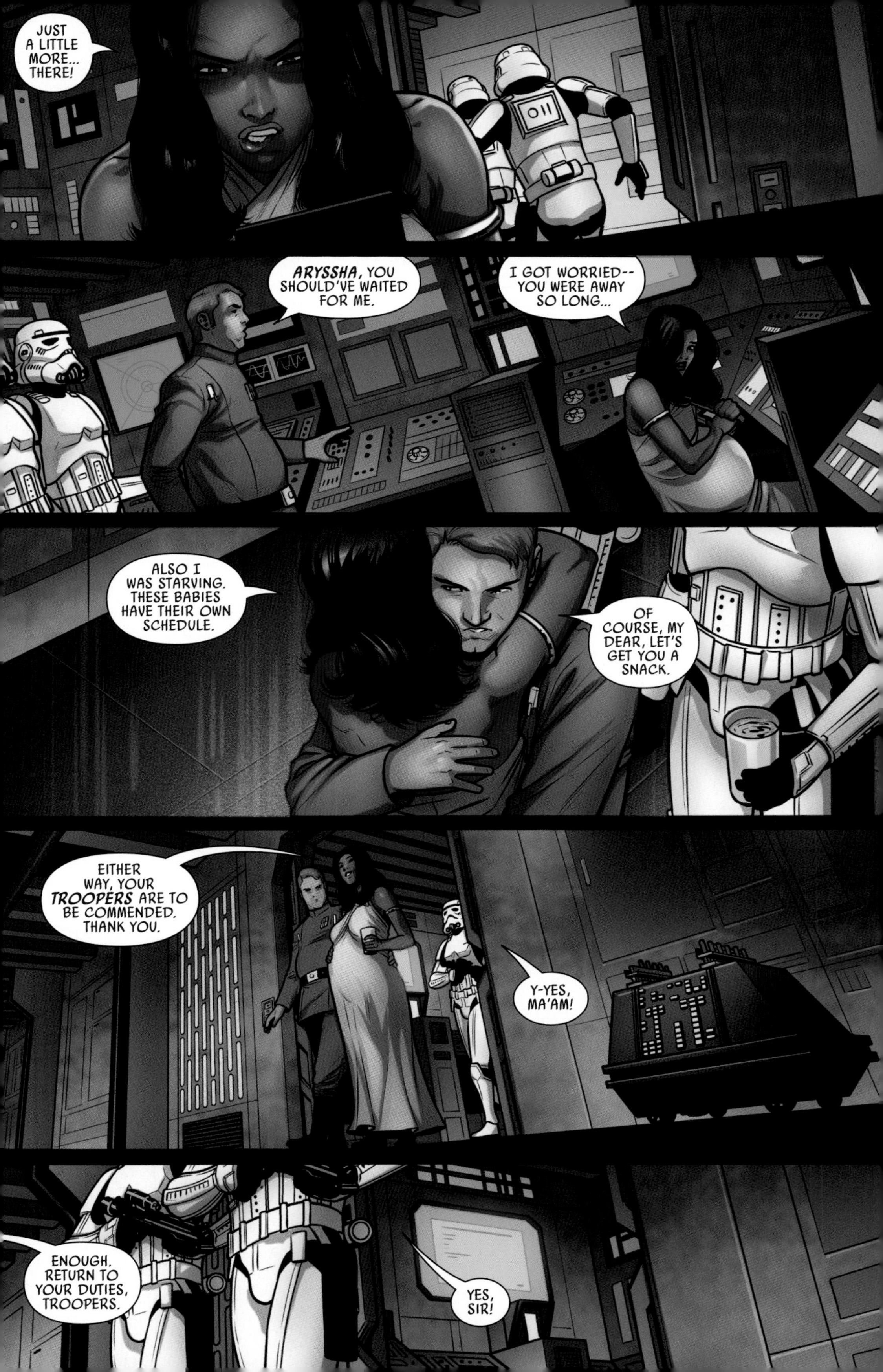
JUST A LITTLE MORE... THERE!
ARYSSHA, YOU SHOULD'VE WAITED FOR ME.
I GOT WORRIED--YOU WERE AWAY SO LONG...
ALSO I WAS STARVING. THESE BABIES HAVE THEIR OWN SCHEDULE.
OF COURSE, MY DEAR, LET'S GET YOU A SNACK.
EITHER WAY, YOUR TROOPERS ARE TO BE COMMENDED. THANK YOU.
Y-YES, MA'AM!
ENOUGH. RETURN TO YOUR DUTIES, TROOPERS.
YES, SIR!

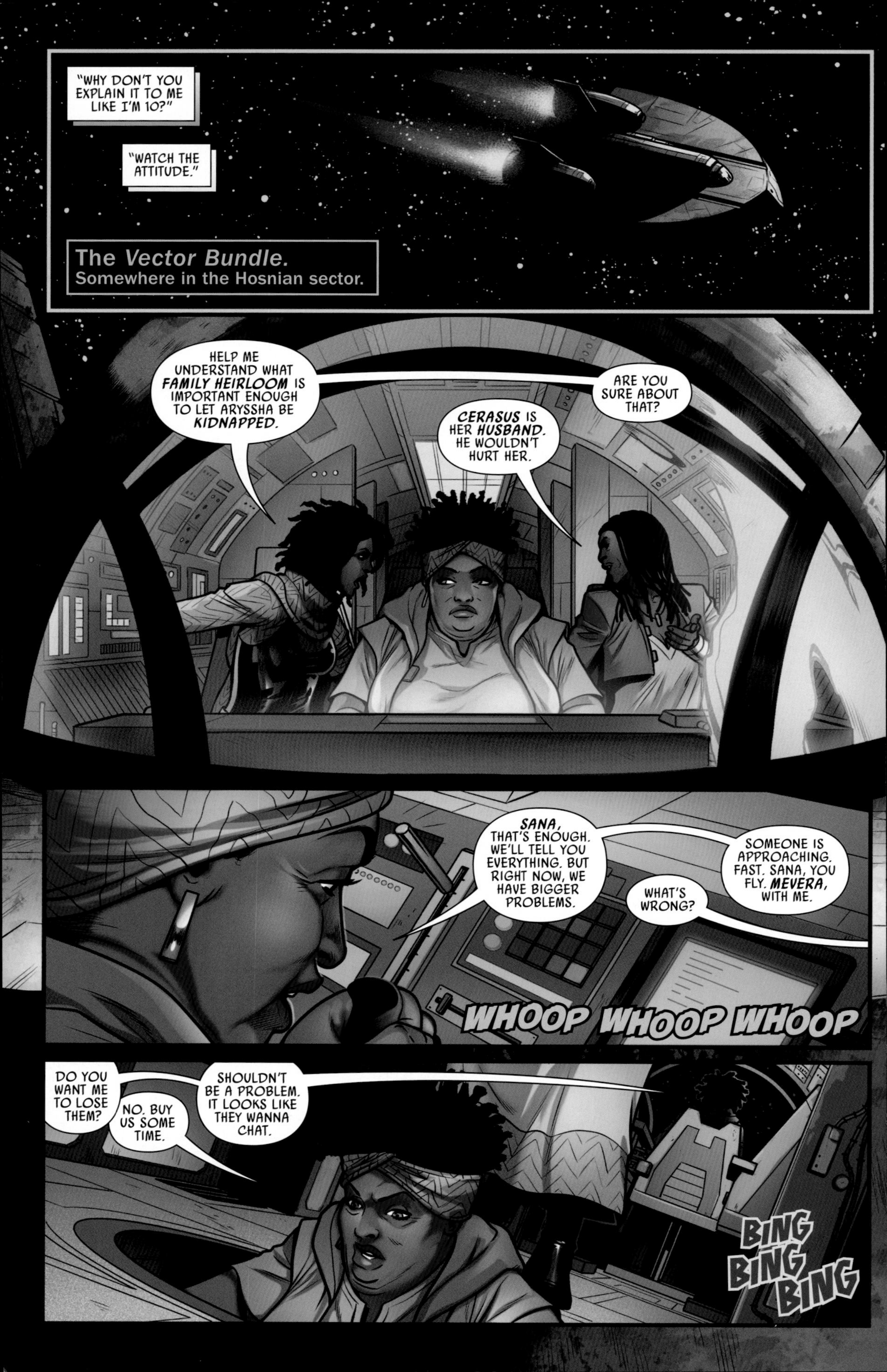
"WHY DON'T YOU EXPLAIN IT TO ME LIKE I'M 10?"
"WATCH THE ATTITUDE."
The Vector Bundle.
Somewhere in the Hosnian sector.
HELP ME UNDERSTAND WHAT FAMILY HEIRLOOM IS IMPORTANT ENOUGH TO LET ARYSSHA BE KIDNAPPED.
CERASUS IS HER HUSBAND. HE WOULDN'T HURT HER.
ARE YOU SURE ABOUT THAT?
SANA, THAT'S ENOUGH. WE'LL TELL YOU EVERYTHING. BUT RIGHT NOW, WE HAVE BIGGER PROBLEMS.
WHAT'S WRONG?
SOMEONE IS APPROACHING. FAST. SANA, YOU FLY. MEVERA, WITH ME.
WHOOP WHOOP WHOOP
DO YOU WANT ME TO LOSE THEM?
NO. BUY US SOME TIME.
SHOULDN'T BE A PROBLEM. IT LOOKS LIKE THEY WANNA CHAT.
BING BING BING

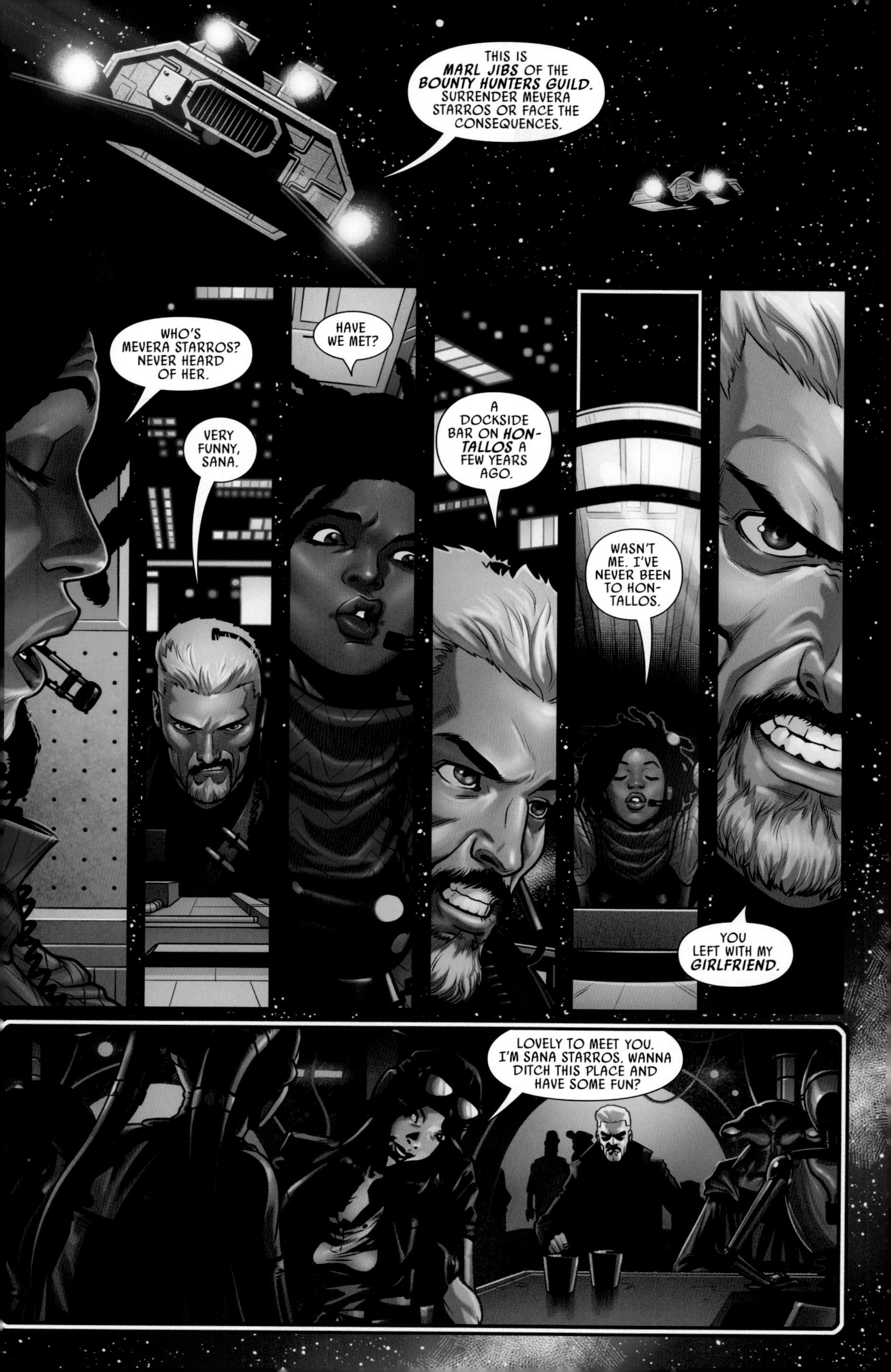
THIS IS MARL JIBS OF THE BOUNTY HUNTERS GUILD. SURRENDER MEVERA STARROS OR FACE THE CONSEQUENCES.
WHO'S MEVERA STARROS? NEVER HEARD OF HER.
VERY FUNNY, SANA.
HAVE WE MET?
A DOCKSIDE BAR ON HON-TALLOS A FEW YEARS AGO.
WASN'T ME. I'VE NEVER BEEN TO HON-TALLOS.
YOU LEFT WITH MY GIRLFRIEND.
LOVELY TO MEET YOU. I'M SANA STARROS. WANNA DITCH THIS PLACE AND HAVE SOME FUN?

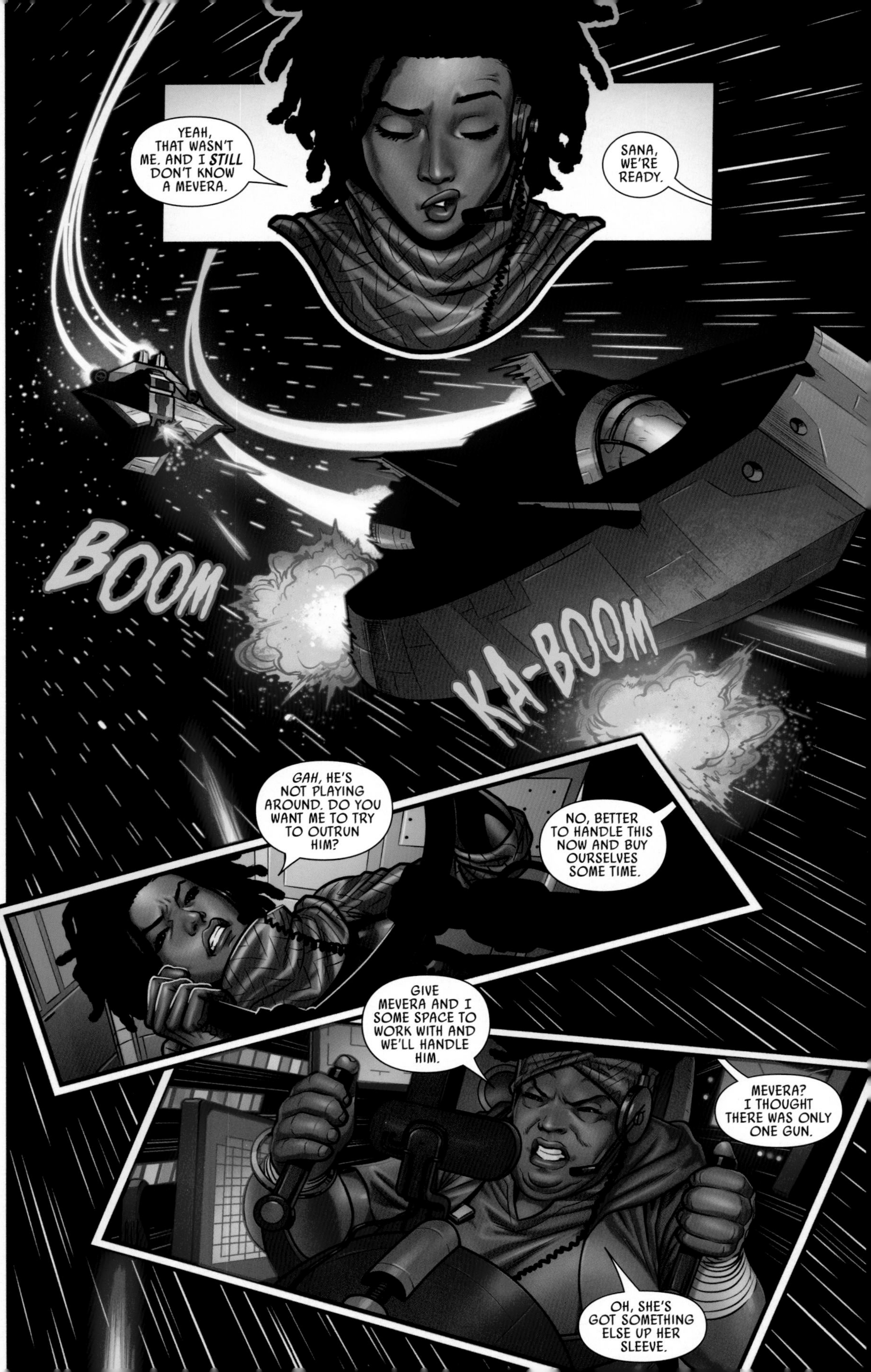
YEAH, THAT WASN'T ME. AND I STILL DON'T KNOW A MEVERA.
SANA, WE'RE READY.
BOOM
KA-BOOM
GAH, HE'S NOT PLAYING AROUND. DO YOU WANT ME TO TRY TO OUTRUN HIM?
NO, BETTER TO HANDLE THIS NOW AND BUY OURSELVES SOME TIME.
GIVE MEVERA AND I SOME SPACE TO WORK WITH AND WE'LL HANDLE HIM.
MEVERA? I THOUGHT THERE WAS ONLY ONE GUN.
OH, SHE'S GOT SOMETHING ELSE UP HER SLEEVE.

WHY IS EVERYONE SO SECRETIVE IN THIS FAMILY?
SURRENDER, STARROS!
NEVER.
SKREEEEEE
BOOM
BA-BROOM
GRAMMY, WHY AREN'T YOU TRYING TO HIT THE SHIP?
HOW DO YOU KNOW I'M NOT?
BECAUSE YOU NEVER MISS.
HA! WELL, YOUR AUNT WANTS TO TRY OUT HER NEW TOY. JUST HOLD THE SHIP STEADY.

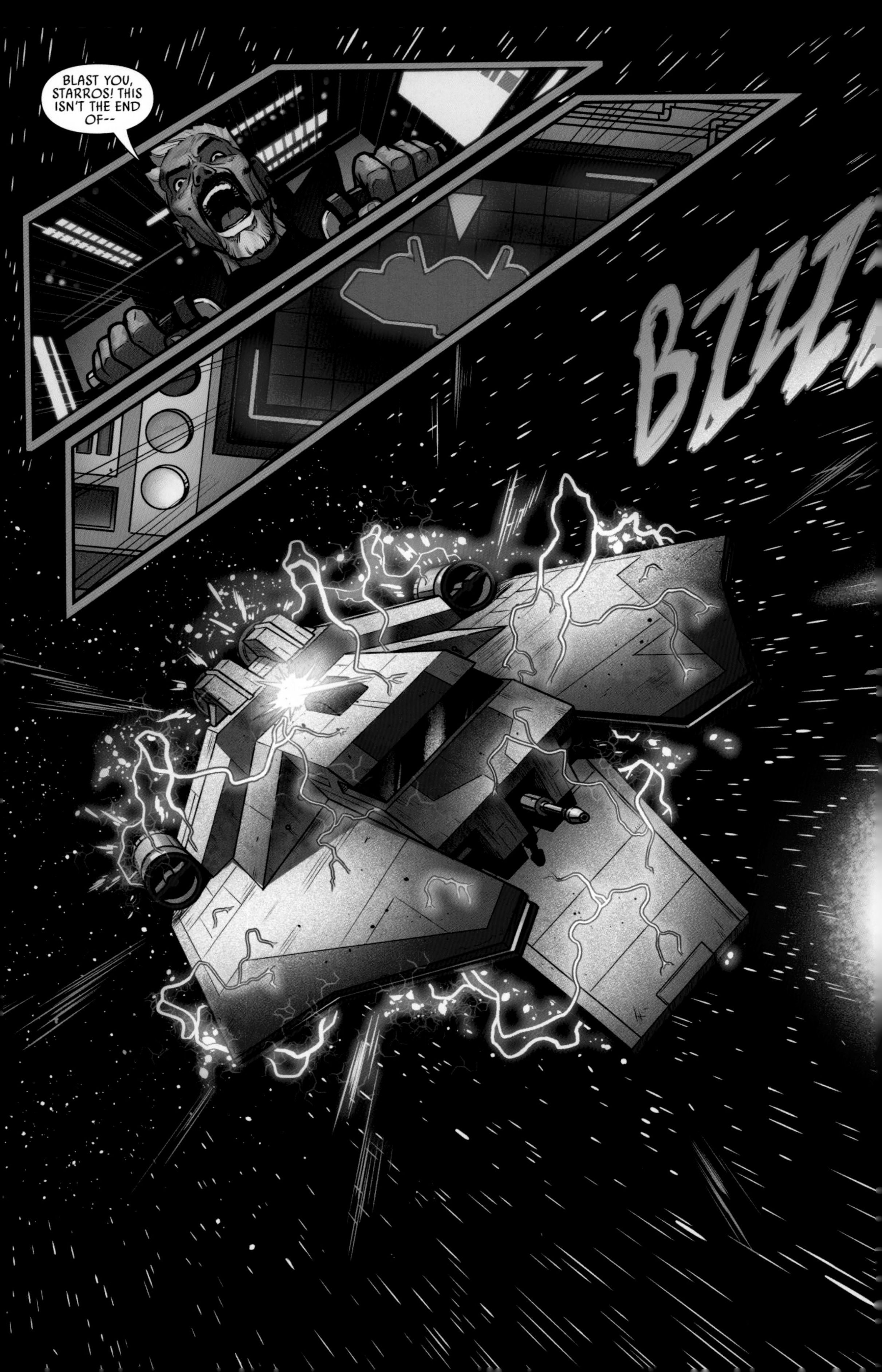
BLAST YOU, STARROS! THIS ISN'T THE END OF--
BZZZ

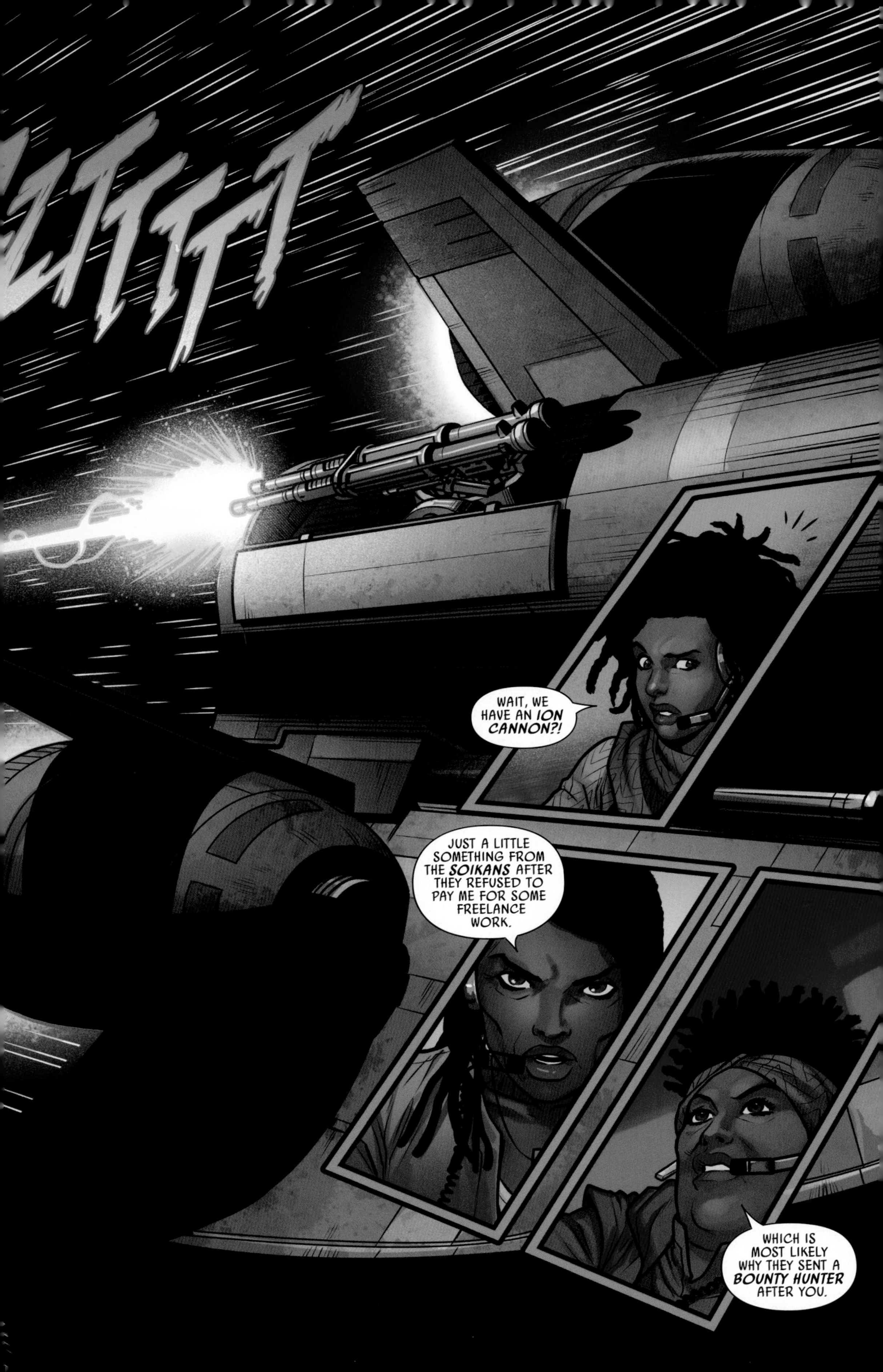
WAIT, WE HAVE AN ION CANNON?!
JUST A LITTLE SOMETHING FROM THE SOIKANS AFTER THEY REFUSED TO PAY ME FOR SOME FREELANCE WORK.
WHICH IS MOST LIKELY WHY THEY SENT A BOUNTY HUNTER AFTER YOU.

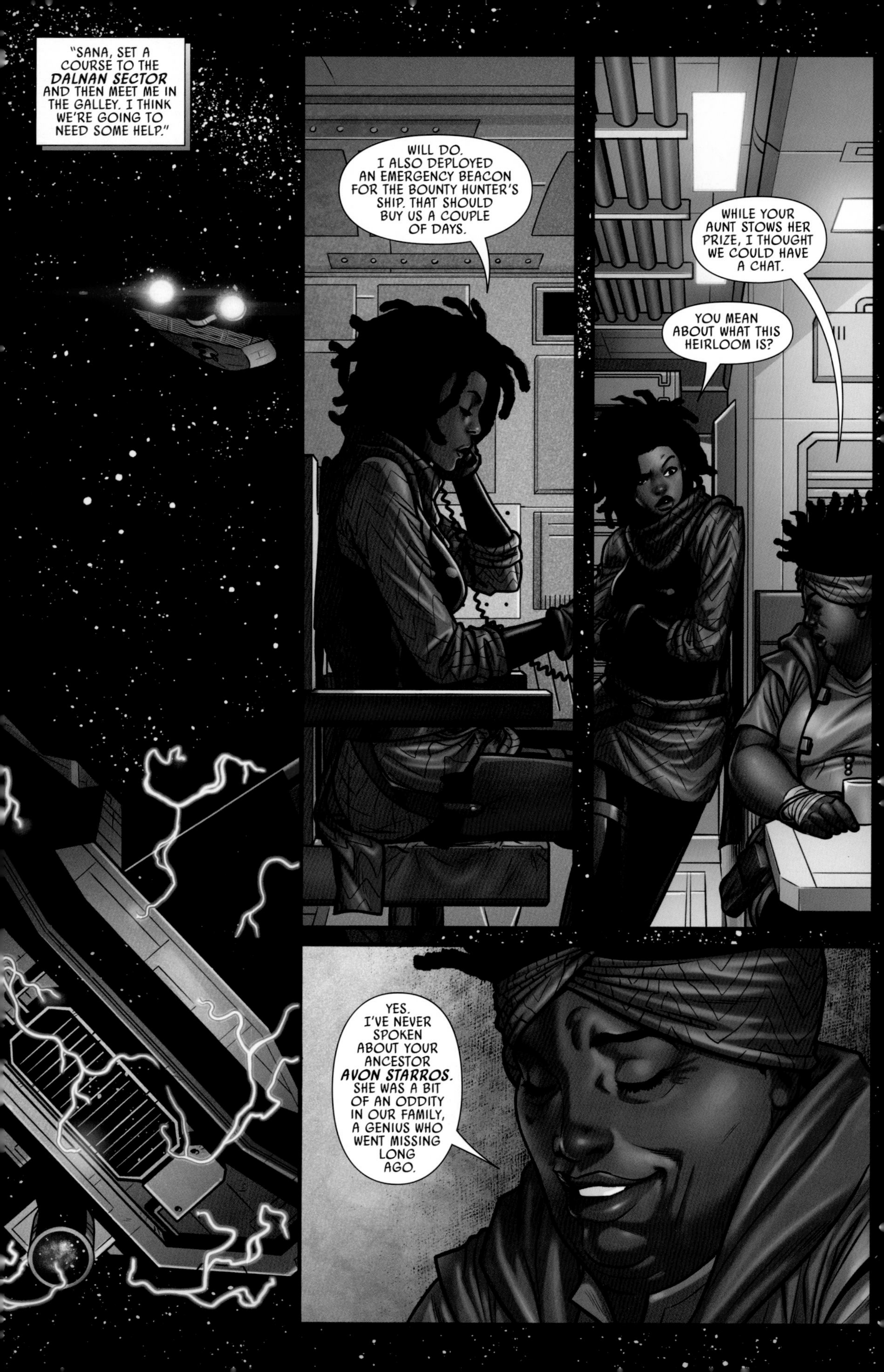
"SANA, SET A COURSE TO THE DALNAN SECTOR AND THEN MEET ME IN THE GALLEY. I THINK WE'RE GOING TO NEED SOME HELP."
WILL DO. I ALSO DEPLOYED AN EMERGENCY BEACON FOR THE BOUNTY HUNTER'S SHIP. THAT SHOULD BUY US A COUPLE OF DAYS.
WHILE YOUR AUNT STOWS HER PRIZE, I THOUGHT WE COULD HAVE A CHAT.
YOU MEAN ABOUT WHAT THIS HEIRLOOM IS?
YES. I'VE NEVER SPOKEN ABOUT YOUR ANCESTOR AVON STARROS. SHE WAS A BIT OF AN ODDITY IN OUR FAMILY, A GENIUS WHO WENT MISSING LONG AGO.

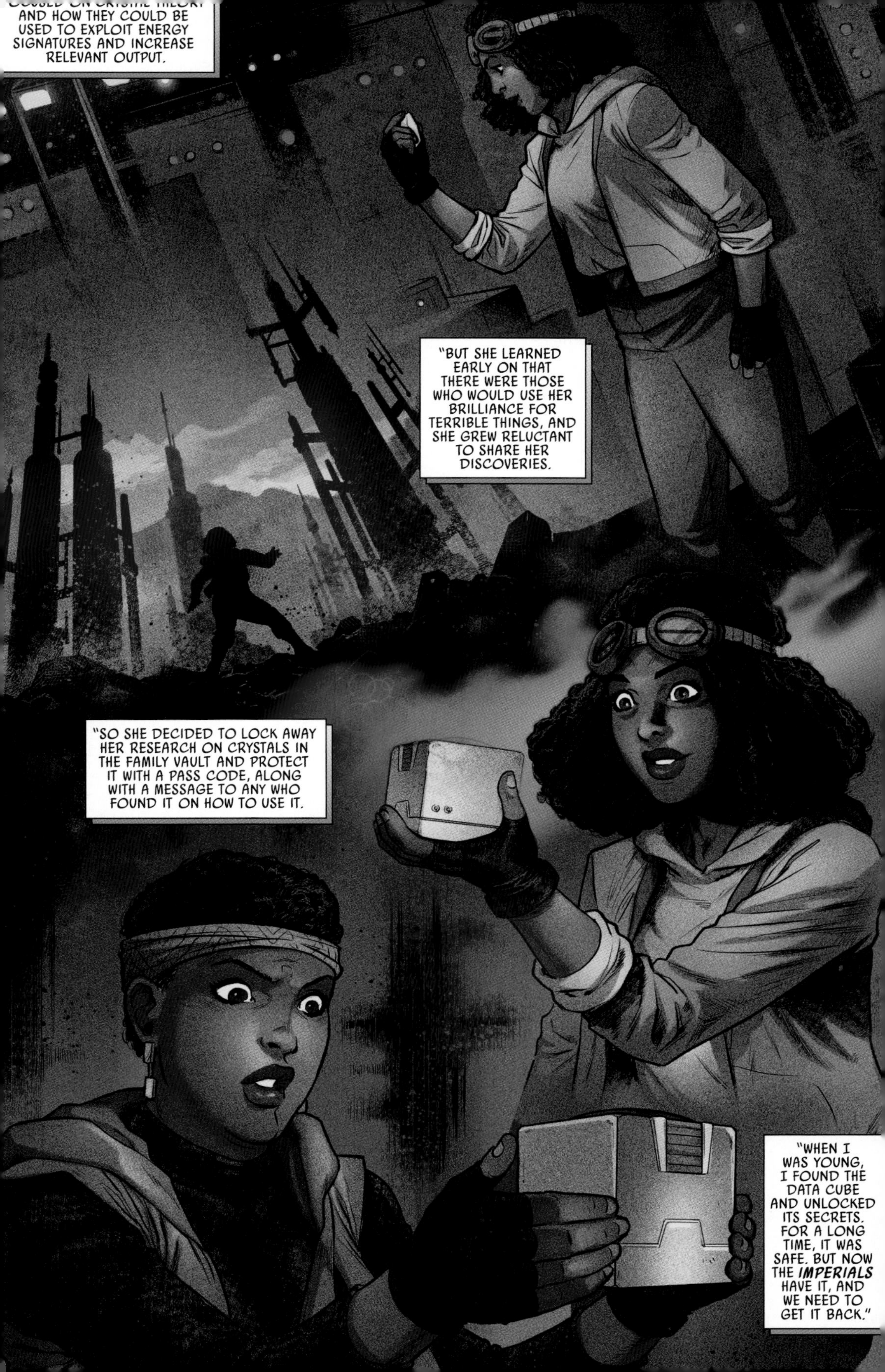
AND HOW THEY COULD BE USED TO EXPLOIT ENERGY SIGNATURES AND INCREASE RELEVANT OUTPUT.
"BUT SHE LEARNED EARLY ON THAT THERE WERE THOSE WHO WOULD USE HER BRILLIANCE FOR TERRIBLE THINGS, AND SHE GREW RELUCTANT TO SHARE HER DISCOVERIES.
"SO SHE DECIDED TO LOCK AWAY HER RESEARCH ON CRYSTALS IN THE FAMILY VAULT AND PROTECT IT WITH A PASS CODE, ALONG WITH A MESSAGE TO ANY WHO FOUND IT ON HOW TO USE IT.
"WHEN I WAS YOUNG, I FOUND THE DATA CUBE AND UNLOCKED ITS SECRETS. FOR A LONG TIME, IT WAS SAFE. BUT NOW THE *IMPERIALS* HAVE IT, AND WE NEED TO GET IT BACK."

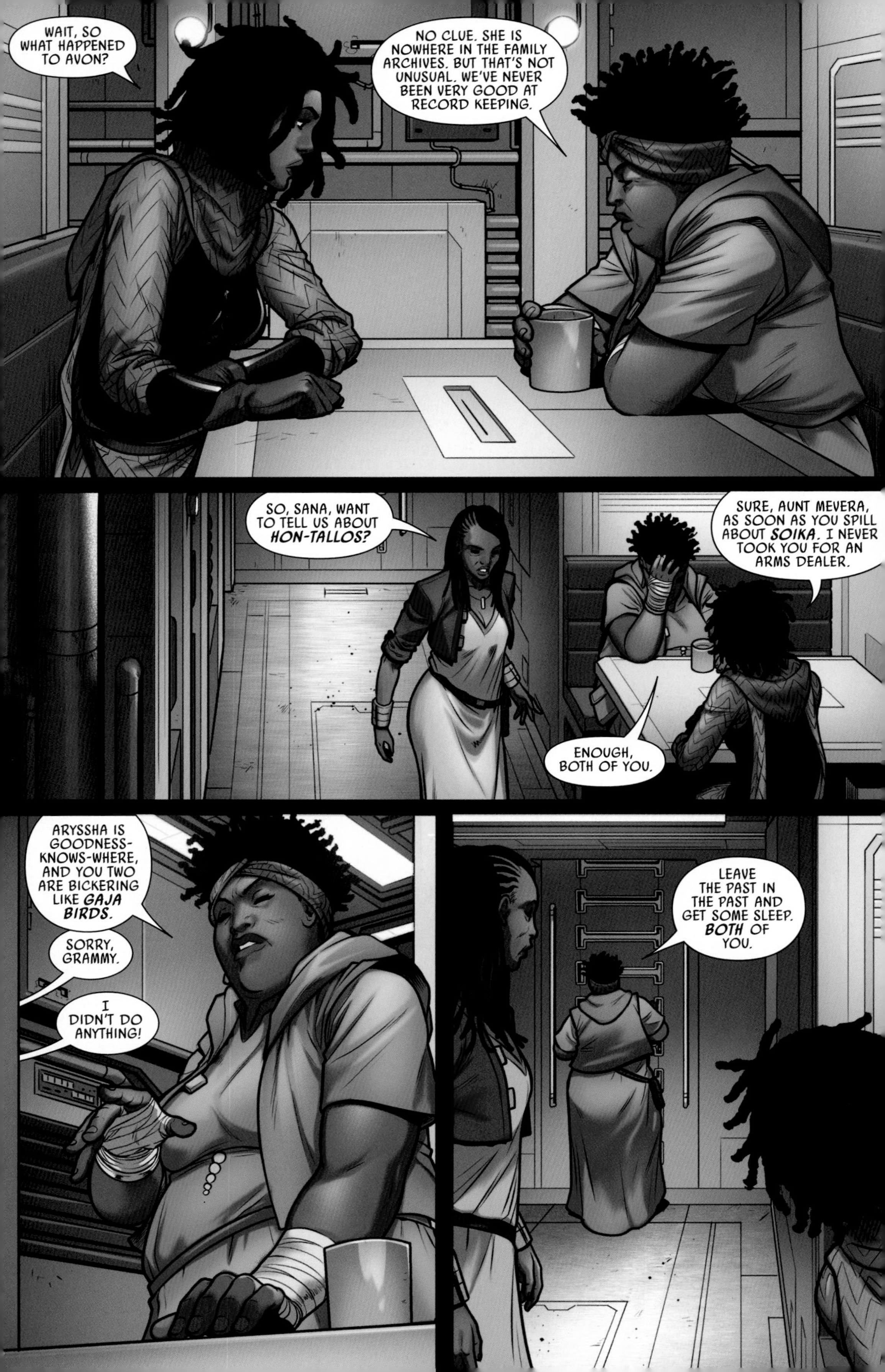
WAIT, SO WHAT HAPPENED TO AVON?
NO CLUE. SHE IS NOWHERE IN THE FAMILY ARCHIVES. BUT THAT'S NOT UNUSUAL. WE'VE NEVER BEEN VERY GOOD AT RECORD KEEPING.
SO, SANA, WANT TO TELL US ABOUT *HON-TALLOS?*
SURE, AUNT MEVERA, AS SOON AS YOU SPILL ABOUT *SOIKA*. I NEVER TOOK YOU FOR AN ARMS DEALER.
ENOUGH, BOTH OF YOU.
ARYSSHA IS GOODNESS-KNOWS-WHERE, AND YOU TWO ARE BICKERING LIKE *GAJA BIRDS*.
SORRY, GRAMMY.
I DIDN'T DO ANYTHING!
LEAVE THE PAST IN THE PAST AND GET SOME SLEEP. *BOTH* OF YOU.

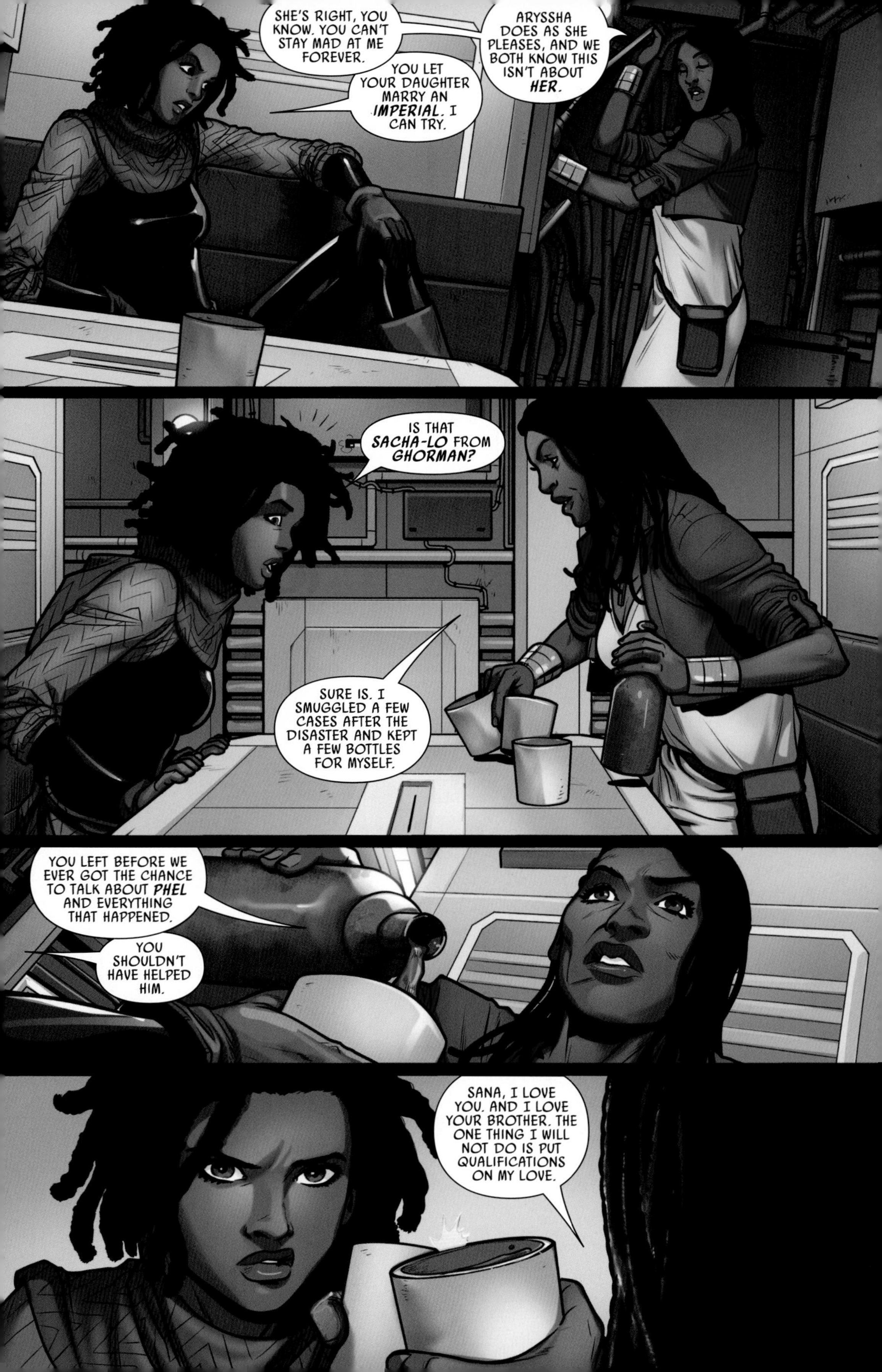
SHE'S RIGHT, YOU KNOW. YOU CAN'T STAY MAD AT ME FOREVER.
YOU LET YOUR DAUGHTER MARRY AN IMPERIAL. I CAN TRY.
ARYSSHA DOES AS SHE PLEASES, AND WE BOTH KNOW THIS ISN'T ABOUT HER.
IS THAT SACHA-LO FROM GHORMAN?
SURE IS. I SMUGGLED A FEW CASES AFTER THE DISASTER AND KEPT A FEW BOTTLES FOR MYSELF.
YOU LEFT BEFORE WE EVER GOT THE CHANCE TO TALK ABOUT PHEL AND EVERYTHING THAT HAPPENED.
YOU SHOULDN'T HAVE HELPED HIM.
SANA, I LOVE YOU. AND I LOVE YOUR BROTHER. THE ONE THING I WILL NOT DO IS PUT QUALIFICATIONS ON MY LOVE.

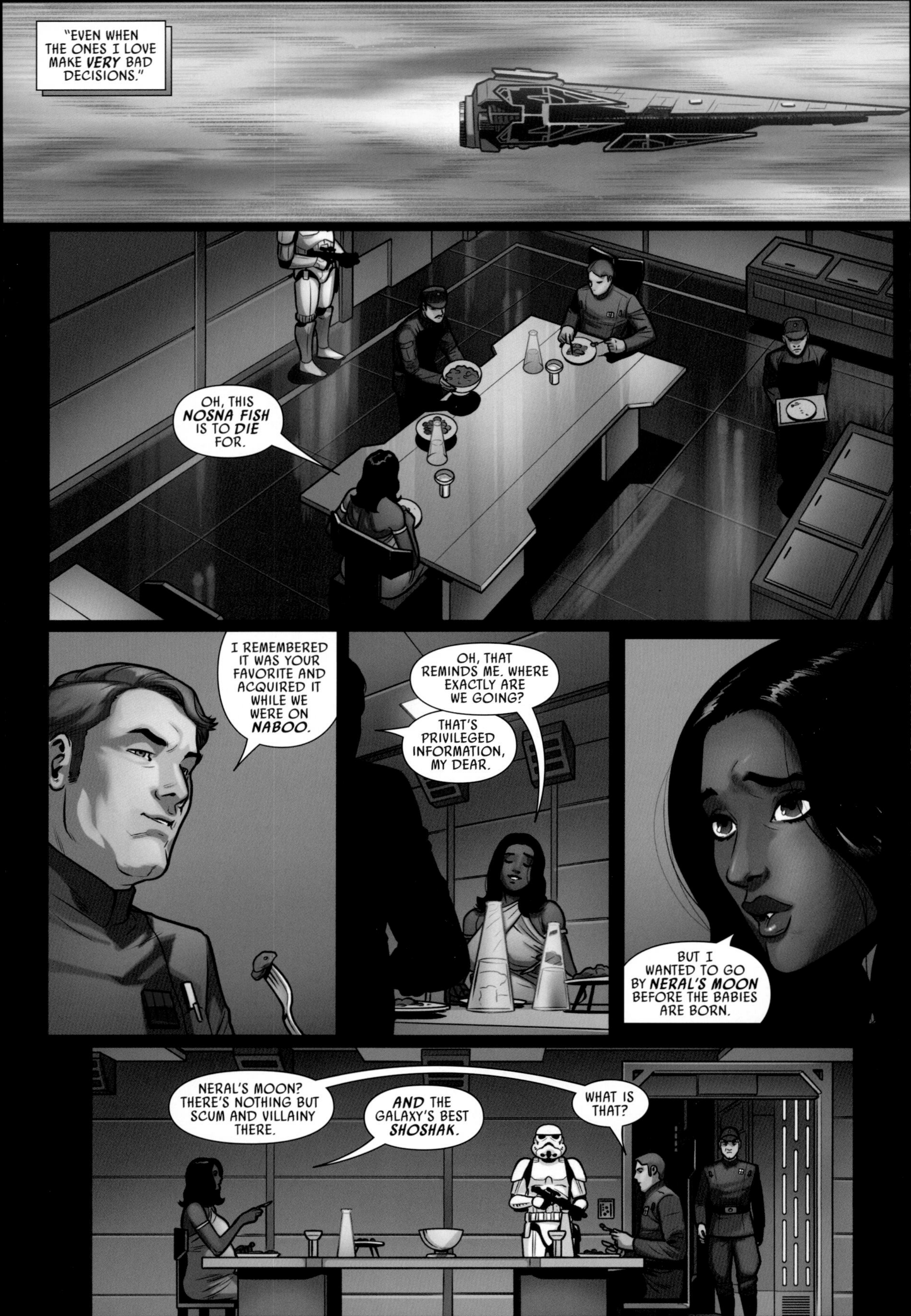
"EVEN WHEN THE ONES I LOVE MAKE *VERY* BAD DECISIONS."
OH, THIS ***NOSNA FISH*** IS TO ***DIE*** FOR.
I REMEMBERED IT WAS YOUR FAVORITE AND ACQUIRED IT WHILE WE WERE ON ***NABOO.***
OH, THAT REMINDS ME. WHERE EXACTLY ARE WE GOING?
THAT'S PRIVILEGED INFORMATION, MY DEAR.
BUT I WANTED TO GO BY ***NERAL'S MOON*** BEFORE THE BABIES ARE BORN.
NERAL'S MOON? THERE'S NOTHING BUT SCUM AND VILLAINY THERE.
AND THE GALAXY'S BEST ***SHOSHAK.***
WHAT IS THAT?

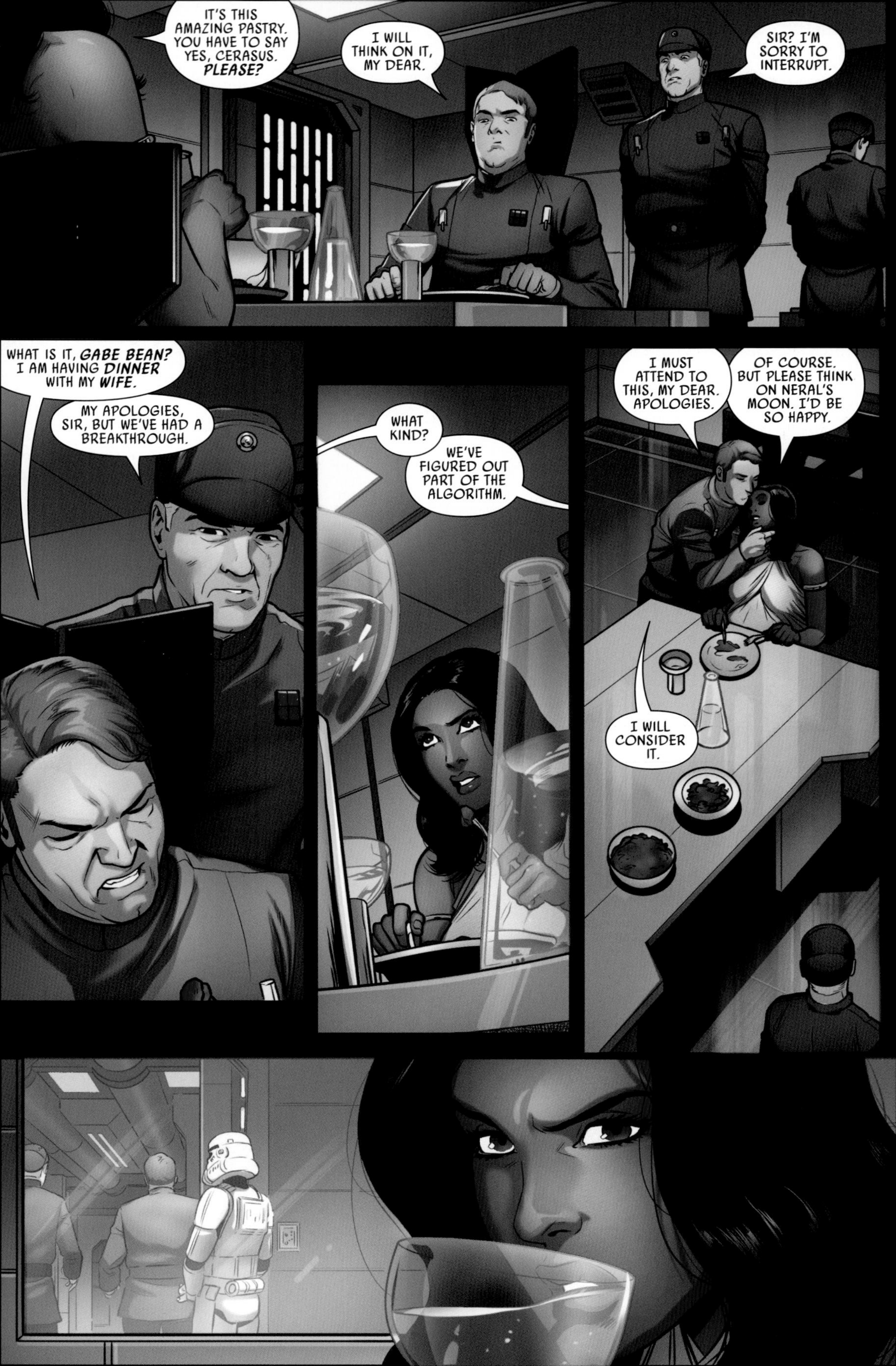
IT'S THIS AMAZING PASTRY. YOU HAVE TO SAY YES, CERASUS. PLEASE?
I WILL THINK ON IT, MY DEAR.
SIR? I'M SORRY TO INTERRUPT.
WHAT IS IT, GABE BEAN? I AM HAVING DINNER WITH MY WIFE.
MY APOLOGIES, SIR, BUT WE'VE HAD A BREAKTHROUGH.
WHAT KIND?
WE'VE FIGURED OUT PART OF THE ALGORITHM.
I MUST ATTEND TO THIS, MY DEAR. APOLOGIES.
OF COURSE. BUT PLEASE THINK ON NERAL'S MOON. I'D BE SO HAPPY.
I WILL CONSIDER IT.

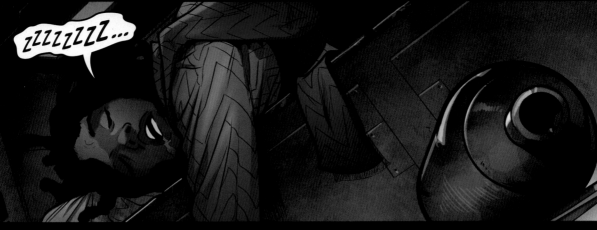

ZZZZZZZ...

SO, THERE I AM IN THE LECTURE ARGUING WITH *TOOB-NIX* BECAUSE HE'S *WRONG.*

THIS IS *AFTER* SHE SNUCK IN LATE THROUGH A WINDOW.

SO I TELL HIM HIS ARGUMENT IS FLAWED. AND GUESS WHO CHIMES IN?

WELL, HE *WAS* WRONG.

AND AFTER THAT DAY, I COULDN'T STOP THINKING ABOUT HER. *MY SANA,* DEFENDER OF ACADEMIC HONOR.

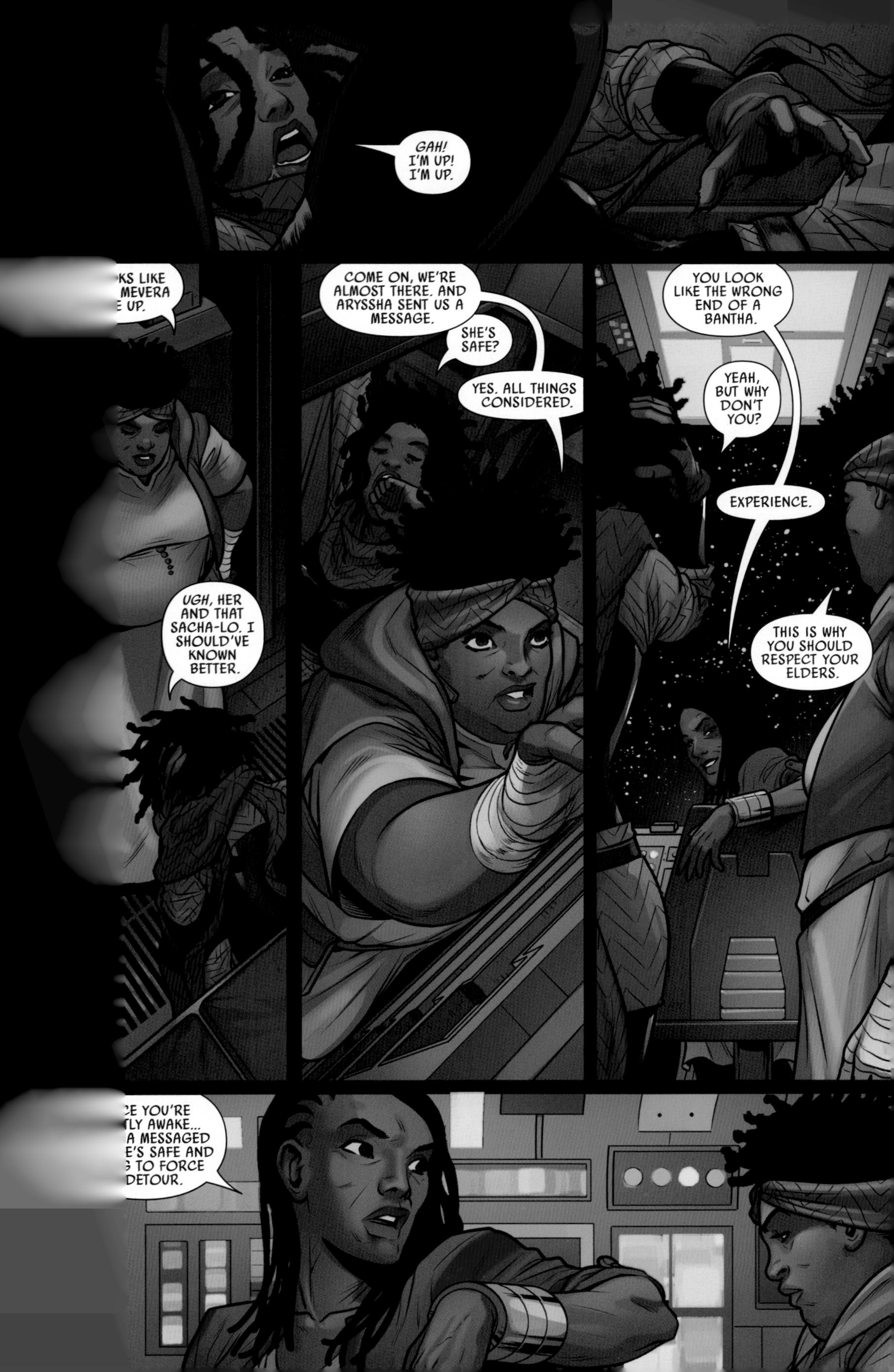
GAH! I'M UP! I'M UP.
KS LIKE MEVERA E UP.
COME ON, WE'RE ALMOST THERE. AND ARYSSHA SENT US A MESSAGE.
SHE'S SAFE?
YES. ALL THINGS CONSIDERED.
UGH, HER AND THAT SACHA-LO. I SHOULD'VE KNOWN BETTER.
YOU LOOK LIKE THE WRONG END OF A BANTHA.
YEAH, BUT WHY DON'T YOU?
EXPERIENCE.
THIS IS WHY YOU SHOULD RESPECT YOUR ELDERS.
CE YOU'RE TLY AWAKE... A MESSAGED E'S SAFE AND G TO FORCE DETOUR.

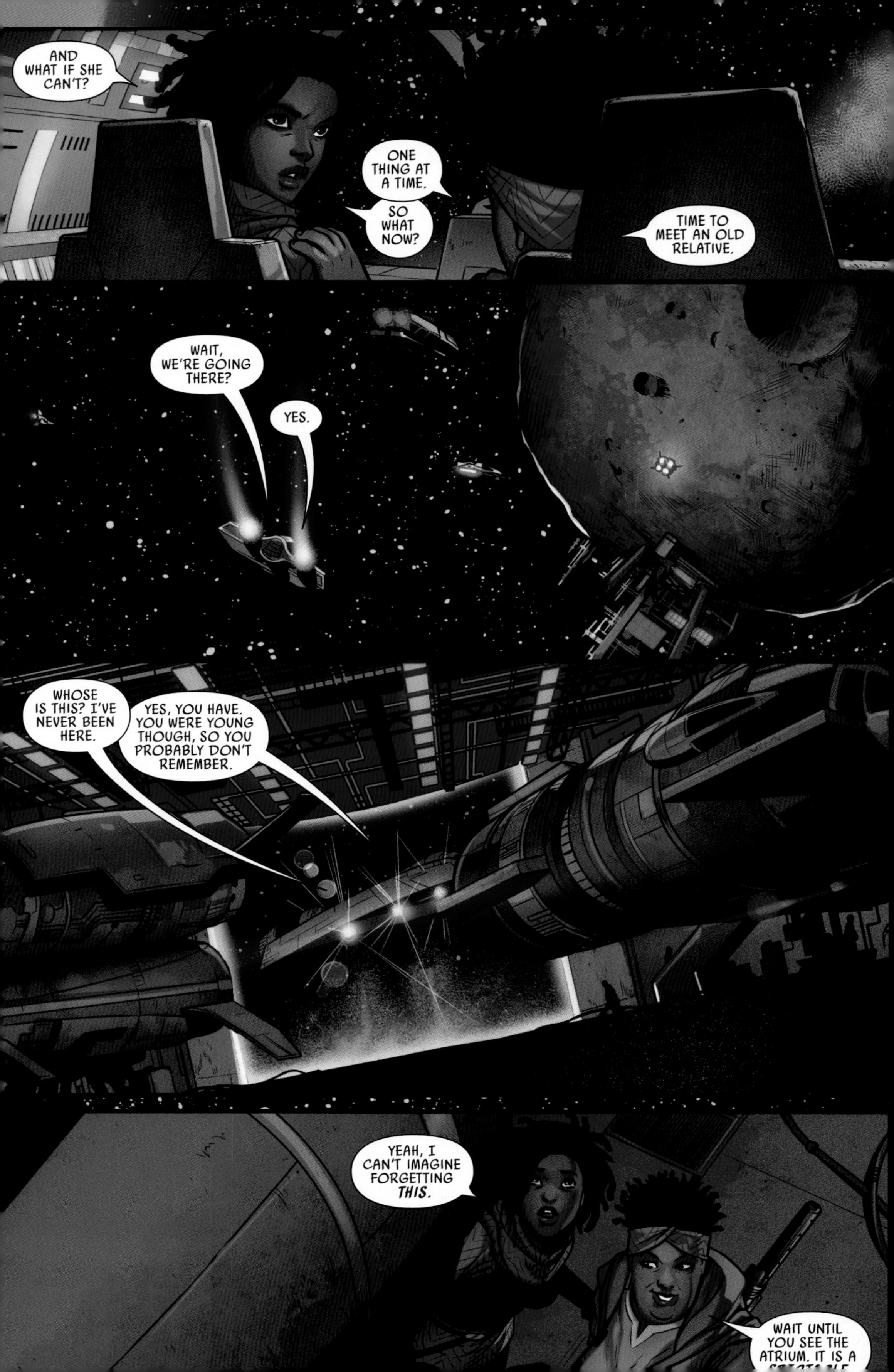
AND WHAT IF SHE CAN'T?
ONE THING AT A TIME.
SO WHAT NOW?
TIME TO MEET AN OLD RELATIVE.
WAIT, WE'RE GOING THERE?
YES.
WHOSE IS THIS? I'VE NEVER BEEN HERE.
YES, YOU HAVE. YOU WERE YOUNG THOUGH, SO YOU PROBABLY DON'T REMEMBER.
YEAH, I CAN'T IMAGINE FORGETTING *THIS.*
WAIT UNTIL YOU SEE THE ATRIUM. IT IS A

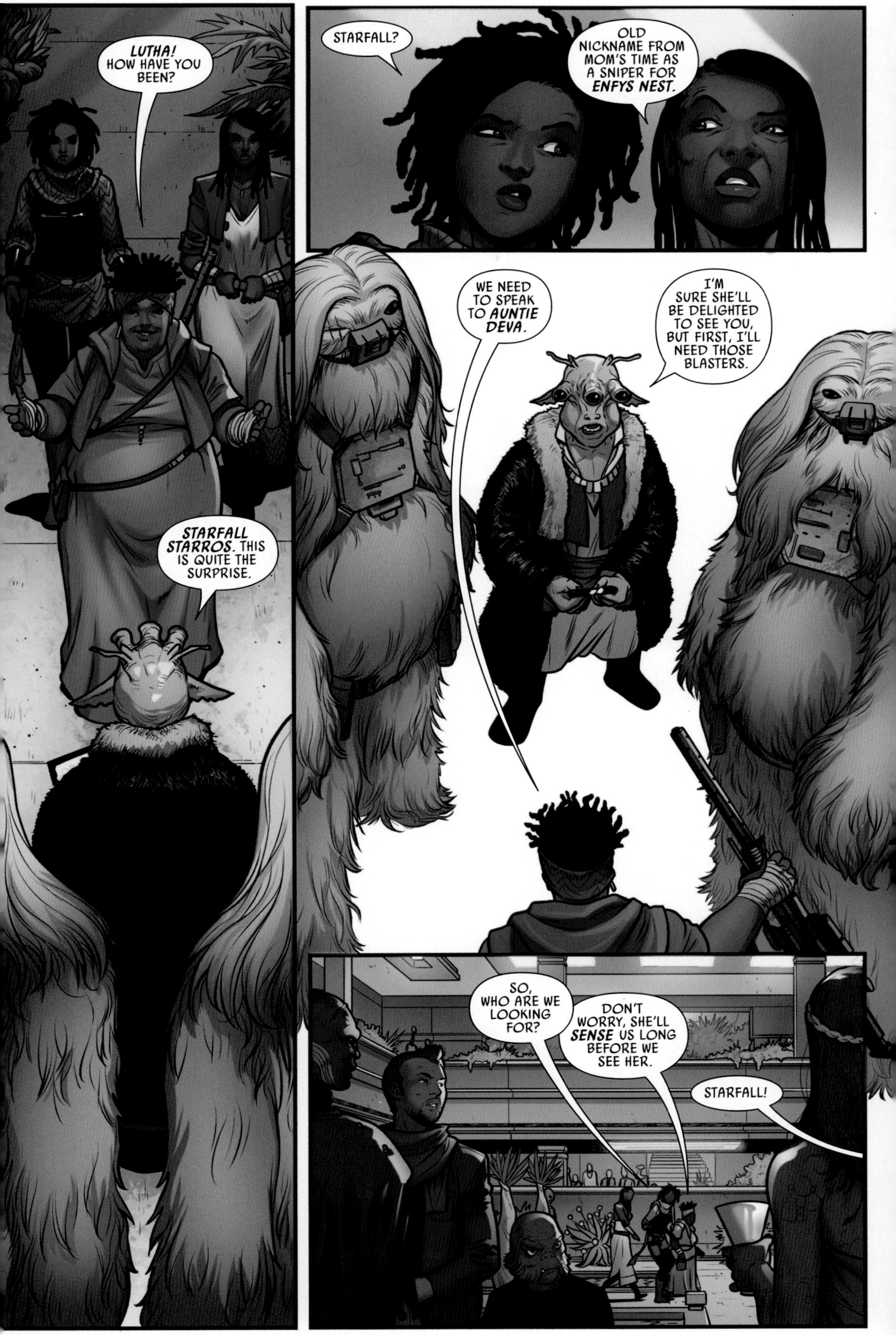
LUTHA! HOW HAVE YOU BEEN?
STARFALL STARROS. THIS IS QUITE THE SURPRISE.
STARFALL?
OLD NICKNAME FROM MOM'S TIME AS A SNIPER FOR ENFYS NEST.
WE NEED TO SPEAK TO AUNTIE DEVA.
I'M SURE SHE'LL BE DELIGHTED TO SEE YOU, BUT FIRST, I'LL NEED THOSE BLASTERS.
SO, WHO ARE WE LOOKING FOR?
DON'T WORRY, SHE'LL SENSE US LONG BEFORE WE SEE HER.
STARFALL!

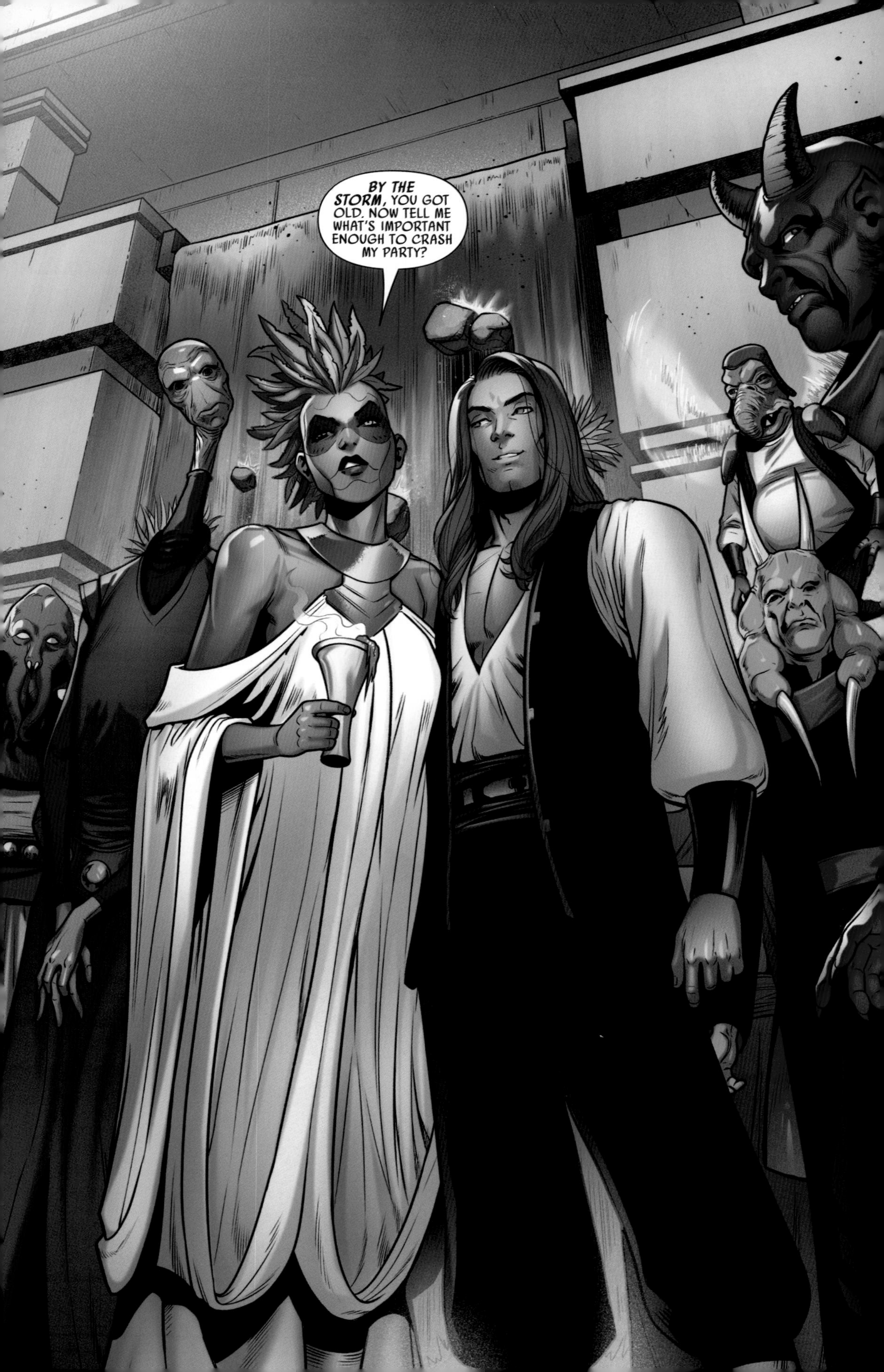
BY THE STORM, YOU GOT OLD. NOW TELL ME WHAT'S IMPORTANT ENOUGH TO CRASH MY PARTY?

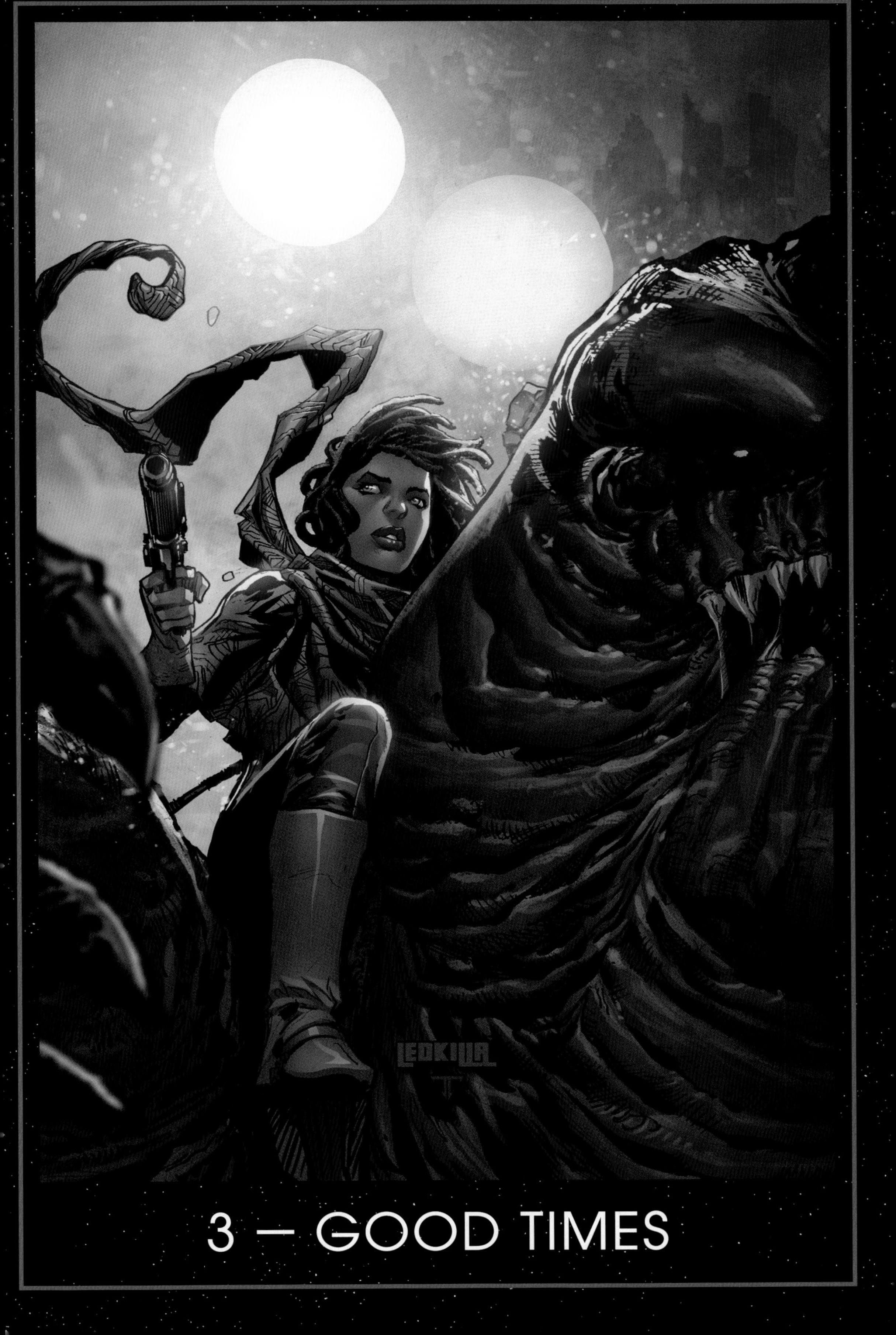

3 — GOOD TIMES

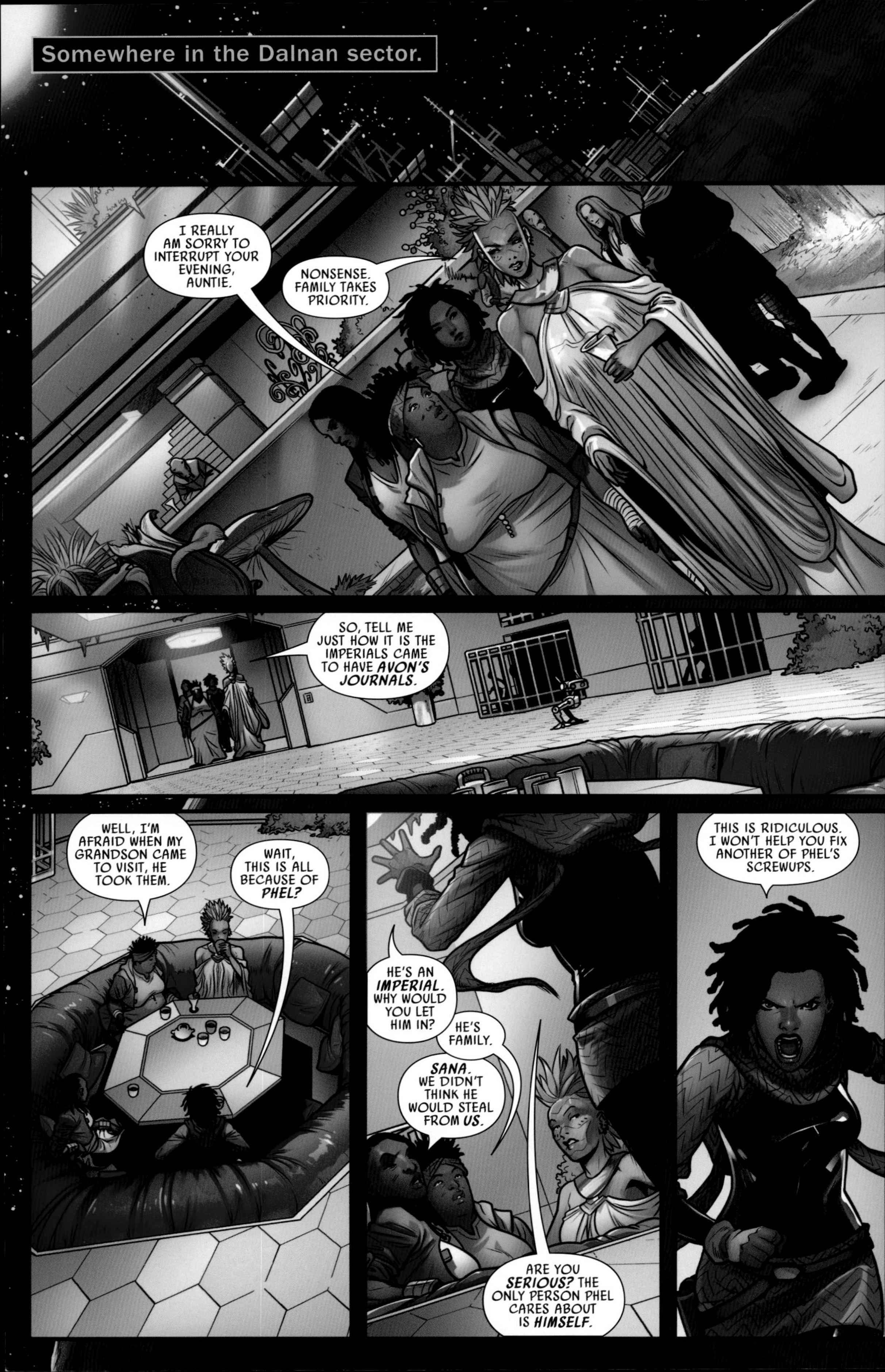
Somewhere in the Dalnan sector.
I REALLY AM SORRY TO INTERRUPT YOUR EVENING, AUNTIE.
NONSENSE. FAMILY TAKES PRIORITY.
SO, TELL ME JUST HOW IT IS THE IMPERIALS CAME TO HAVE AVON'S JOURNALS.
WELL, I'M AFRAID WHEN MY GRANDSON CAME TO VISIT, HE TOOK THEM.
WAIT, THIS IS ALL BECAUSE OF PHEL?
HE'S AN IMPERIAL. WHY WOULD YOU LET HIM IN?
HE'S FAMILY.
SANA. WE DIDN'T THINK HE WOULD STEAL FROM US.
ARE YOU SERIOUS? THE ONLY PERSON PHEL CARES ABOUT IS HIMSELF.
THIS IS RIDICULOUS. I WON'T HELP YOU FIX ANOTHER OF PHEL'S SCREWUPS.

MURMUR MURMUR

HAHA HAHAHA

PHEL! ALWAYS PHEL. I SHOULD'VE GONE TO VISIT *MY DADS* INSTEAD.

JORU, PLEASE. NEAT.

THAT BAD?

THE USUAL. FAMILY, YOU KNOW?

MORE THAN JUST ABOUT ANYONE. I'M *LANITRA*, BY THE WAY.

A PLEASURE.

YES. IT IS.

WHAT BRINGS YOU TO THIS ROCK?

I HAVE A FAVOR TO ASK OF *MISTRESS LOMPOP.* YOU?

I'M ACTUALLY NOT ALL THAT SURE RIGHT NOW.

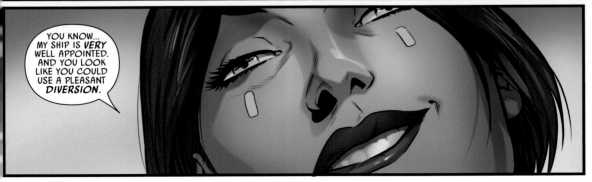

YOU KNOW... MY SHIP IS *VERY* WELL APPOINTED. AND YOU LOOK LIKE YOU COULD USE A PLEASANT *DIVERSION.*

YOU KNOW, THAT ACTUALLY SOUNDS REALLY, REALLY NICE.

OH GOOD, YOU TWO HAVE MET. WE LEAVE FOR HON-TALLOS IN THREE HOURS.

I THOUGHT YOU SAID IT WAS TOO RISKY.

EH, I FOUND HELP.

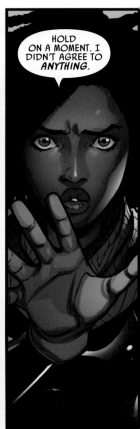

HOLD ON A MOMENT. I DIDN'T AGREE TO ANYTHING.

SANA, HAVE ANOTHER DRINK AND RELAX. LANITRA?

YES?

TELL YOUR FRIENDS.

BE CAREFUL WITH THAT ONE--SHE'S A HANDFUL.

SO SHE WORKS FOR YOU.

EVERYONE HERE WORKS FOR ME. MOST OF THEM JUST DON'T KNOW IT YET.

DID MY AUNT AND GRANDMOTHER SEND YOU OUT HERE?

NOPE. THEY TOLD ME TO LEAVE YOU BE. SOMETHING ABOUT A HARD HEAD.

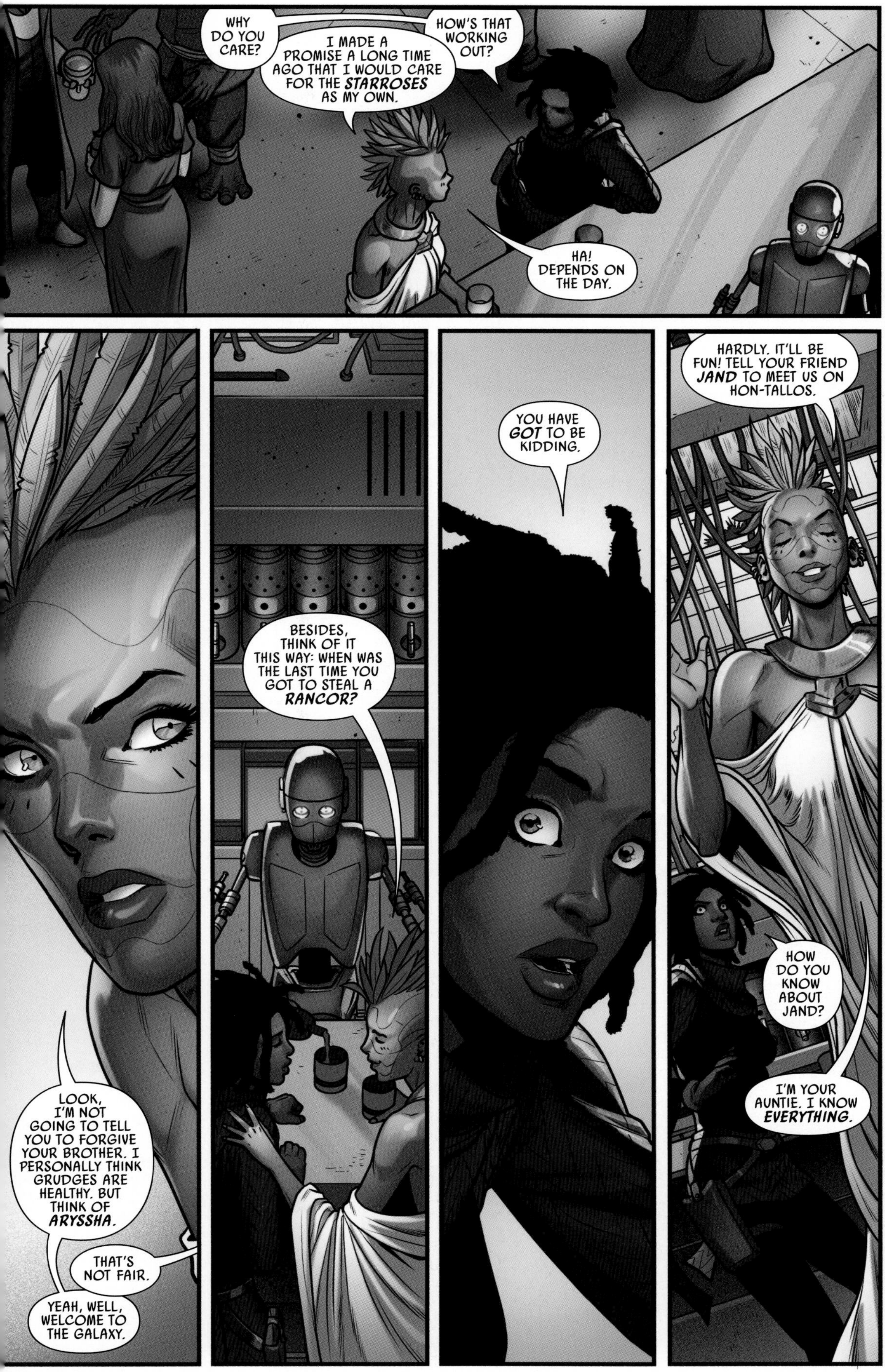
WHY DO YOU CARE?
I MADE A PROMISE A LONG TIME AGO THAT I WOULD CARE FOR THE STARROSES AS MY OWN.
HOW'S THAT WORKING OUT?
HA! DEPENDS ON THE DAY.
LOOK, I'M NOT GOING TO TELL YOU TO FORGIVE YOUR BROTHER. I PERSONALLY THINK GRUDGES ARE HEALTHY. BUT THINK OF ARYSSHA.
THAT'S NOT FAIR.
YEAH, WELL, WELCOME TO THE GALAXY.
BESIDES, THINK OF IT THIS WAY: WHEN WAS THE LAST TIME YOU GOT TO STEAL A RANCOR?
YOU HAVE GOT TO BE KIDDING.
HARDLY. IT'LL BE FUN! TELL YOUR FRIEND JAND TO MEET US ON HON-TALLOS.
HOW DO YOU KNOW ABOUT JAND?
I'M YOUR AUNTIE. I KNOW EVERYTHING.

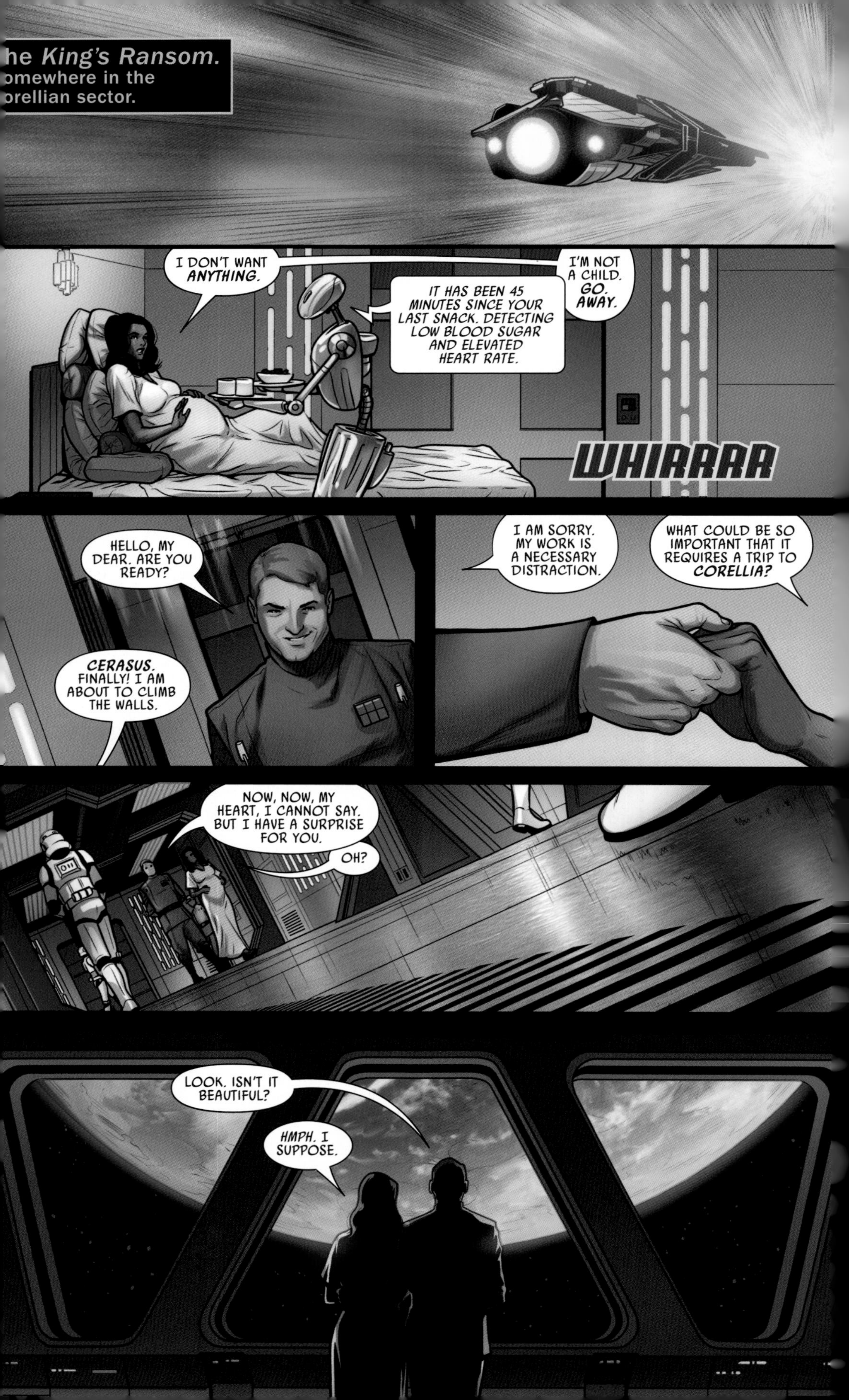

he King's Ransom.
omewhere in the
orellian sector.
I DON'T WANT ANYTHING.
IT HAS BEEN 45 MINUTES SINCE YOUR LAST SNACK. DETECTING LOW BLOOD SUGAR AND ELEVATED HEART RATE.
I'M NOT A CHILD. GO. AWAY.
WHIRRRR
HELLO, MY DEAR. ARE YOU READY?
CERASUS. FINALLY! I AM ABOUT TO CLIMB THE WALLS.
I AM SORRY. MY WORK IS A NECESSARY DISTRACTION.
WHAT COULD BE SO IMPORTANT THAT IT REQUIRES A TRIP TO CORELLIA?
NOW, NOW, MY HEART, I CANNOT SAY. BUT I HAVE A SURPRISE FOR YOU.
OH?
LOOK. ISN'T IT BEAUTIFUL?
HMPH. I SUPPOSE.

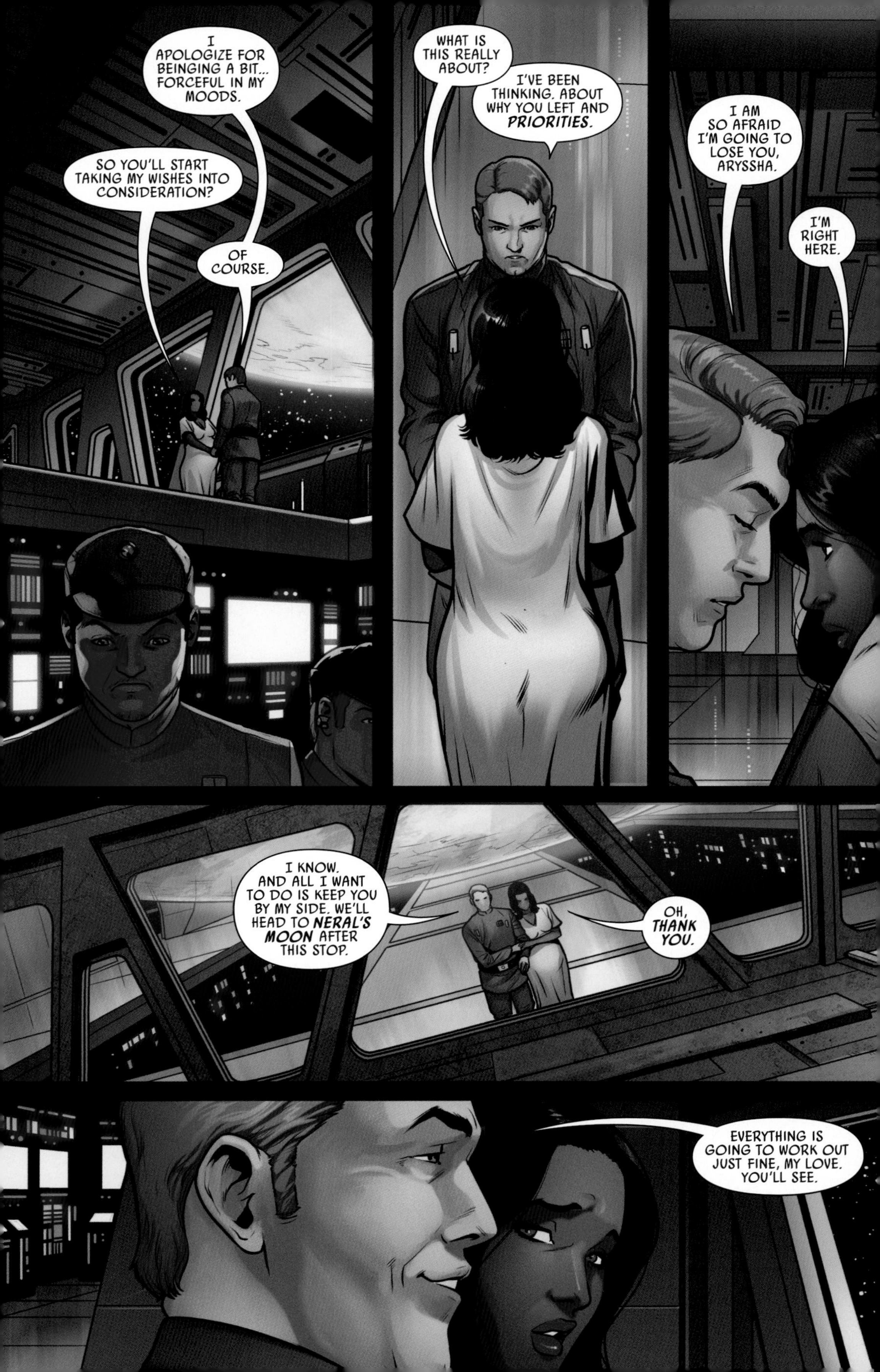
I APOLOGIZE FOR BEINGING A BIT... FORCEFUL IN MY MOODS.
SO YOU'LL START TAKING MY WISHES INTO CONSIDERATION?
OF COURSE.
WHAT IS THIS REALLY ABOUT?
I'VE BEEN THINKING. ABOUT WHY YOU LEFT AND PRIORITIES.
I AM SO AFRAID I'M GOING TO LOSE YOU, ARYSSHA.
I'M RIGHT HERE.
I KNOW. AND ALL I WANT TO DO IS KEEP YOU BY MY SIDE. WE'LL HEAD TO NERAL'S MOON AFTER THIS STOP.
OH, THANK YOU.
EVERYTHING IS GOING TO WORK OUT JUST FINE, MY LOVE. YOU'LL SEE.

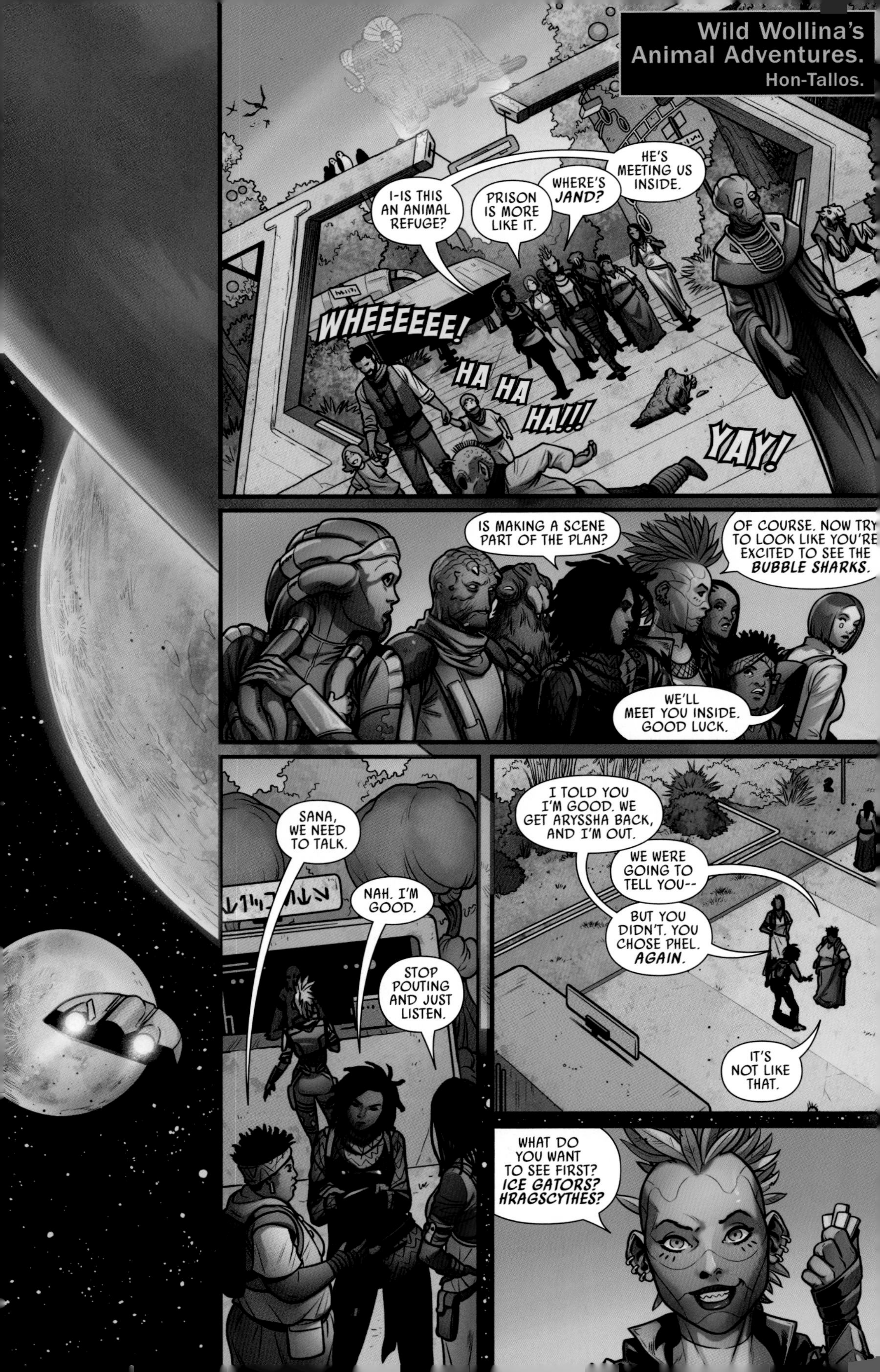
Wild Wollina's Animal Adventures.
Hon-Tallos.
I-IS THIS AN ANIMAL REFUGE?
PRISON IS MORE LIKE IT.
WHERE'S JAND?
HE'S MEETING US INSIDE.
WHEEEEEE!
HA HA HA!!!
YAY!
IS MAKING A SCENE PART OF THE PLAN?
OF COURSE. NOW TRY TO LOOK LIKE YOU'RE EXCITED TO SEE THE BUBBLE SHARKS.
WE'LL MEET YOU INSIDE. GOOD LUCK.
SANA, WE NEED TO TALK.
NAH. I'M GOOD.
STOP POUTING AND JUST LISTEN.
I TOLD YOU I'M GOOD. WE GET ARYSSHA BACK, AND I'M OUT.
WE WERE GOING TO TELL YOU--
BUT YOU DIDN'T. YOU CHOSE PHEL. AGAIN.
IT'S NOT LIKE THAT.
WHAT DO YOU WANT TO SEE FIRST? ICE GATORS? HRAGSCYTHES?

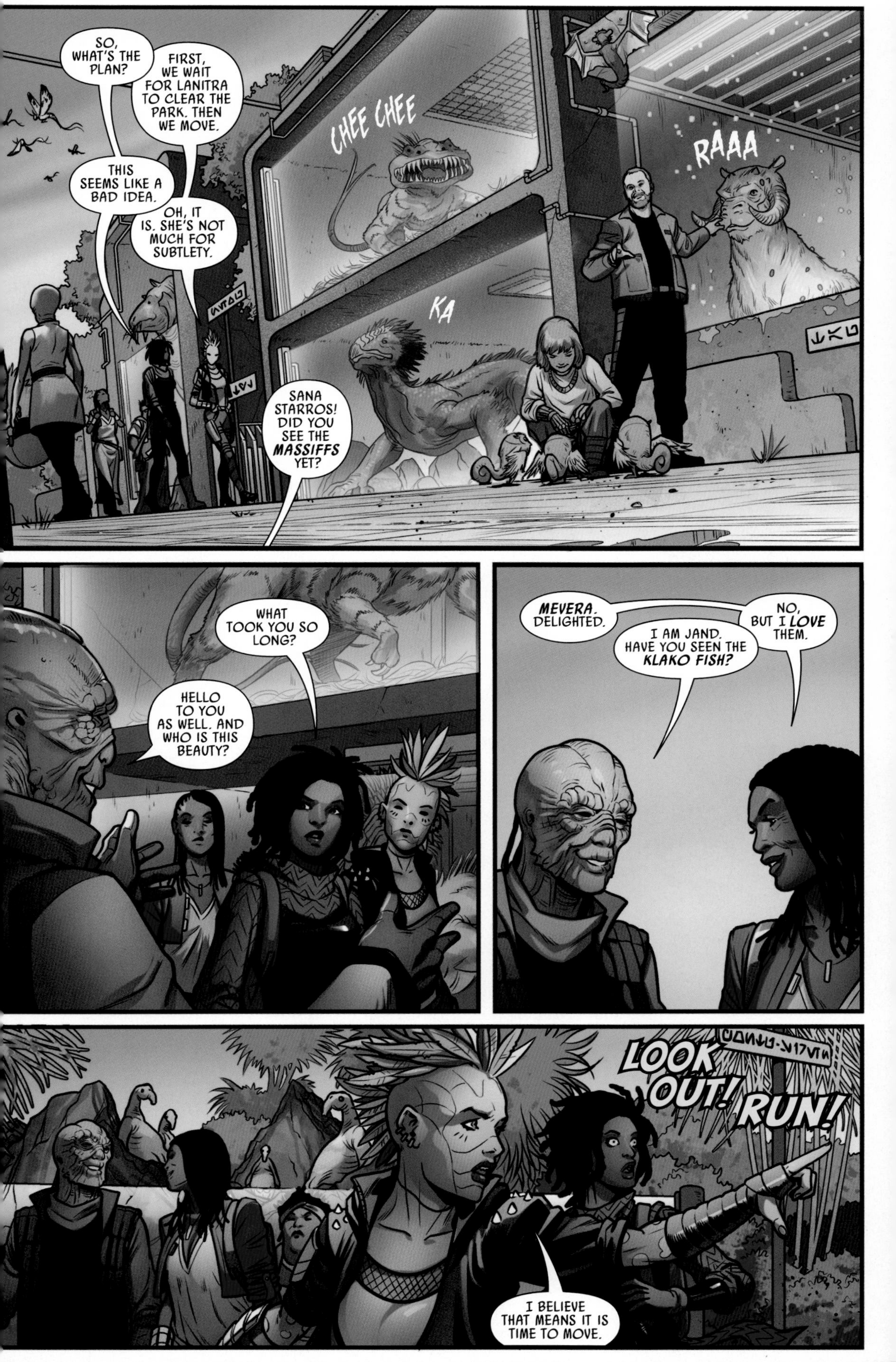
SO, WHAT'S THE PLAN?
FIRST, WE WAIT FOR LANITRA TO CLEAR THE PARK. THEN WE MOVE.
CHEE CHEE
RAAA
THIS SEEMS LIKE A BAD IDEA.
OH, IT IS. SHE'S NOT MUCH FOR SUBTLETY.
KA
SANA STARROS! DID YOU SEE THE MASSIFFS YET?
WHAT TOOK YOU SO LONG?
HELLO TO YOU AS WELL. AND WHO IS THIS BEAUTY?
MEVERA. DELIGHTED.
I AM JAND. HAVE YOU SEEN THE KLAKO FISH?
NO, BUT I LOVE THEM.
LOOK OUT! RUN!
I BELIEVE THAT MEANS IT IS TIME TO MOVE.

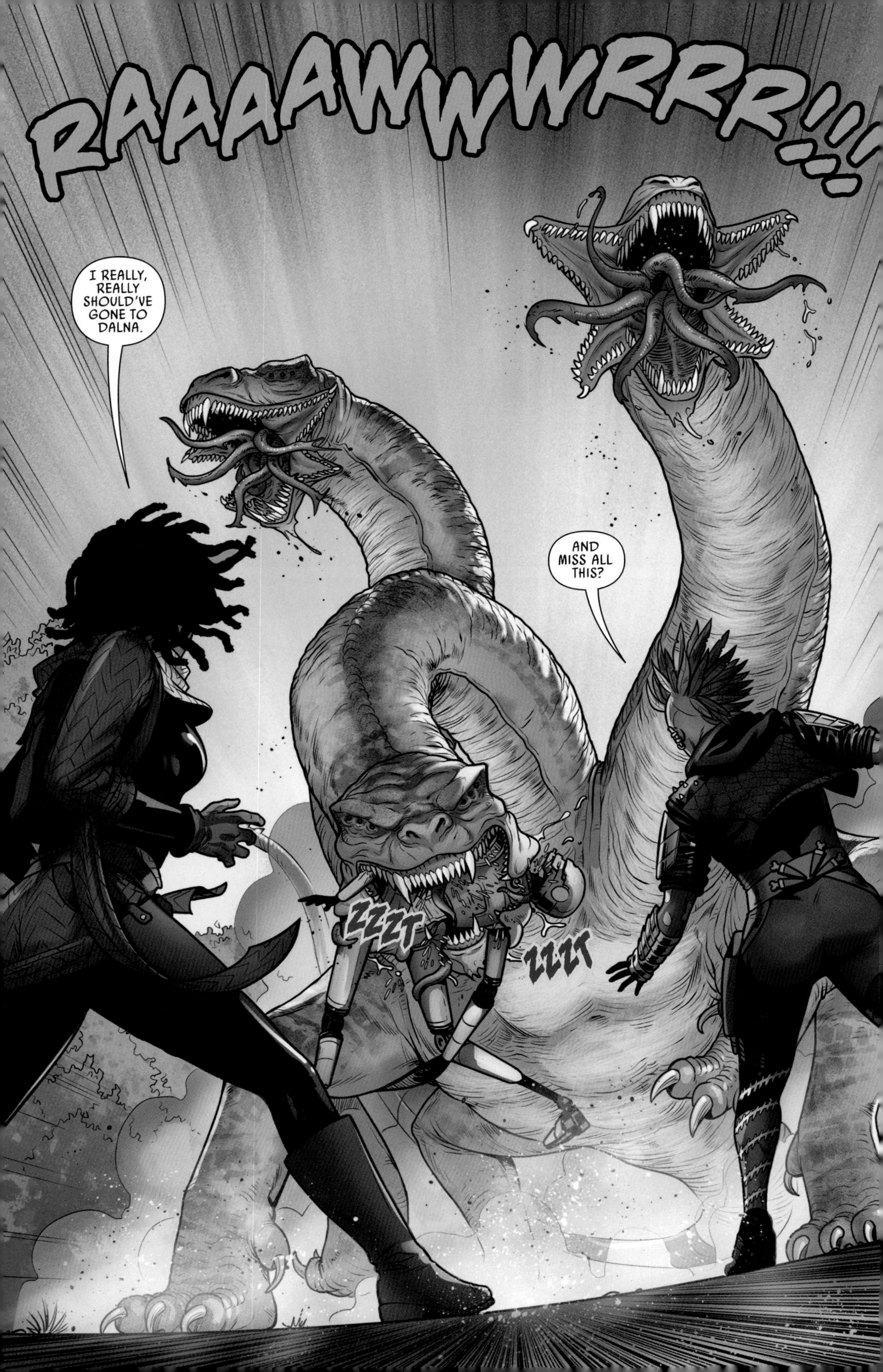
RAAAAWWWRRR!!!!
I REALLY, REALLY SHOULD'VE GONE TO DALNA.
AND MISS ALL THIS?
ZZZT
ZZZT

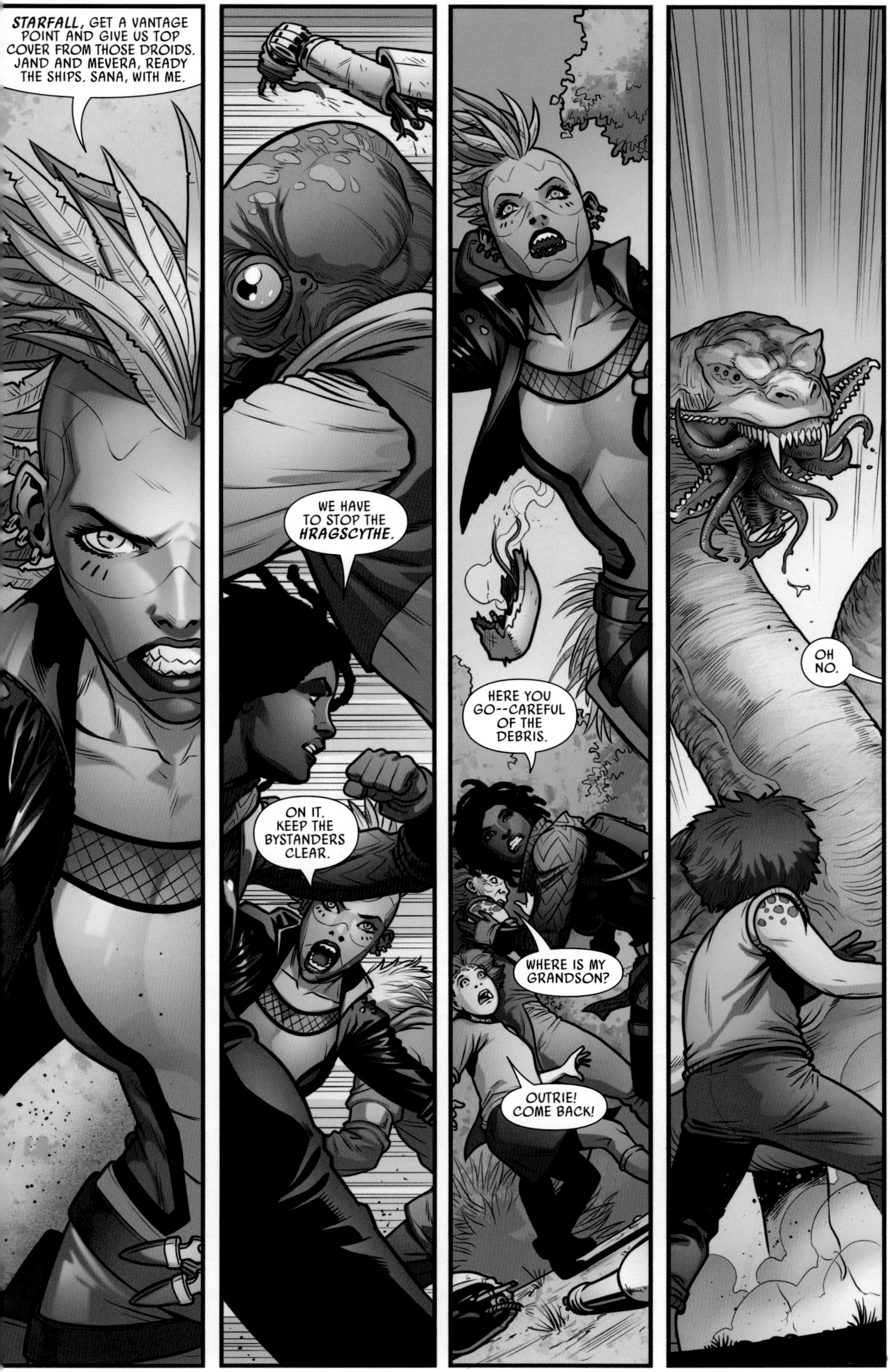
STARFALL, GET A VANTAGE POINT AND GIVE US TOP COVER FROM THOSE DROIDS. JAND AND MEVERA, READY THE SHIPS. SANA, WITH ME.
WE HAVE TO STOP THE HRAGSCYTHE.
ON IT. KEEP THE BYSTANDERS CLEAR.
HERE YOU GO--CAREFUL OF THE DEBRIS.
WHERE IS MY GRANDSON?
OUTRIE! COME BACK!
OH NO.

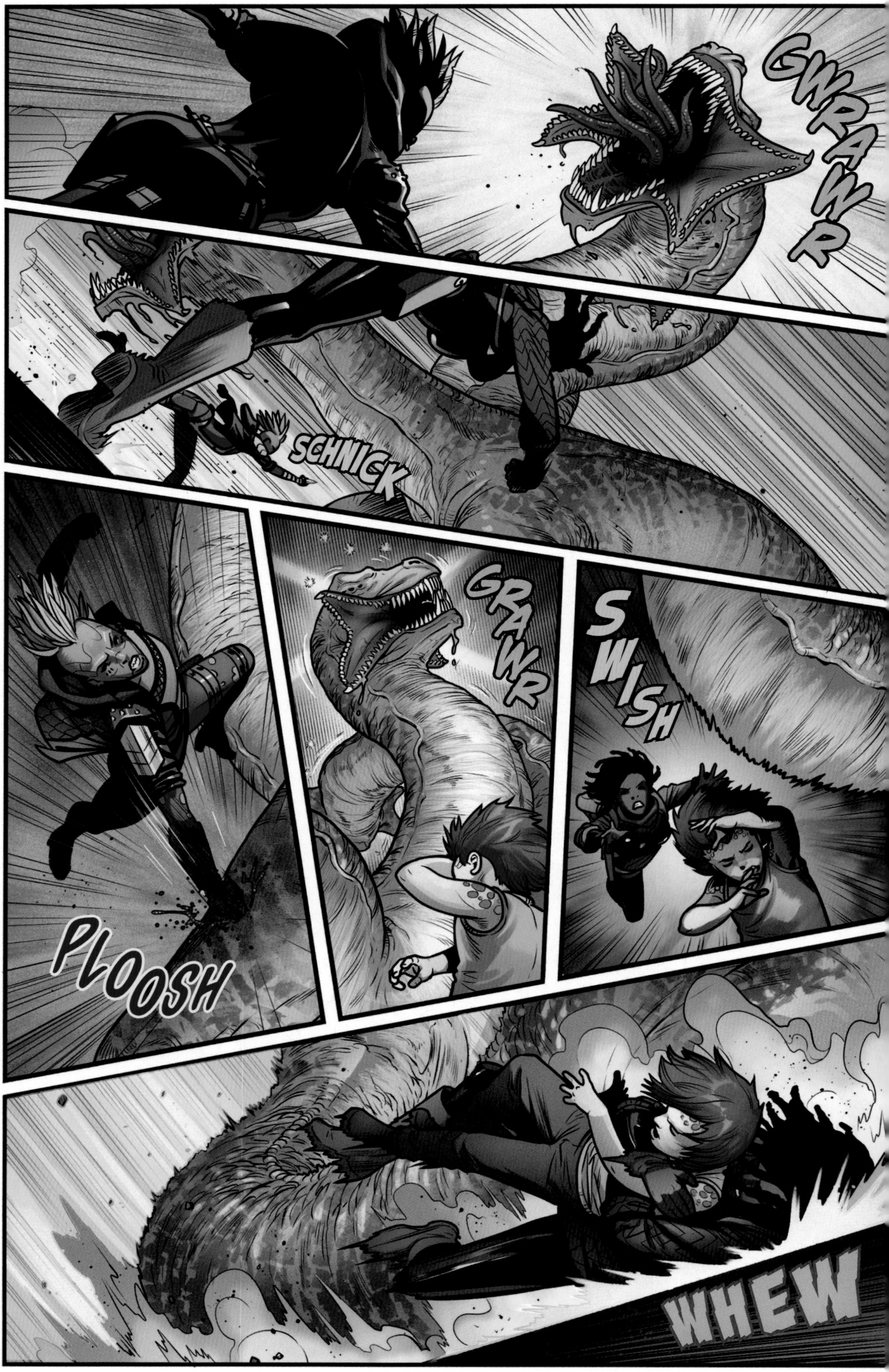
GWRAWR
SCHNICK
PLOOSH
GRAWR
SWISH
WHEW

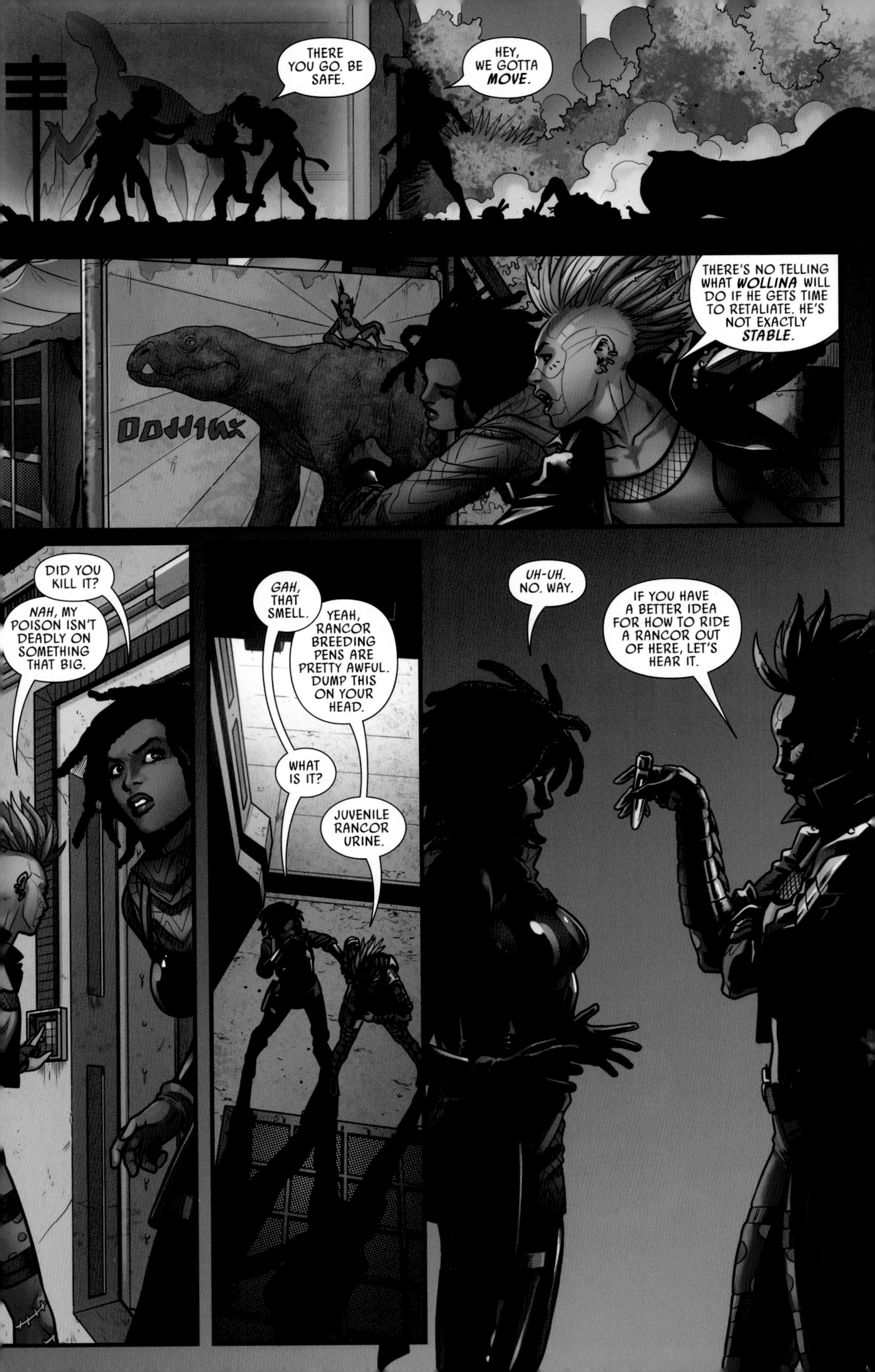
THERE YOU GO. BE SAFE.
HEY, WE GOTTA MOVE.
THERE'S NO TELLING WHAT WOLLINA WILL DO IF HE GETS TIME TO RETALIATE. HE'S NOT EXACTLY STABLE.
DID YOU KILL IT?
NAH, MY POISON ISN'T DEADLY ON SOMETHING THAT BIG.
GAH, THAT SMELL.
YEAH, RANCOR BREEDING PENS ARE PRETTY AWFUL. DUMP THIS ON YOUR HEAD.
WHAT IS IT?
JUVENILE RANCOR URINE.
UH-UH. NO. WAY.
IF YOU HAVE A BETTER IDEA FOR HOW TO RIDE A RANCOR OUT OF HERE, LET'S HEAR IT.

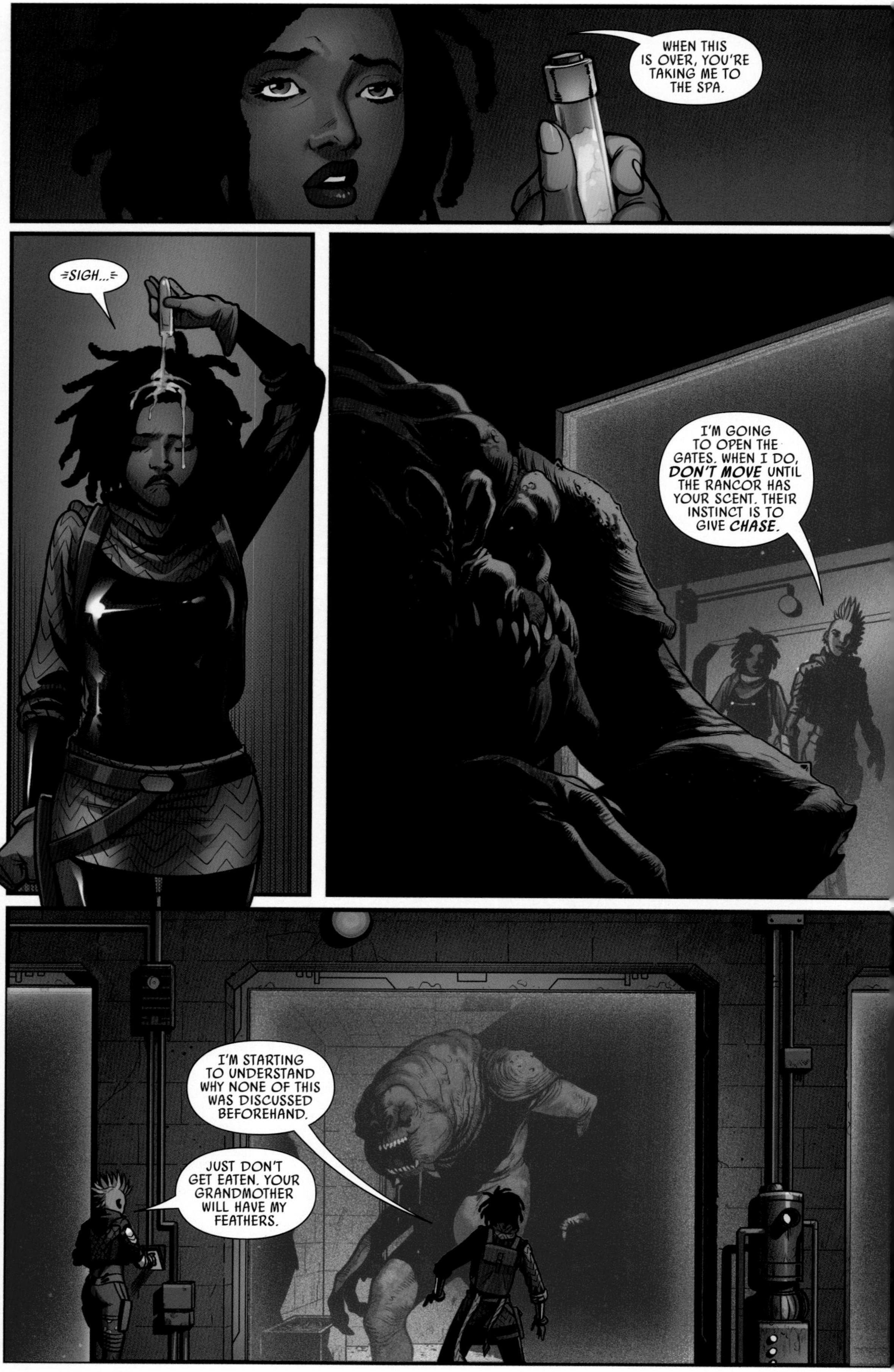
WHEN THIS IS OVER, YOU'RE TAKING ME TO THE SPA.
≡SIGH...≡
I'M GOING TO OPEN THE GATES. WHEN I DO, DON'T MOVE UNTIL THE RANCOR HAS YOUR SCENT. THEIR INSTINCT IS TO GIVE CHASE.
I'M STARTING TO UNDERSTAND WHY NONE OF THIS WAS DISCUSSED BEFOREHAND.
JUST DON'T GET EATEN. YOUR GRANDMOTHER WILL HAVE MY FEATHERS.

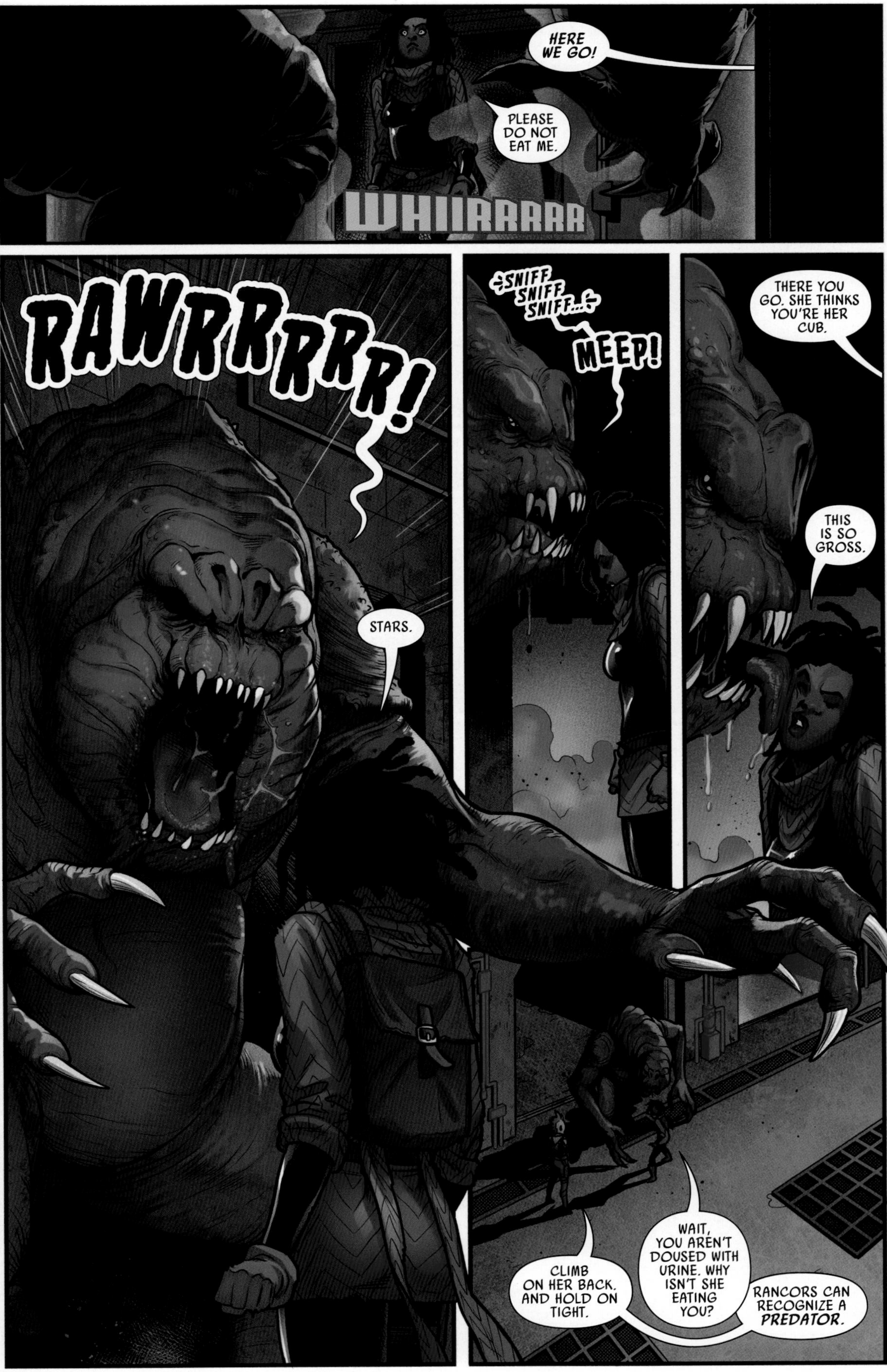
HERE WE GO!
PLEASE DO NOT EAT ME.
WHIIRRRRR
RAWRRRRRR!
STARS.
SNIFF SNIFF SNIFF...
MEEP!
THERE YOU GO. SHE THINKS YOU'RE HER CUB.
THIS IS SO GROSS.
CLIMB ON HER BACK. AND HOLD ON TIGHT.
WAIT, YOU AREN'T DOUSED WITH URINE. WHY ISN'T SHE EATING YOU?
RANCORS CAN RECOGNIZE A *PREDATOR*.

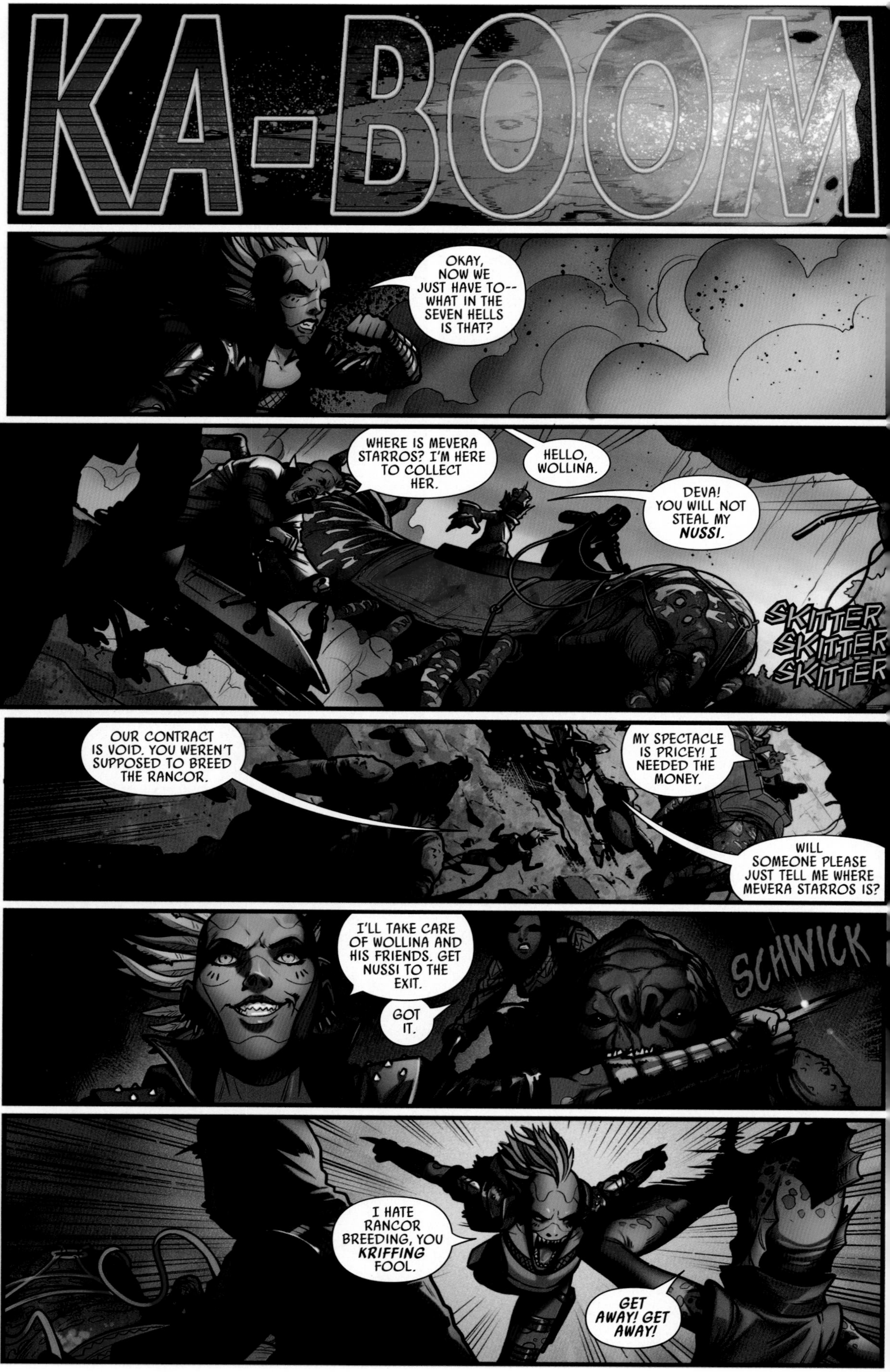
KA-BOOM
OKAY, NOW WE JUST HAVE TO-- WHAT IN THE SEVEN HELLS IS THAT?
WHERE IS MEVERA STARROS? I'M HERE TO COLLECT HER.
HELLO, WOLLINA.
DEVA! YOU WILL NOT STEAL MY NUSSI.
SKITTER SKITTER SKITTER
OUR CONTRACT IS VOID. YOU WEREN'T SUPPOSED TO BREED THE RANCOR.
MY SPECTACLE IS PRICEY! I NEEDED THE MONEY.
WILL SOMEONE PLEASE JUST TELL ME WHERE MEVERA STARROS IS?
I'LL TAKE CARE OF WOLLINA AND HIS FRIENDS. GET NUSSI TO THE EXIT.
GOT IT.
SCHWICK
I HATE RANCOR BREEDING, YOU KRIFFING FOOL.
GET AWAY! GET AWAY!

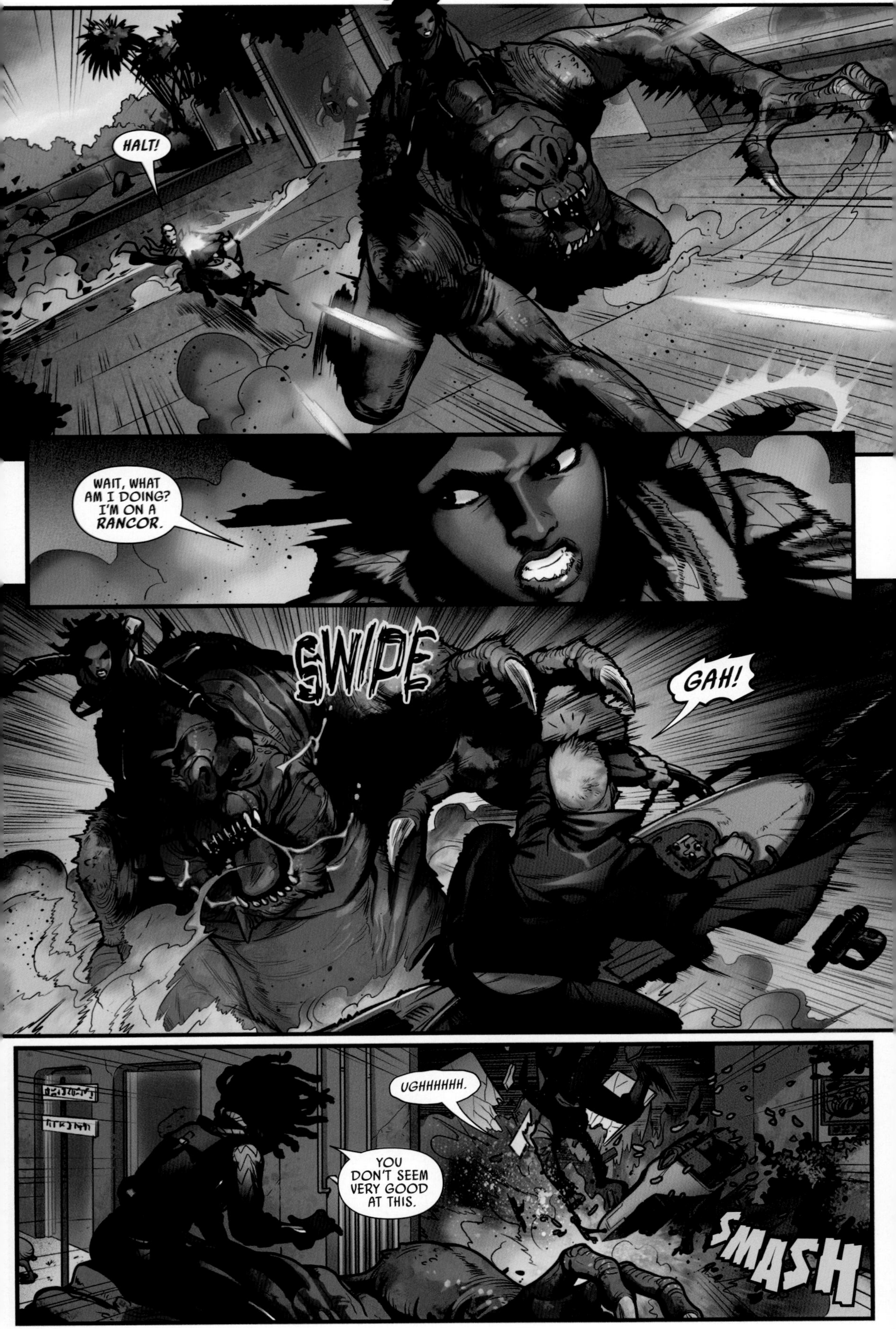
HALT!
WAIT, WHAT AM I DOING? I'M ON A RANCOR.
SWIPE
GAH!
UGHHHHHH.
YOU DON'T SEEM VERY GOOD AT THIS.
SMASH

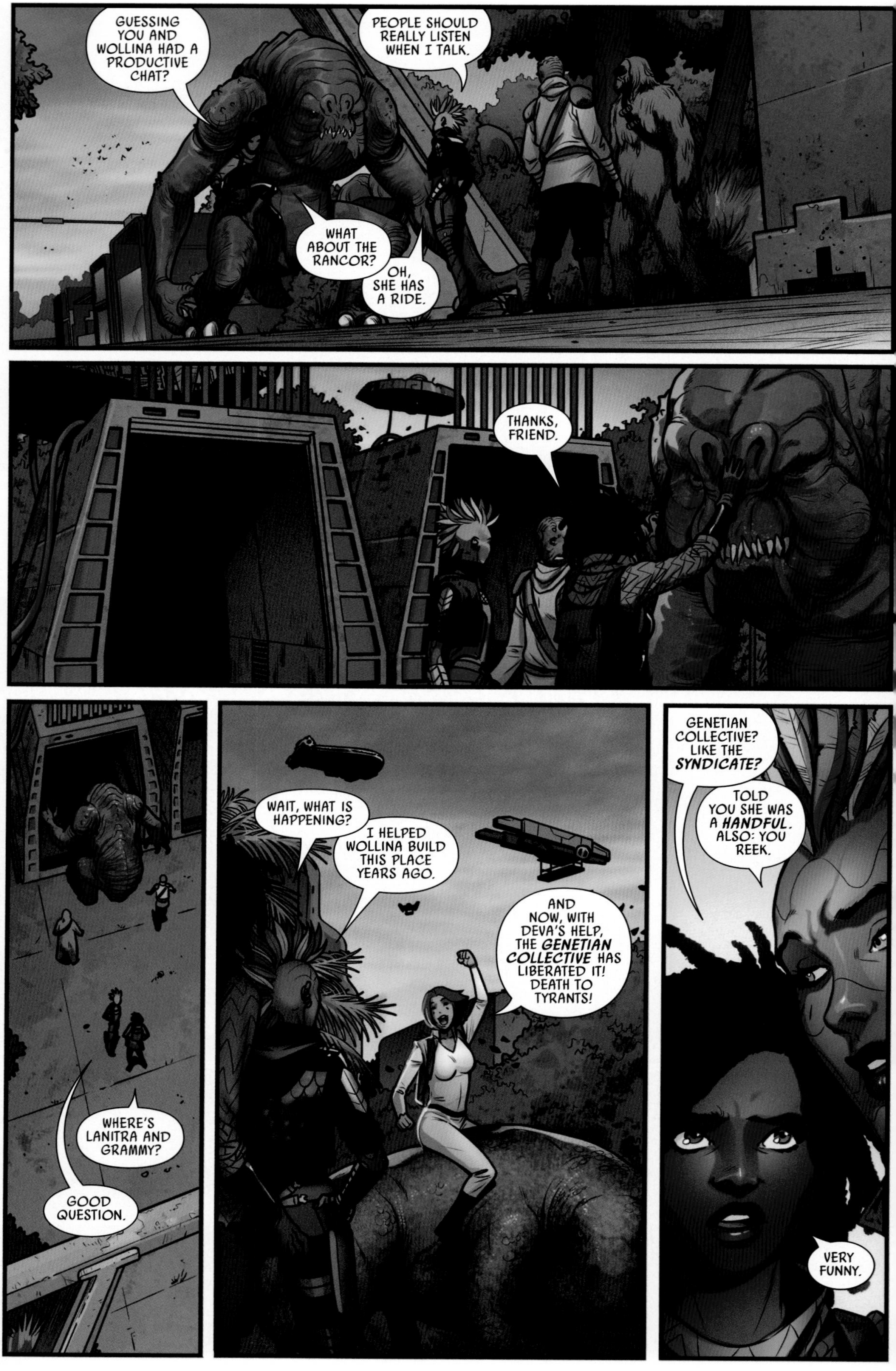
GUESSING YOU AND WOLLINA HAD A PRODUCTIVE CHAT?
PEOPLE SHOULD REALLY LISTEN WHEN I TALK.
WHAT ABOUT THE RANCOR?
OH, SHE HAS A RIDE.
THANKS, FRIEND.
WHERE'S LANITRA AND GRAMMY?
GOOD QUESTION.
WAIT, WHAT IS HAPPENING?
I HELPED WOLLINA BUILD THIS PLACE YEARS AGO.
AND NOW, WITH DEVA'S HELP, THE ***GENETIAN COLLECTIVE*** HAS LIBERATED IT! DEATH TO TYRANTS!
GENETIAN COLLECTIVE? LIKE THE ***SYNDICATE?***
TOLD YOU SHE WAS A ***HANDFUL.*** ALSO: YOU REEK.
VERY FUNNY.

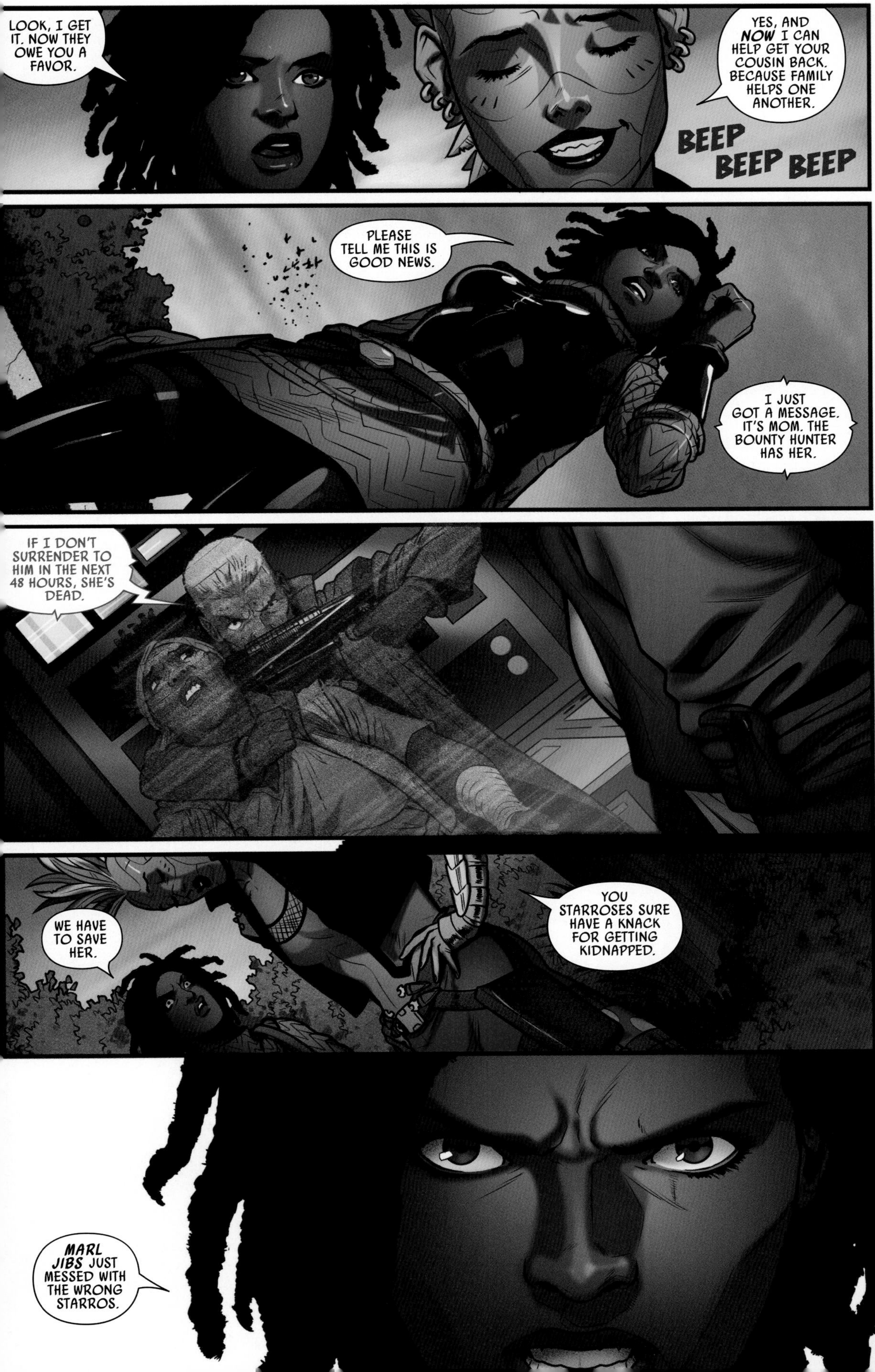
LOOK, I GET IT. NOW THEY OWE YOU A FAVOR.
YES, AND *NOW* I CAN HELP GET YOUR COUSIN BACK. BECAUSE FAMILY HELPS ONE ANOTHER.
BEEP BEEP BEEP
PLEASE TELL ME THIS IS GOOD NEWS.
I JUST GOT A MESSAGE. IT'S MOM. THE BOUNTY HUNTER HAS HER.
IF I DON'T SURRENDER TO HIM IN THE NEXT 48 HOURS, SHE'S DEAD.
WE HAVE TO SAVE HER.
YOU STARROSES SURE HAVE A KNACK FOR GETTING KIDNAPPED.
MARL JIBS JUST MESSED WITH THE WRONG STARROS.

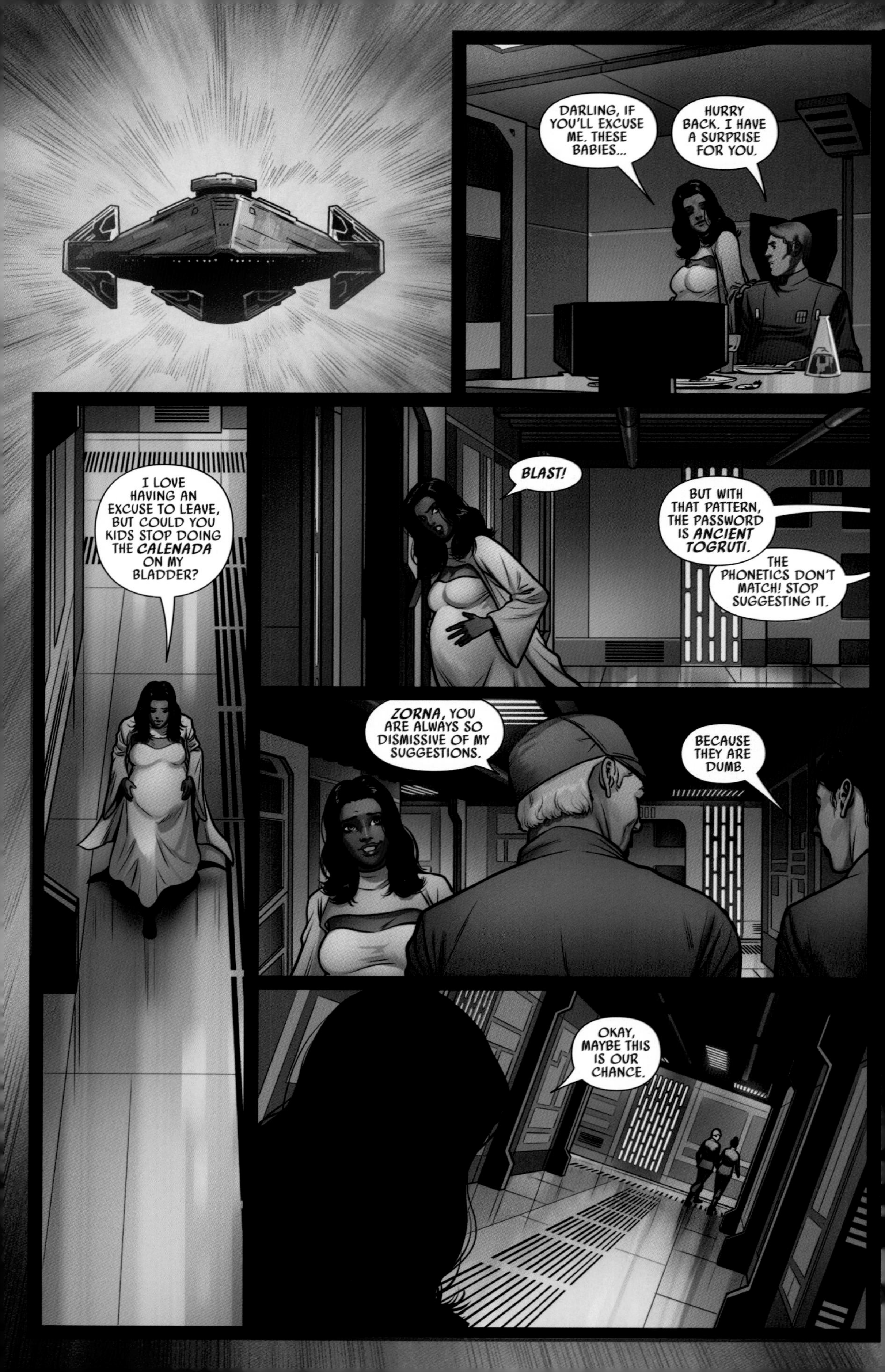
DARLING, IF YOU'LL EXCUSE ME. THESE BABIES...
HURRY BACK. I HAVE A SURPRISE FOR YOU.
I LOVE HAVING AN EXCUSE TO LEAVE, BUT COULD YOU KIDS STOP DOING THE *CALENADA* ON MY BLADDER?
BLAST!
BUT WITH THAT PATTERN, THE PASSWORD IS *ANCIENT TOGRUTI*.
THE PHONETICS DON'T MATCH! STOP SUGGESTING IT.
ZORNA, YOU ARE ALWAYS SO DISMISSIVE OF MY SUGGESTIONS.
BECAUSE THEY ARE DUMB.
OKAY, MAYBE THIS IS OUR CHANCE.

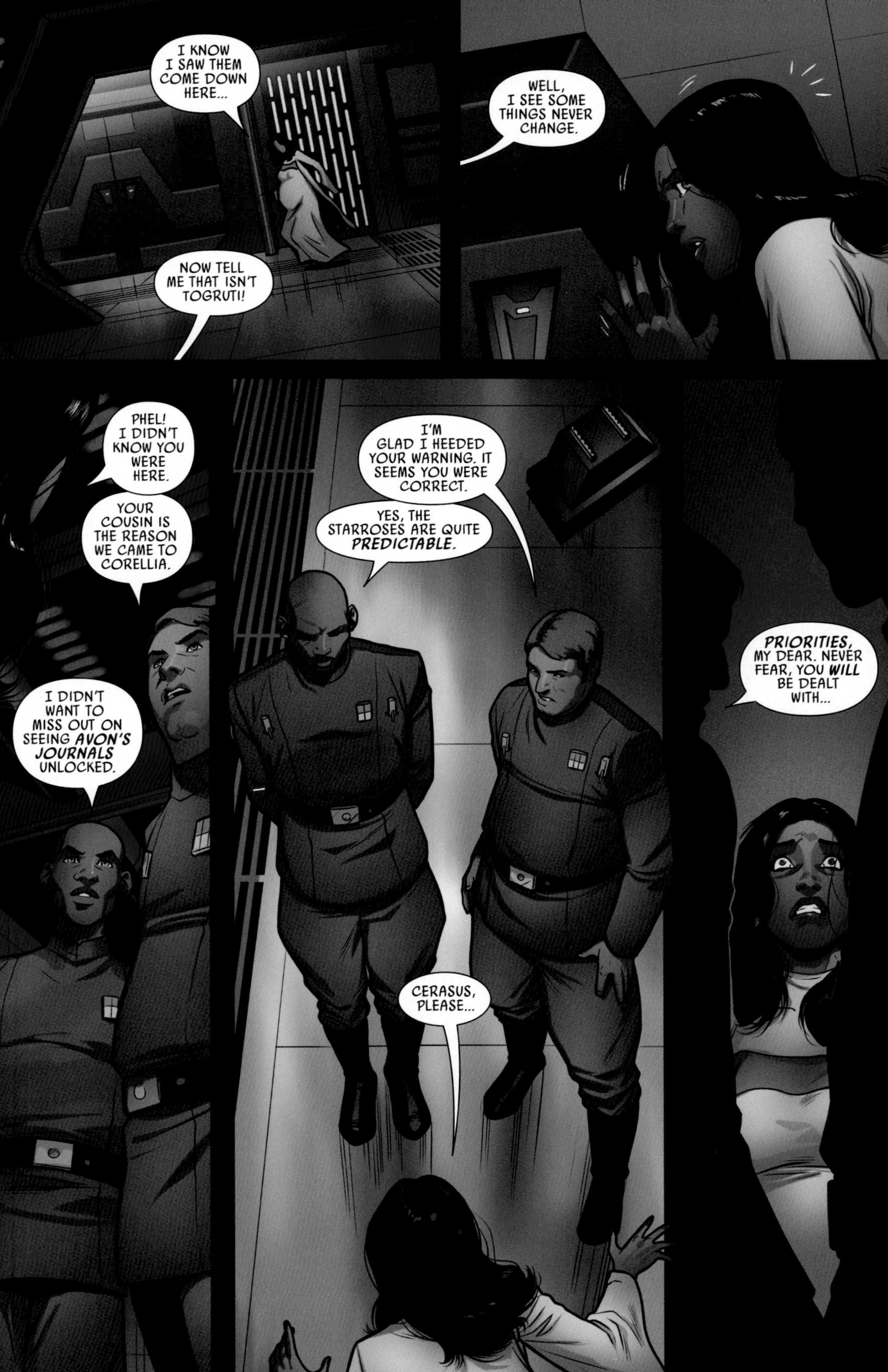
I KNOW I SAW THEM COME DOWN HERE...
NOW TELL ME THAT ISN'T TOGRUTI!
WELL, I SEE SOME THINGS NEVER CHANGE.
PHEL! I DIDN'T KNOW YOU WERE HERE.
YOUR COUSIN IS THE REASON WE CAME TO CORELLIA.
I DIDN'T WANT TO MISS OUT ON SEEING AVON'S JOURNALS UNLOCKED.
I'M GLAD I HEEDED YOUR WARNING. IT SEEMS YOU WERE CORRECT.
YES, THE STARROSES ARE QUITE PREDICTABLE.
CERASUS, PLEASE...
PRIORITIES, MY DEAR. NEVER FEAR, YOU WILL BE DEALT WITH...

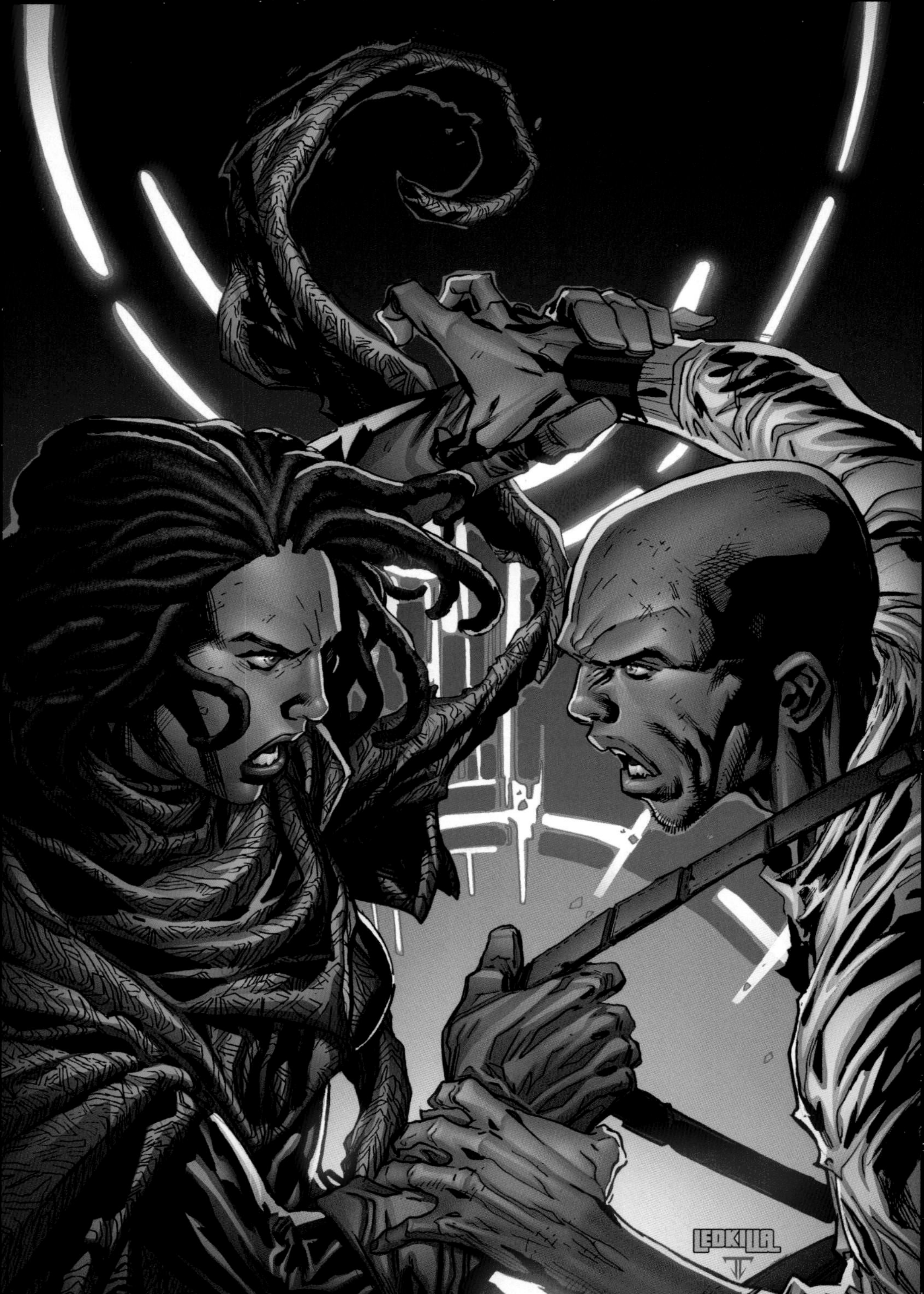
LEDKILLA

4 — PERFECT STRANGERS

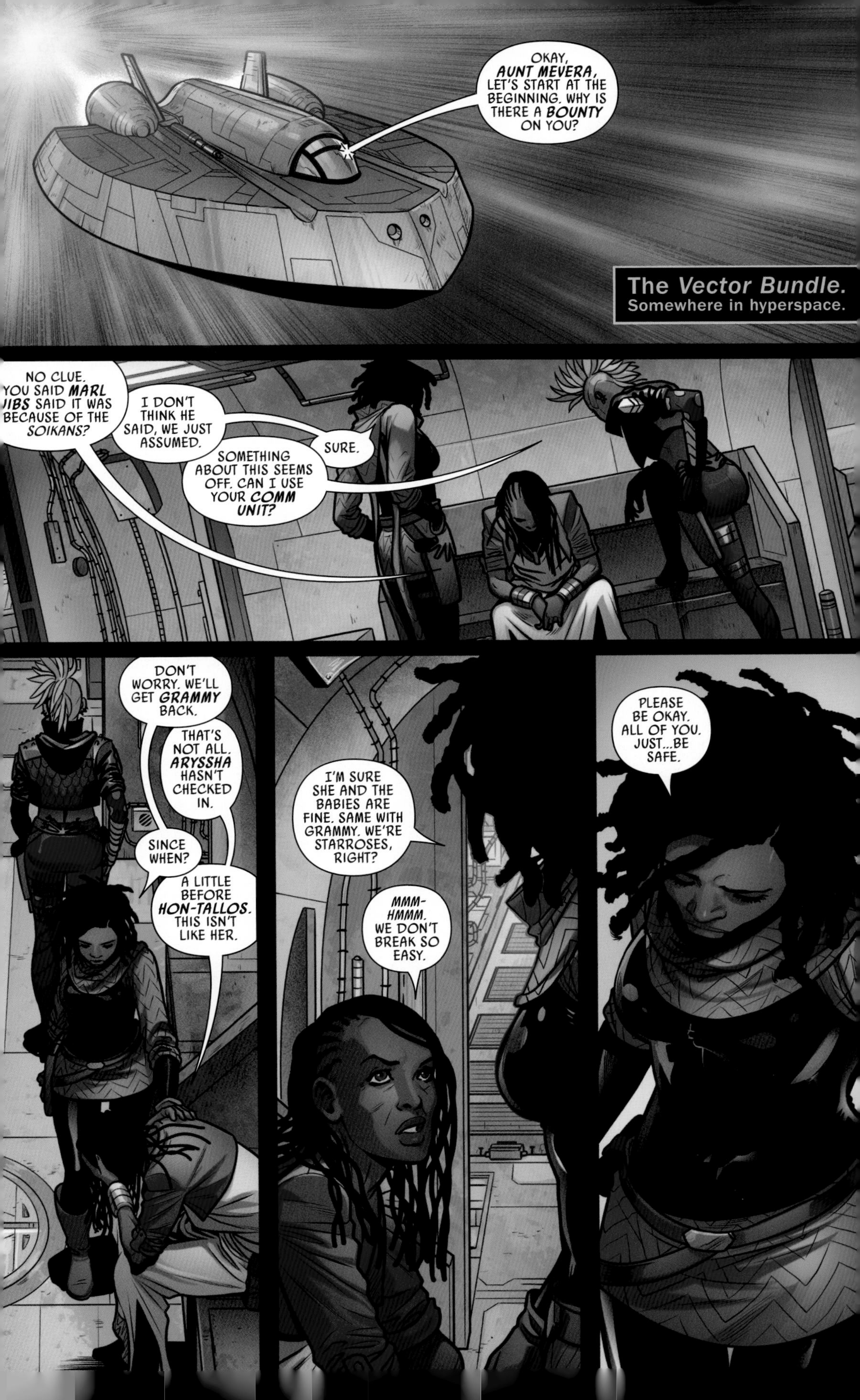

OKAY, AUNT MEVERA, LET'S START AT THE BEGINNING. WHY IS THERE A BOUNTY ON YOU?
The Vector Bundle.
Somewhere in hyperspace.
NO CLUE. YOU SAID MARL JIBS SAID IT WAS BECAUSE OF THE SOIKANS?
I DON'T THINK HE SAID, WE JUST ASSUMED.
SURE.
SOMETHING ABOUT THIS SEEMS OFF. CAN I USE YOUR COMM UNIT?
DON'T WORRY. WE'LL GET GRAMMY BACK.
THAT'S NOT ALL. ARYSSHA HASN'T CHECKED IN.
SINCE WHEN?
A LITTLE BEFORE HON-TALLOS. THIS ISN'T LIKE HER.
I'M SURE SHE AND THE BABIES ARE FINE. SAME WITH GRAMMY. WE'RE STARROSES, RIGHT?
MMM-HMMM. WE DON'T BREAK SO EASY.
PLEASE BE OKAY. ALL OF YOU. JUST...BE SAFE.

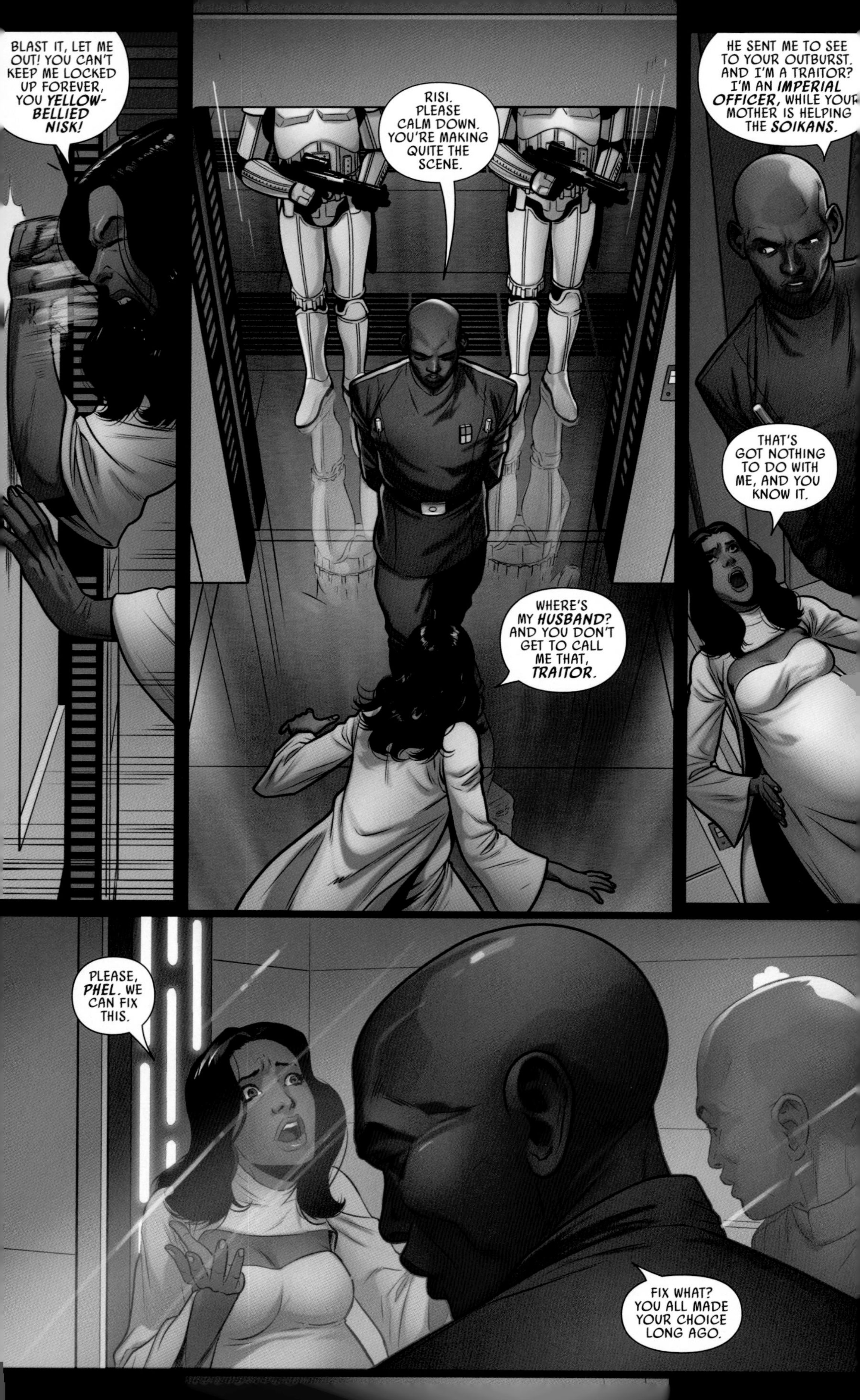
BLAST IT, LET ME OUT! YOU CAN'T KEEP ME LOCKED UP FOREVER, YOU YELLOW-BELLIED NISK!
RISI. PLEASE CALM DOWN. YOU'RE MAKING QUITE THE SCENE.
WHERE'S MY HUSBAND? AND YOU DON'T GET TO CALL ME THAT, TRAITOR.
HE SENT ME TO SEE TO YOUR OUTBURST. AND I'M A TRAITOR? I'M AN IMPERIAL OFFICER, WHILE YOUR MOTHER IS HELPING THE SOIKANS.
THAT'S GOT NOTHING TO DO WITH ME, AND YOU KNOW IT.
PLEASE, PHEL. WE CAN FIX THIS.
FIX WHAT? YOU ALL MADE YOUR CHOICE LONG AGO.

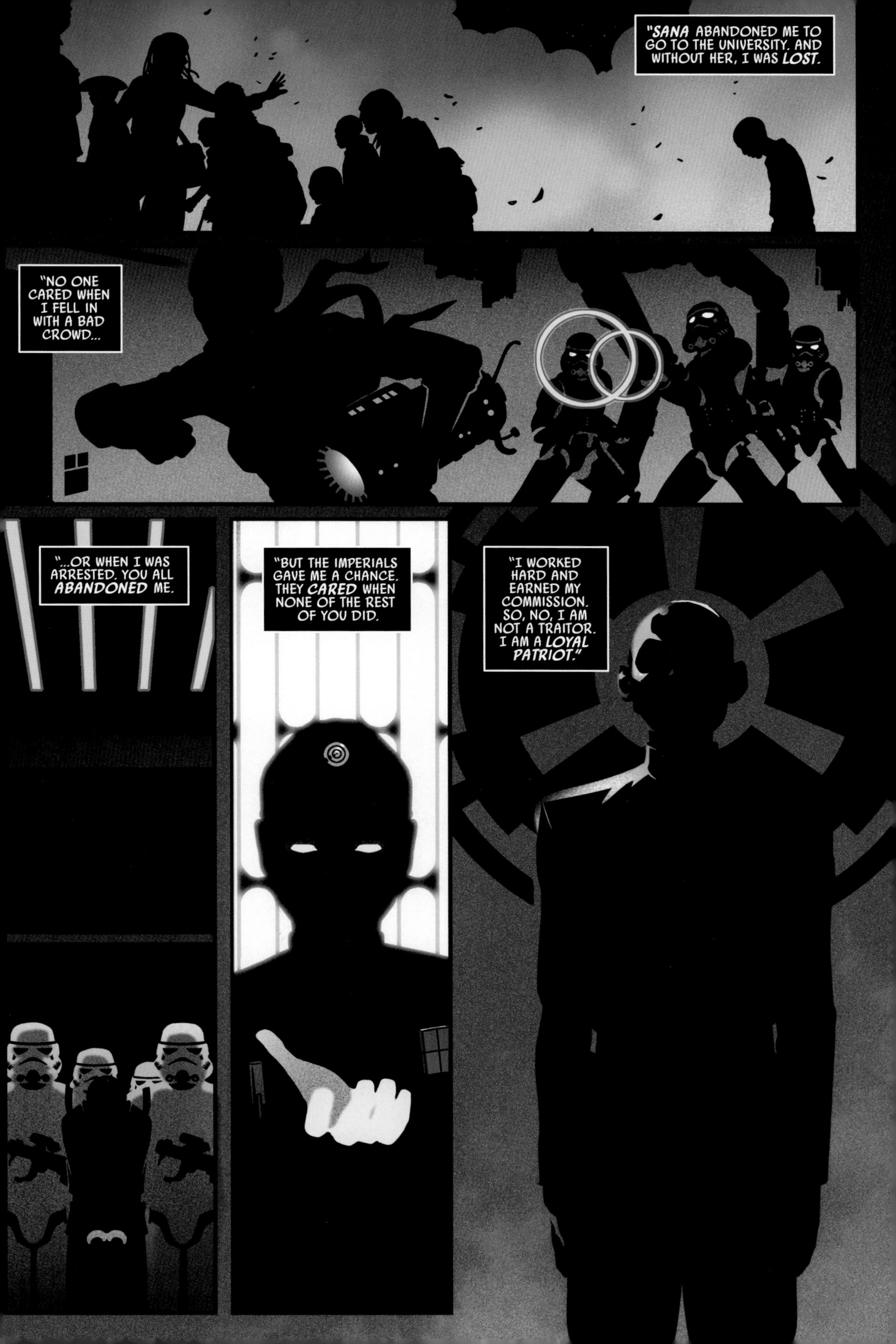
"SANA ABANDONED ME TO GO TO THE UNIVERSITY. AND WITHOUT HER, I WAS LOST.
"NO ONE CARED WHEN I FELL IN WITH A BAD CROWD...
"...OR WHEN I WAS ARRESTED. YOU ALL ABANDONED ME.
"BUT THE IMPERIALS GAVE ME A CHANCE. THEY CARED WHEN NONE OF THE REST OF YOU DID.
"I WORKED HARD AND EARNED MY COMMISSION. SO, NO, I AM NOT A TRAITOR. I AM A LOYAL PATRIOT."

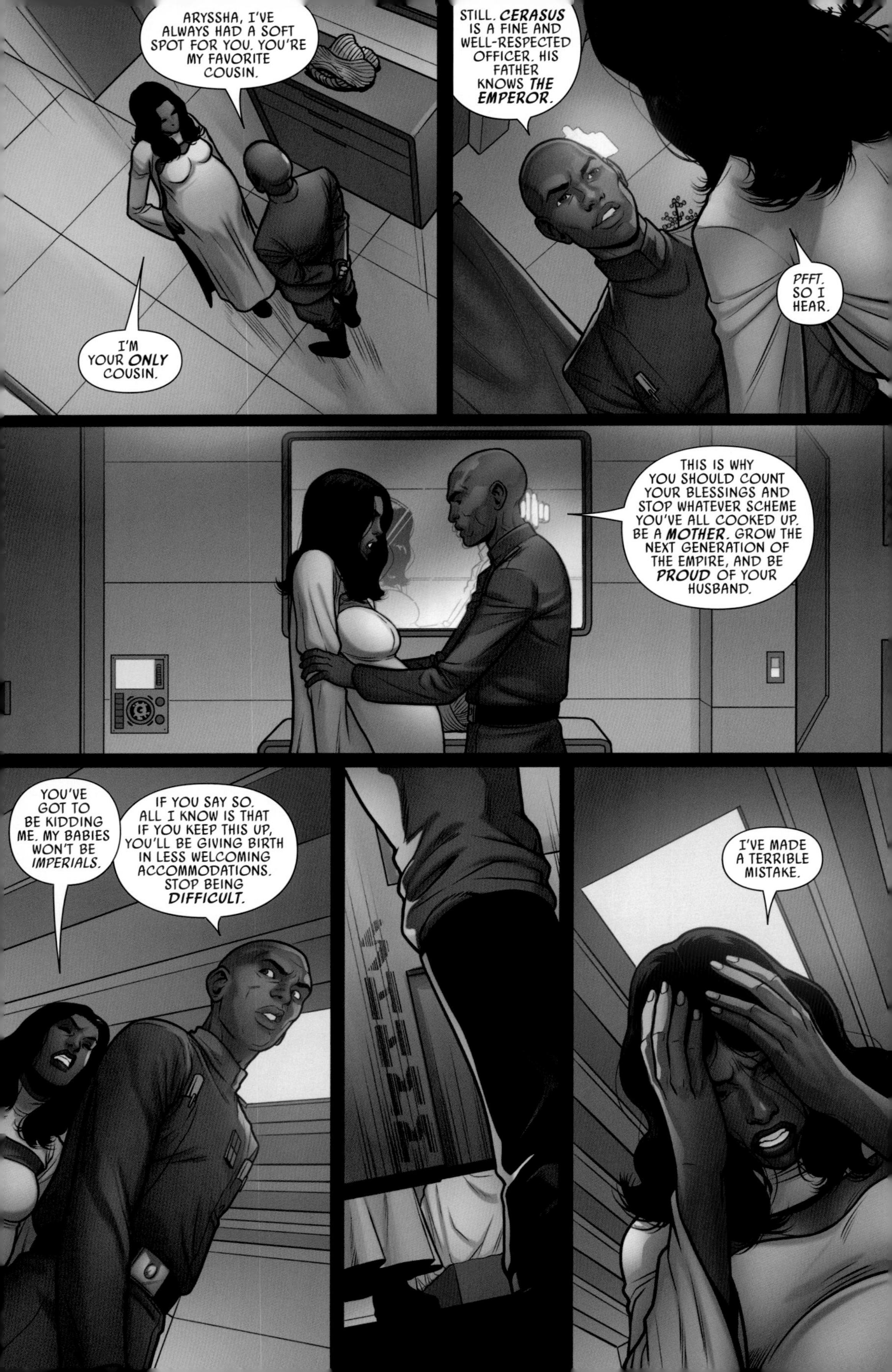
ARYSSHA, I'VE ALWAYS HAD A SOFT SPOT FOR YOU. YOU'RE MY FAVORITE COUSIN.
I'M YOUR ONLY COUSIN.
STILL. CERASUS IS A FINE AND WELL-RESPECTED OFFICER. HIS FATHER KNOWS THE EMPEROR.
PFFT. SO I HEAR.
THIS IS WHY YOU SHOULD COUNT YOUR BLESSINGS AND STOP WHATEVER SCHEME YOU'VE ALL COOKED UP. BE A MOTHER. GROW THE NEXT GENERATION OF THE EMPIRE, AND BE PROUD OF YOUR HUSBAND.
YOU'VE GOT TO BE KIDDING ME. MY BABIES WON'T BE IMPERIALS.
IF YOU SAY SO. ALL I KNOW IS THAT IF YOU KEEP THIS UP, YOU'LL BE GIVING BIRTH IN LESS WELCOMING ACCOMMODATIONS. STOP BEING DIFFICULT.
I'VE MADE A TERRIBLE MISTAKE.

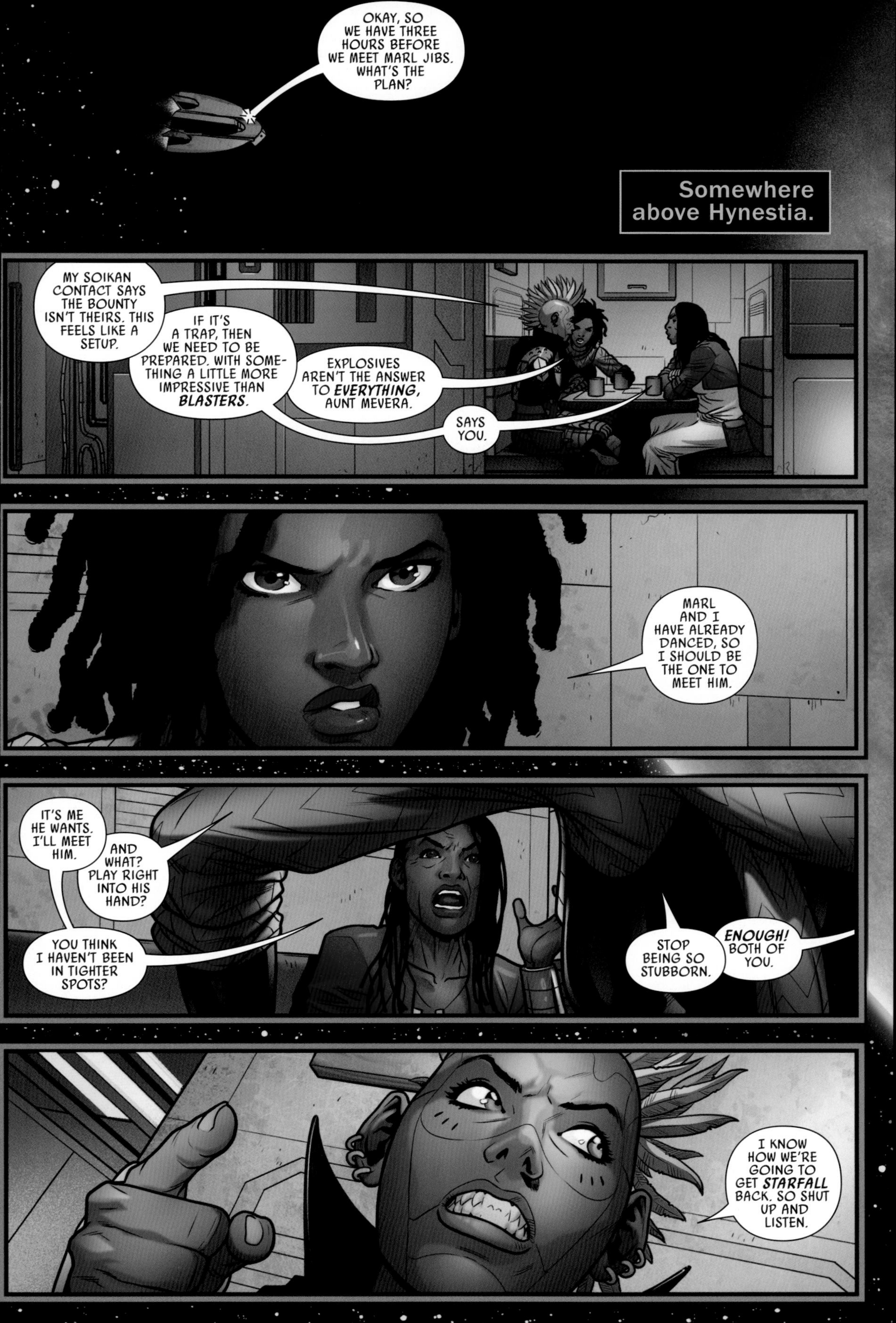
OKAY, SO WE HAVE THREE HOURS BEFORE WE MEET MARL JIBS. WHAT'S THE PLAN?
Somewhere above Hynestia.
MY SOIKAN CONTACT SAYS THE BOUNTY ISN'T THEIRS. THIS FEELS LIKE A SETUP.
IF IT'S A TRAP, THEN WE NEED TO BE PREPARED. WITH SOMETHING A LITTLE MORE IMPRESSIVE THAN BLASTERS.
EXPLOSIVES AREN'T THE ANSWER TO EVERYTHING, AUNT MEVERA.
SAYS YOU.
MARL AND I HAVE ALREADY DANCED, SO I SHOULD BE THE ONE TO MEET HIM.
IT'S ME HE WANTS. I'LL MEET HIM.
AND WHAT? PLAY RIGHT INTO HIS HAND?
YOU THINK I HAVEN'T BEEN IN TIGHTER SPOTS?
STOP BEING SO STUBBORN.
ENOUGH! BOTH OF YOU.
I KNOW HOW WE'RE GOING TO GET STARFALL BACK. SO SHUT UP AND LISTEN.

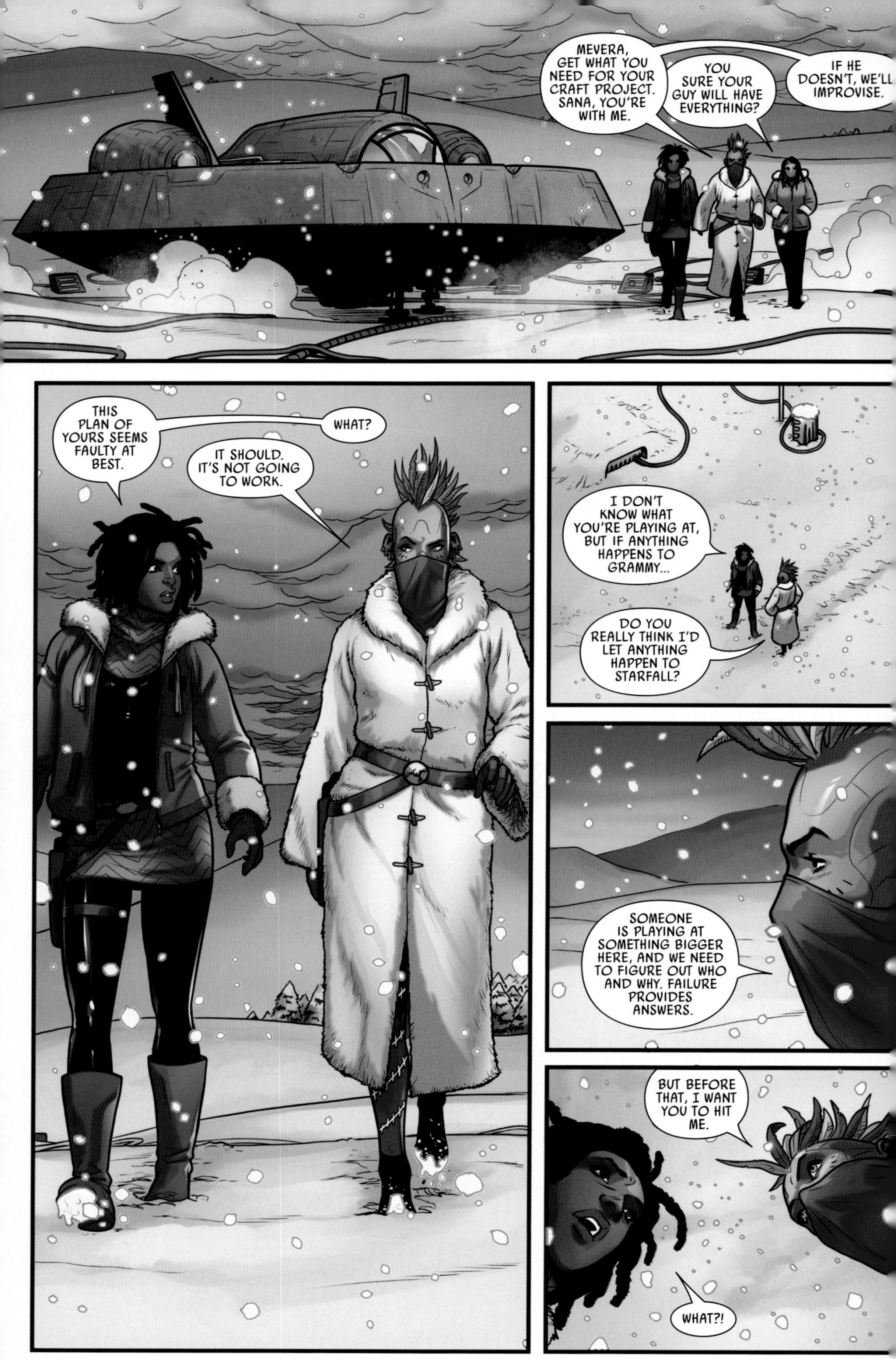
MEVERA, GET WHAT YOU NEED FOR YOUR CRAFT PROJECT. SANA, YOU'RE WITH ME.
YOU SURE YOUR GUY WILL HAVE EVERYTHING?
IF HE DOESN'T, WE'LL IMPROVISE.
THIS PLAN OF YOURS SEEMS FAULTY AT BEST.
IT SHOULD. IT'S NOT GOING TO WORK.
WHAT?
I DON'T KNOW WHAT YOU'RE PLAYING AT, BUT IF ANYTHING HAPPENS TO GRAMMY...
DO YOU REALLY THINK I'D LET ANYTHING HAPPEN TO STARFALL?
SOMEONE IS PLAYING AT SOMETHING BIGGER HERE, AND WE NEED TO FIGURE OUT WHO AND WHY. FAILURE PROVIDES ANSWERS.
BUT BEFORE THAT, I WANT YOU TO HIT ME.
WHAT?!

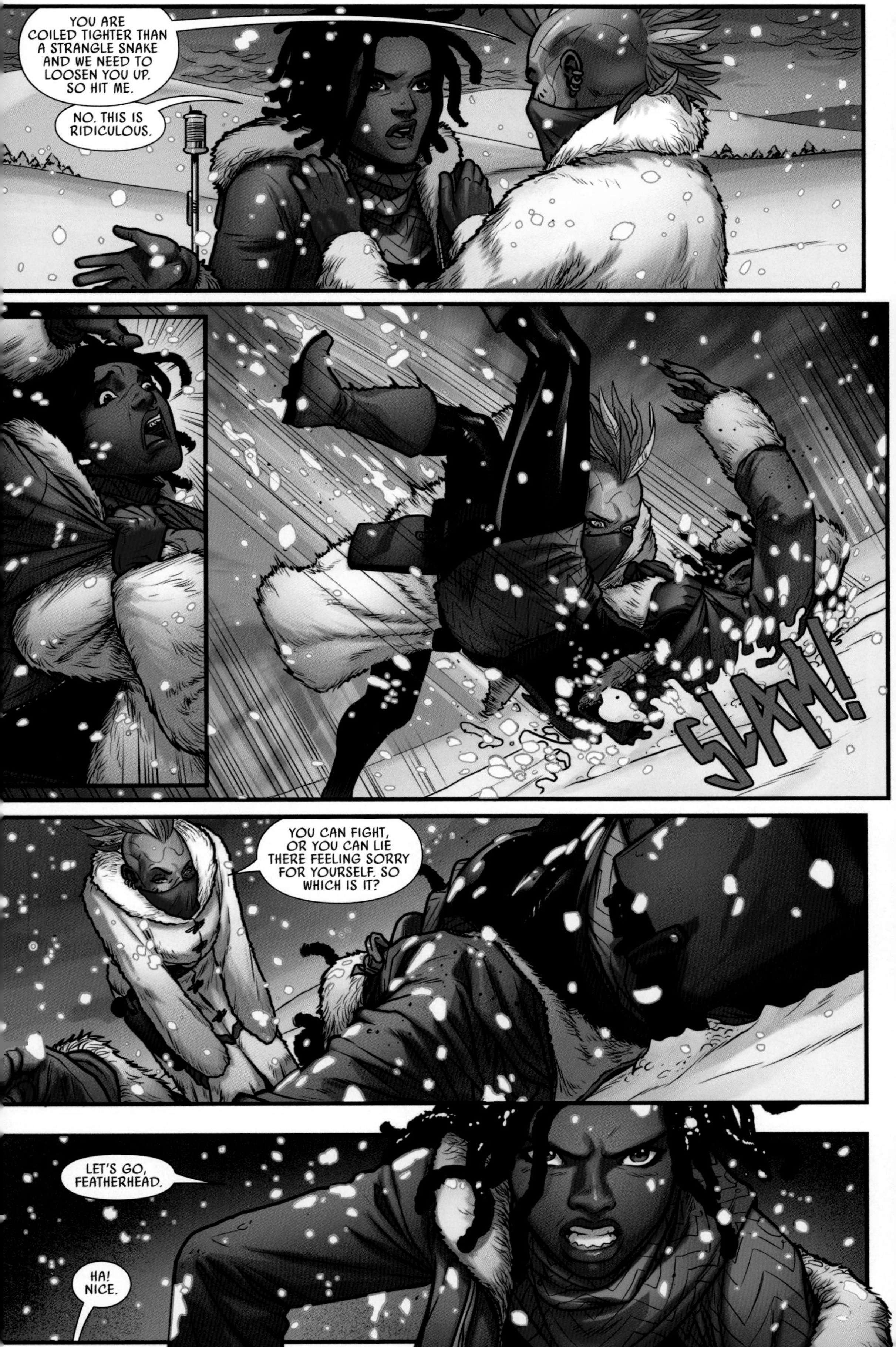

YOU ARE COILED TIGHTER THAN A STRANGLE SNAKE AND WE NEED TO LOOSEN YOU UP. SO HIT ME.
NO. THIS IS RIDICULOUS.
SLAM!
YOU CAN FIGHT, OR YOU CAN LIE THERE FEELING SORRY FOR YOURSELF. SO WHICH IS IT?
LET'S GO, FEATHERHEAD.
HA! NICE.

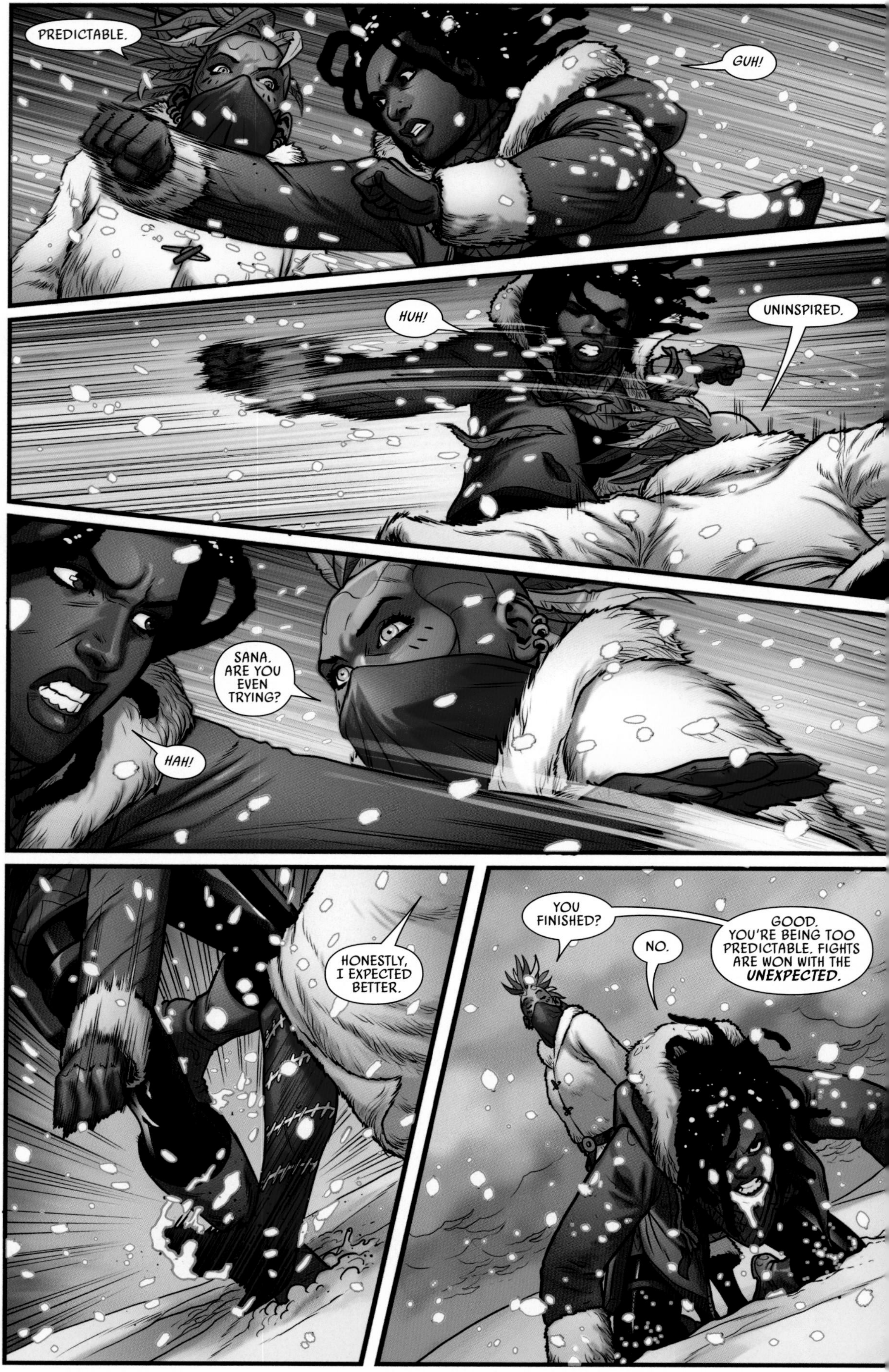
PREDICTABLE.
GUH!
HUH!
UNINSPIRED.
SANA. ARE YOU EVEN TRYING?
HAH!
HONESTLY, I EXPECTED BETTER.
YOU FINISHED?
NO.
GOOD. YOU'RE BEING TOO PREDICTABLE. FIGHTS ARE WON WITH THE *UNEXPECTED.*

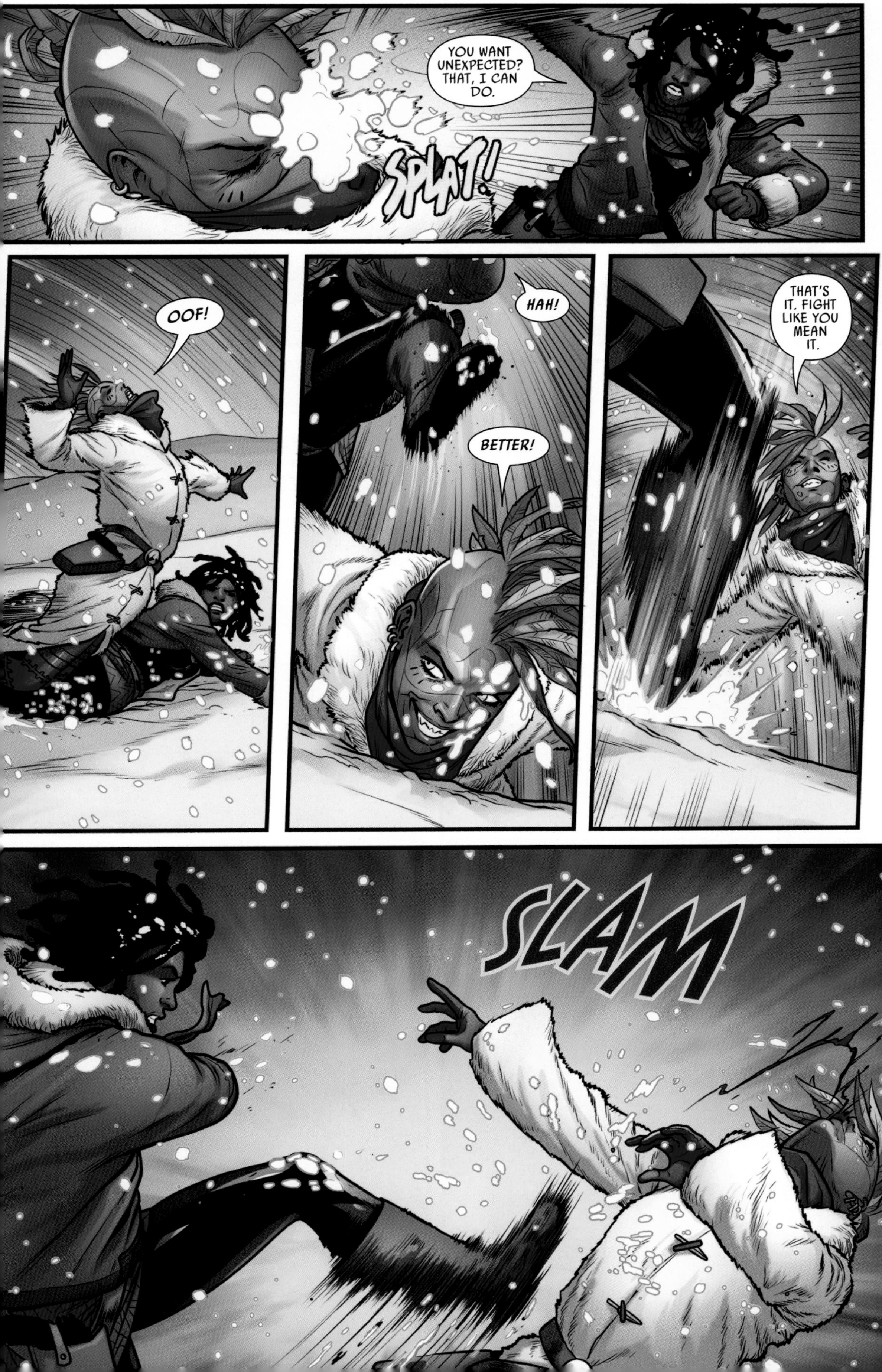
YOU WANT UNEXPECTED? THAT, I CAN DO.
SPLAT!
OOF!
HAH!
BETTER!
THAT'S IT. FIGHT LIKE YOU MEAN IT.
SLAM

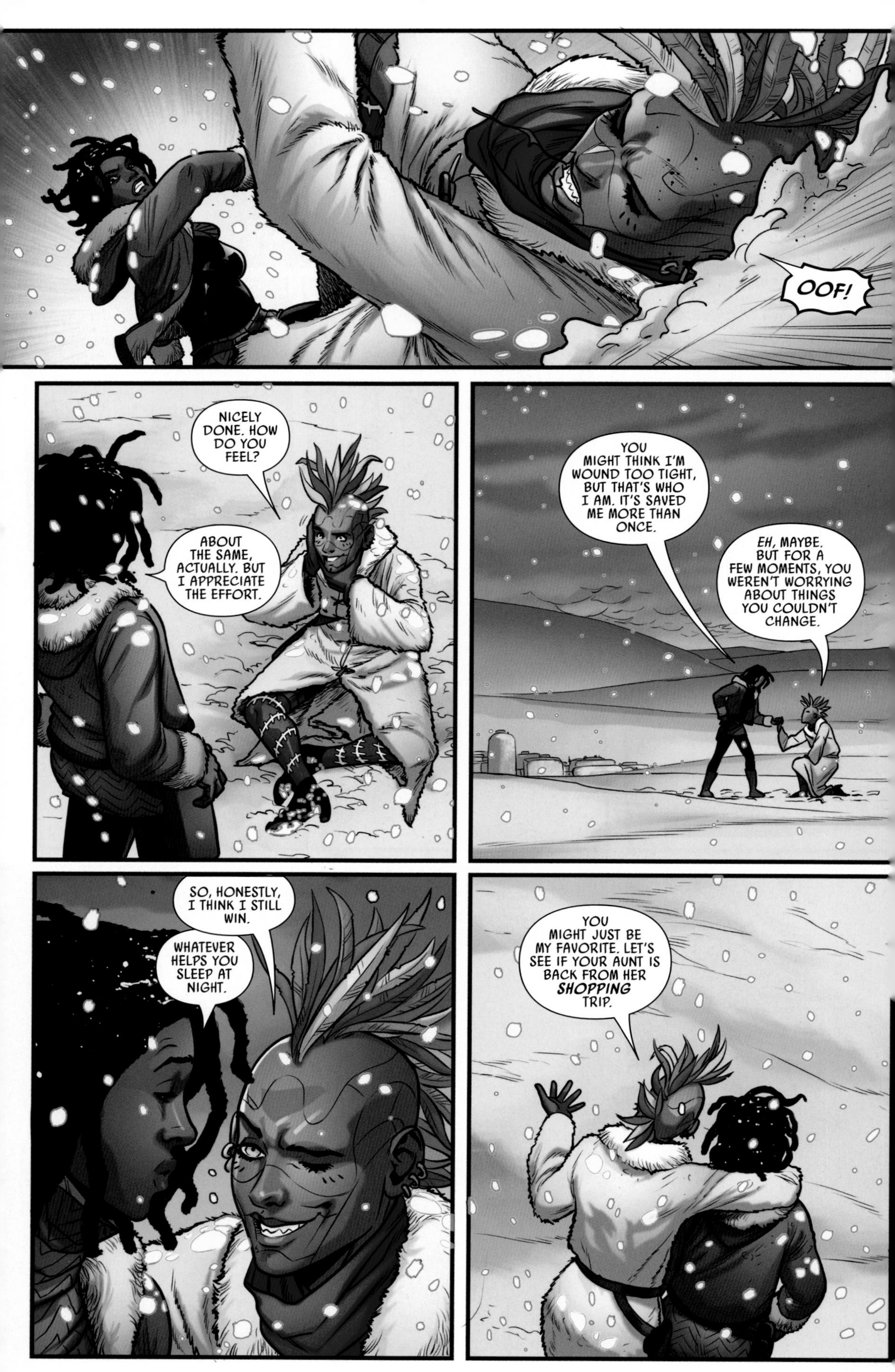
OOF!
NICELY DONE. HOW DO YOU FEEL?
ABOUT THE SAME, ACTUALLY. BUT I APPRECIATE THE EFFORT.
YOU MIGHT THINK I'M WOUND TOO TIGHT, BUT THAT'S WHO I AM. IT'S SAVED ME MORE THAN ONCE.
EH, MAYBE. BUT FOR A FEW MOMENTS, YOU WEREN'T WORRYING ABOUT THINGS YOU COULDN'T CHANGE.
SO, HONESTLY, I THINK I STILL WIN.
WHATEVER HELPS YOU SLEEP AT NIGHT.
YOU MIGHT JUST BE MY FAVORITE. LET'S SEE IF YOUR AUNT IS BACK FROM HER SHOPPING TRIP.

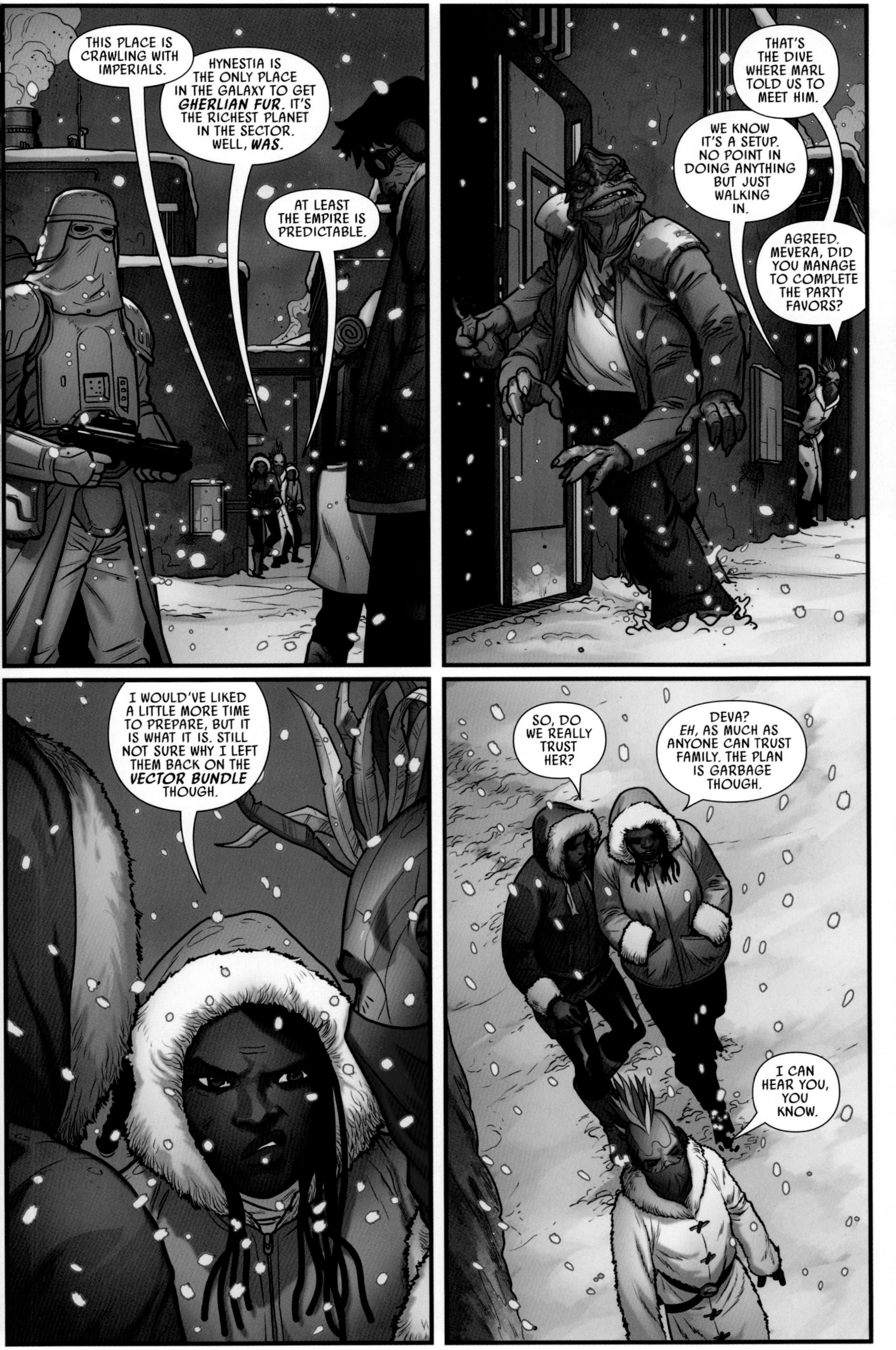
THIS PLACE IS CRAWLING WITH IMPERIALS.
HYNESTIA IS THE ONLY PLACE IN THE GALAXY TO GET **GHERLIAN FUR**. IT'S THE RICHEST PLANET IN THE SECTOR. WELL, ***WAS***.
AT LEAST THE EMPIRE IS PREDICTABLE.
THAT'S THE DIVE WHERE MARL TOLD US TO MEET HIM.
WE KNOW IT'S A SETUP. NO POINT IN DOING ANYTHING BUT JUST WALKING IN.
AGREED. MEVERA, DID YOU MANAGE TO COMPLETE THE PARTY FAVORS?
I WOULD'VE LIKED A LITTLE MORE TIME TO PREPARE, BUT IT IS WHAT IT IS. STILL NOT SURE WHY I LEFT THEM BACK ON THE ***VECTOR BUNDLE*** THOUGH.
SO, DO WE REALLY TRUST HER?
DEVA? *EH*, AS MUCH AS ANYONE CAN TRUST FAMILY. THE PLAN IS GARBAGE THOUGH.
I CAN HEAR YOU, YOU KNOW.

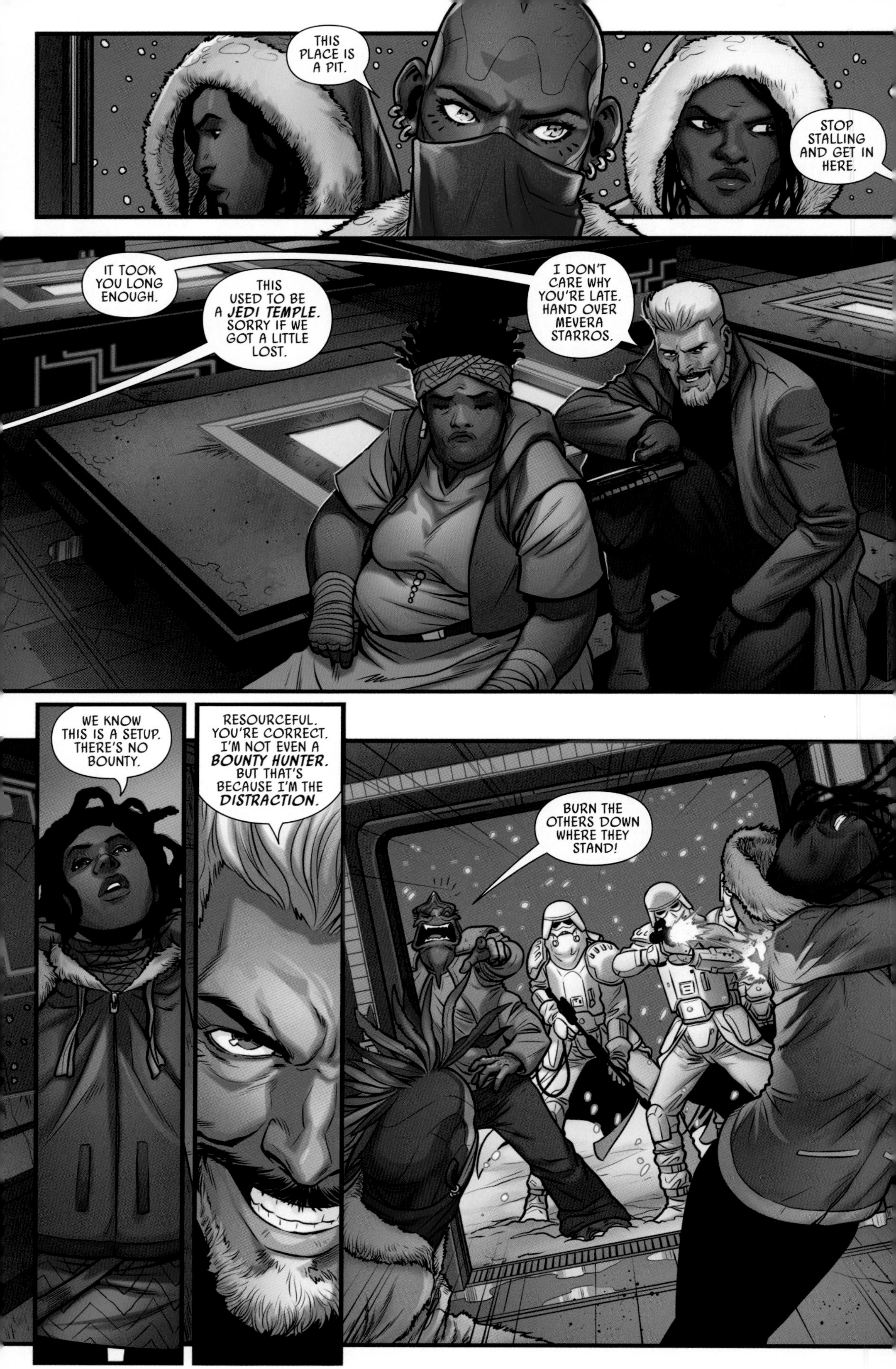
THIS PLACE IS A PIT.
STOP STALLING AND GET IN HERE.
IT TOOK YOU LONG ENOUGH.
THIS USED TO BE A JEDI TEMPLE. SORRY IF WE GOT A LITTLE LOST.
I DON'T CARE WHY YOU'RE LATE. HAND OVER MEVERA STARROS.
WE KNOW THIS IS A SETUP. THERE'S NO BOUNTY.
RESOURCEFUL. YOU'RE CORRECT. I'M NOT EVEN A BOUNTY HUNTER. BUT THAT'S BECAUSE I'M THE DISTRACTION.
BURN THE OTHERS DOWN WHERE THEY STAND!

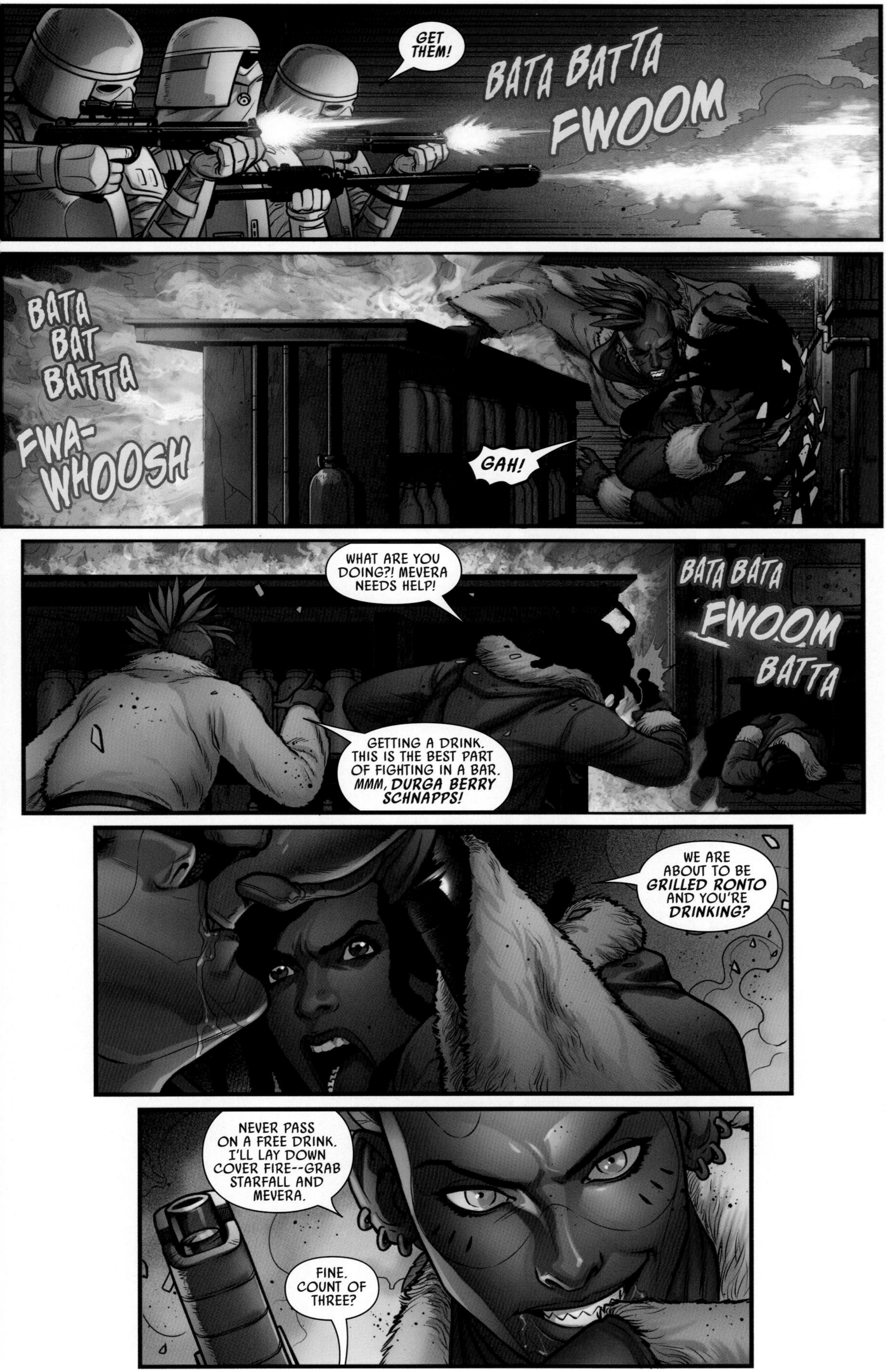
GET THEM!
BATA BATTA FWOOM
BATA BAT BATTA FWA-WHOOSH
GAH!
WHAT ARE YOU DOING?! MEVERA NEEDS HELP!
BATA BATA FWOOM BATTA
GETTING A DRINK. THIS IS THE BEST PART OF FIGHTING IN A BAR. MMM, DURGA BERRY SCHNAPPS!
WE ARE ABOUT TO BE GRILLED RONTO AND YOU'RE DRINKING?
NEVER PASS ON A FREE DRINK. I'LL LAY DOWN COVER FIRE--GRAB STARFALL AND MEVERA.
FINE. COUNT OF THREE?

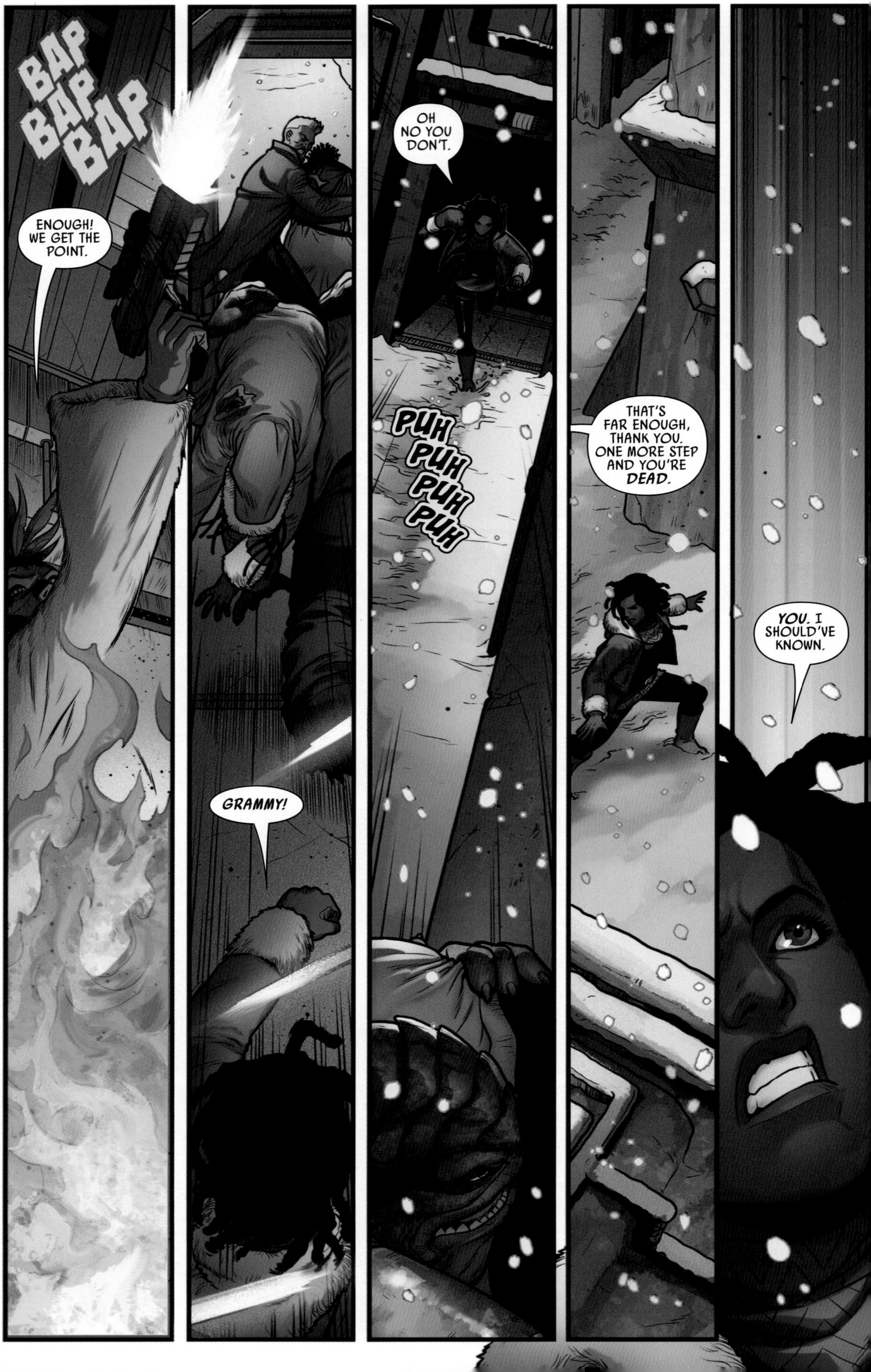
BAP BAP BAP
ENOUGH! WE GET THE POINT.
GRAMMY!
OH NO YOU DON'T.
PUH PUH PUH PUH
THAT'S FAR ENOUGH, THANK YOU. ONE MORE STEP AND YOU'RE DEAD.
YOU. I SHOULD'VE KNOWN.

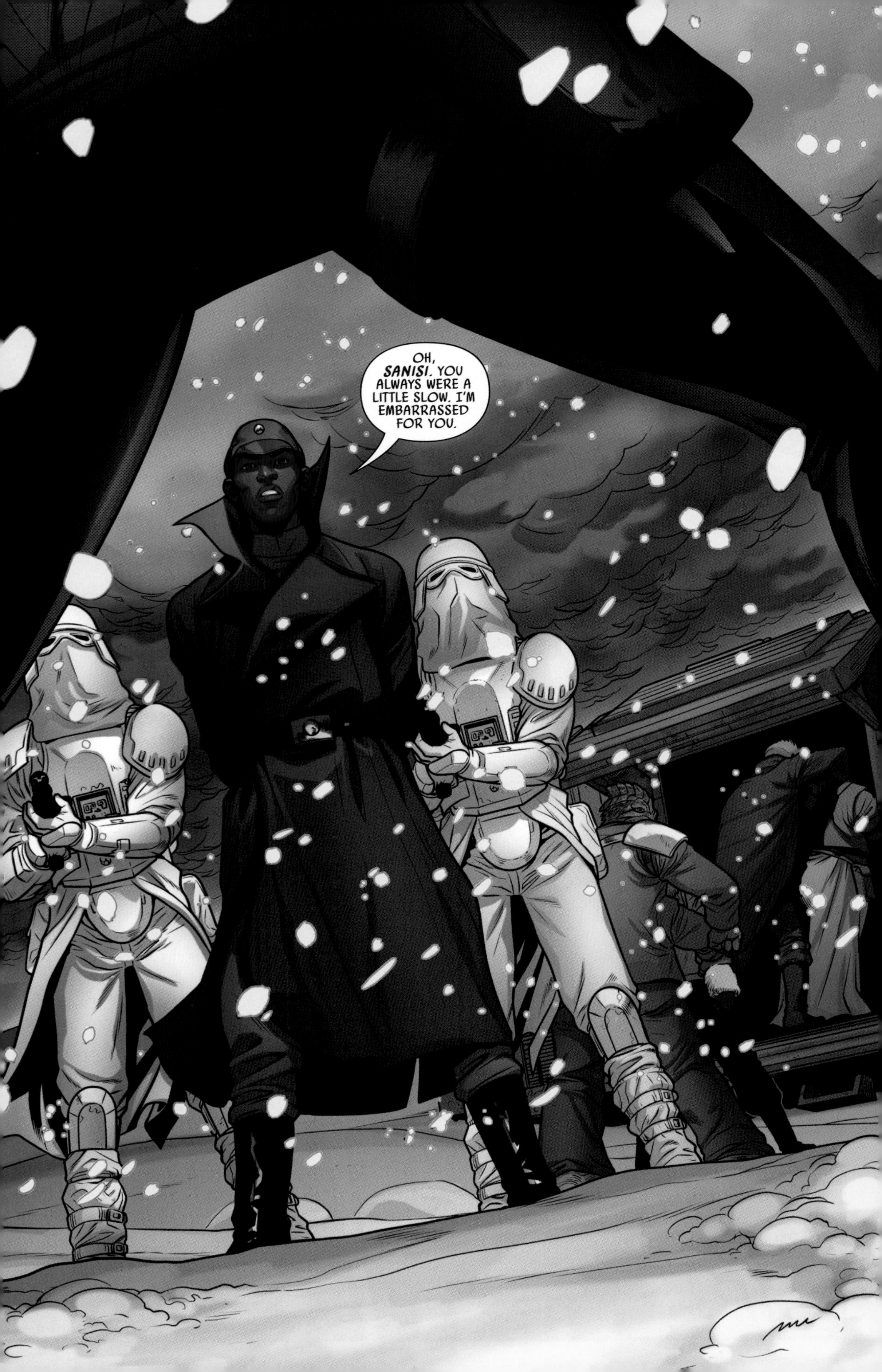
OH, SANISI. YOU ALWAYS WERE A LITTLE SLOW. I'M EMBARRASSED FOR YOU.

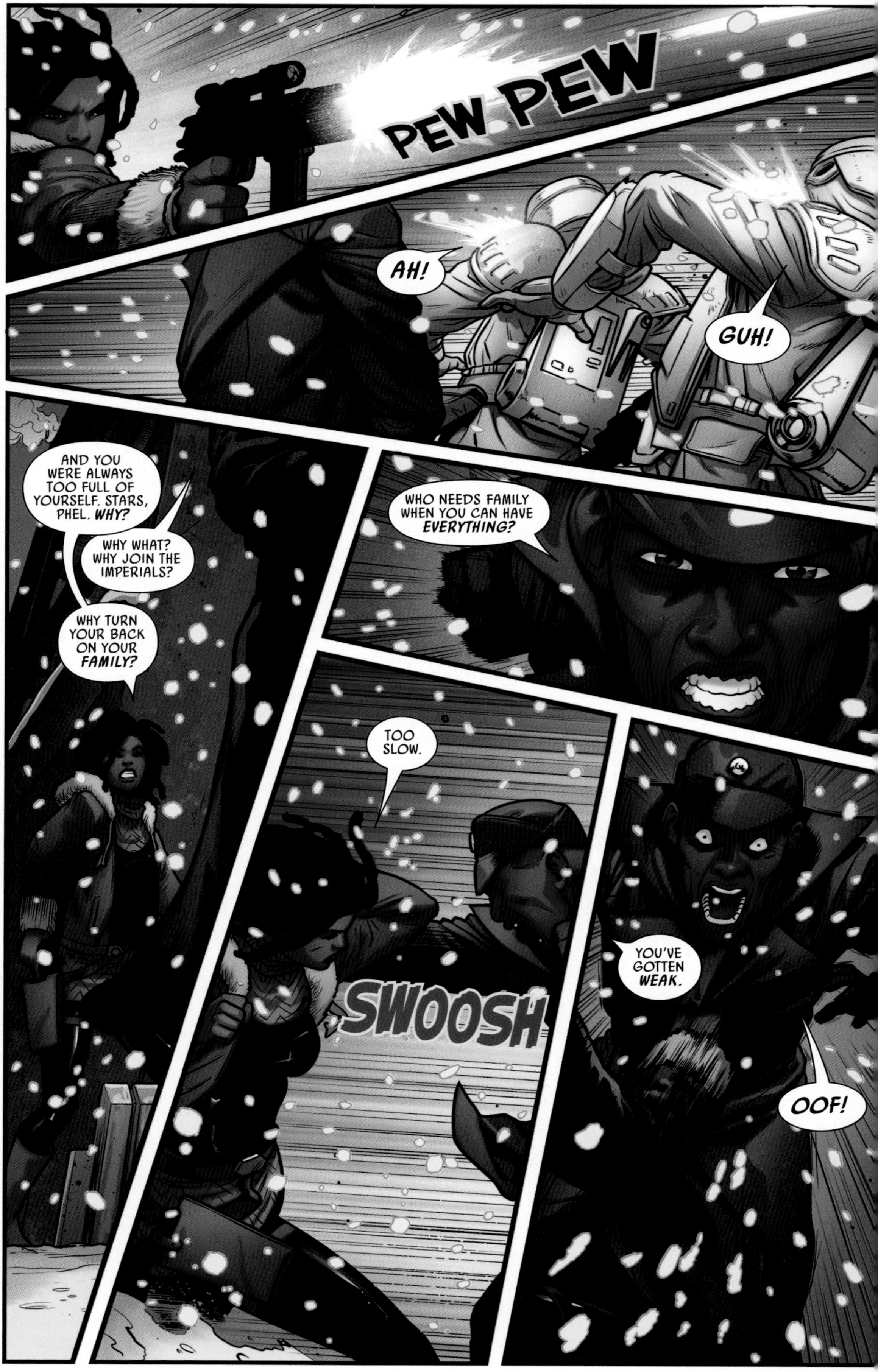
PEW PEW
AH!
GUH!
AND YOU WERE ALWAYS TOO FULL OF YOURSELF. STARS, PHEL. WHY?
WHY WHAT? WHY JOIN THE IMPERIALS?
WHY TURN YOUR BACK ON YOUR FAMILY?
WHO NEEDS FAMILY WHEN YOU CAN HAVE EVERYTHING?
TOO SLOW.
SWOOSH
YOU'VE GOTTEN WEAK.
OOF!

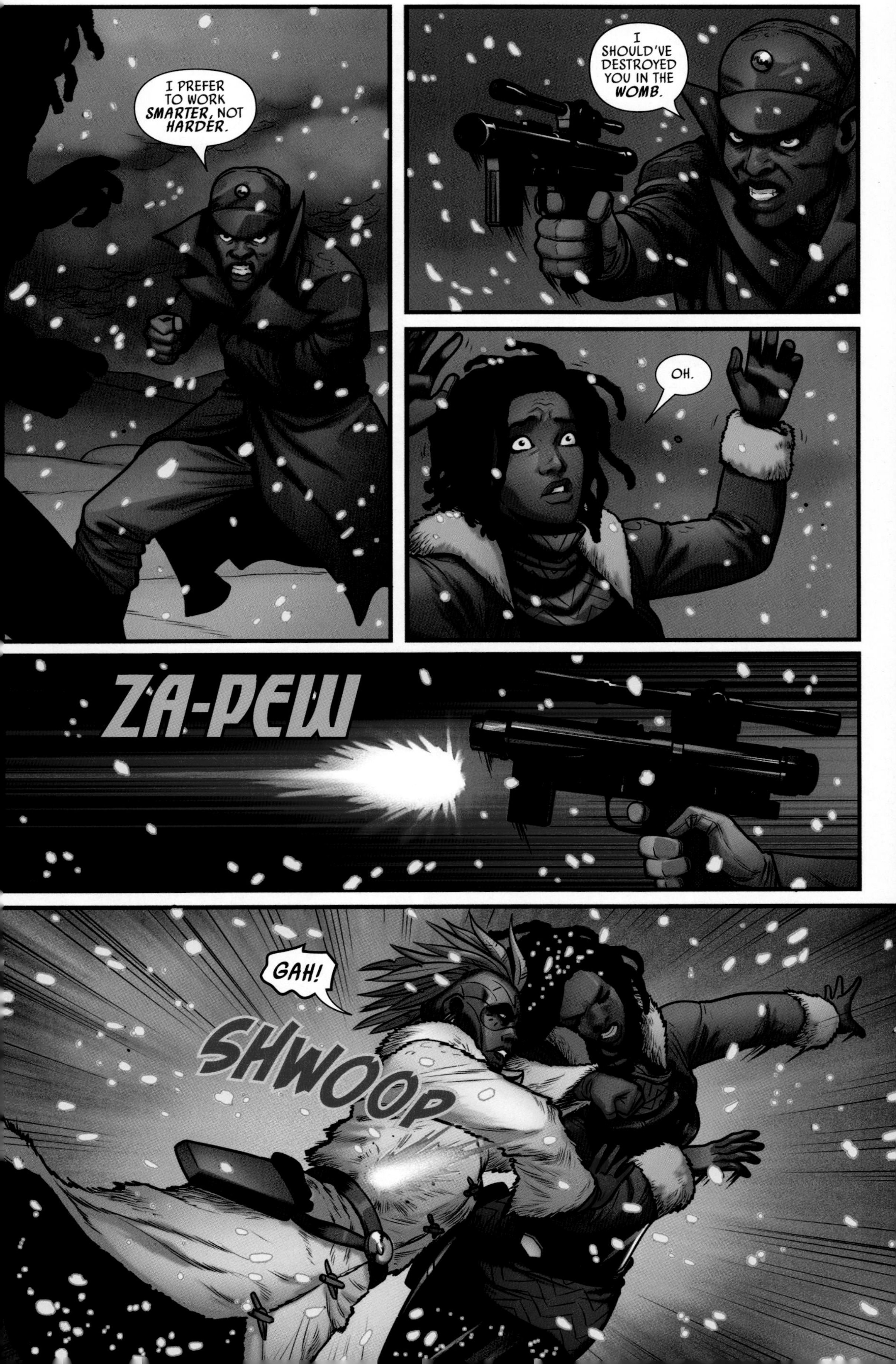
I PREFER TO WORK SMARTER, NOT HARDER.
I SHOULD'VE DESTROYED YOU IN THE WOMB.
OH.
ZA-PEW
GAH!
SHWOOP

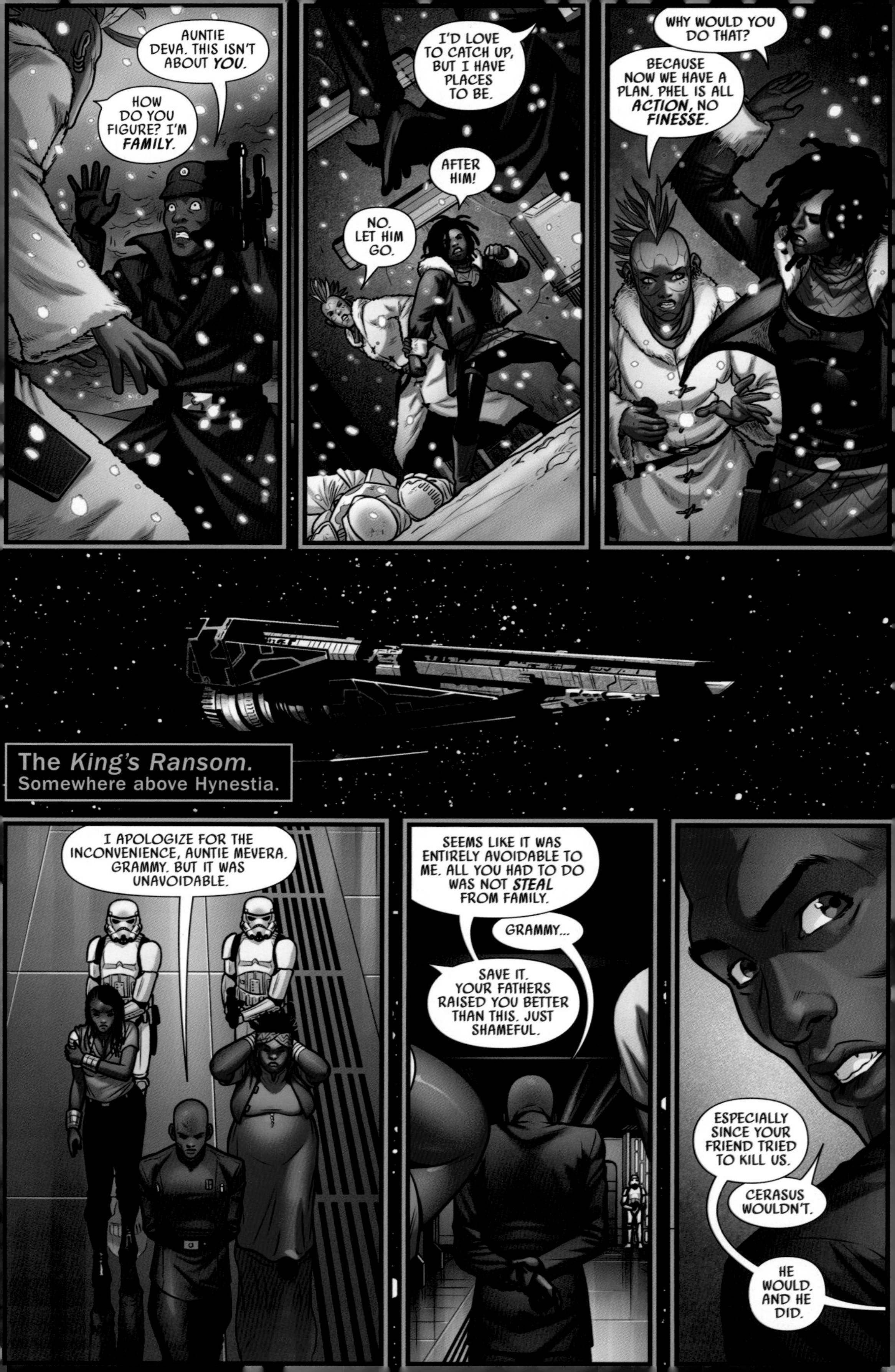
AUNTIE DEVA. THIS ISN'T ABOUT *YOU*.
HOW DO YOU FIGURE? I'M *FAMILY*.
I'D LOVE TO CATCH UP, BUT I HAVE PLACES TO BE.
AFTER HIM!
NO. LET HIM GO.
WHY WOULD YOU DO THAT?
BECAUSE NOW WE HAVE A PLAN. PHEL IS ALL *ACTION*, NO *FINESSE*.
The *King's Ransom*.
Somewhere above Hynestia.
I APOLOGIZE FOR THE INCONVENIENCE, AUNTIE MEVERA. GRAMMY. BUT IT WAS UNAVOIDABLE.
SEEMS LIKE IT WAS ENTIRELY AVOIDABLE TO ME. ALL YOU HAD TO DO WAS NOT *STEAL* FROM FAMILY.
GRAMMY...
SAVE IT. YOUR FATHERS RAISED YOU BETTER THAN THIS. JUST SHAMEFUL.
ESPECIALLY SINCE YOUR FRIEND TRIED TO KILL US.
CERASUS WOULDN'T.
HE WOULD. AND HE DID.

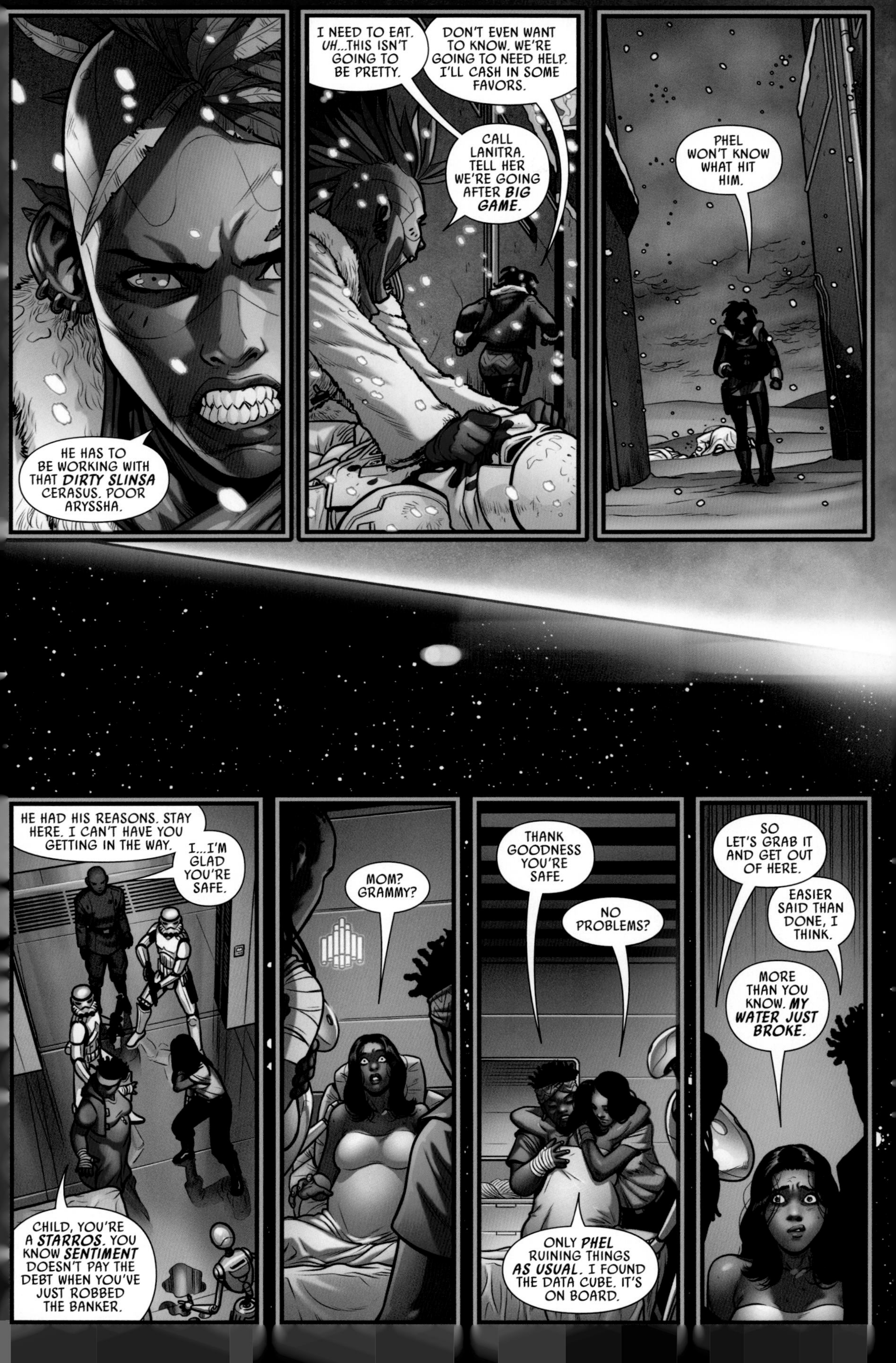
HE HAS TO BE WORKING WITH THAT DIRTY SLINSA CERASUS. POOR ARYSSHA.
I NEED TO EAT. UH...THIS ISN'T GOING TO BE PRETTY.
DON'T EVEN WANT TO KNOW. WE'RE GOING TO NEED HELP. I'LL CASH IN SOME FAVORS.
CALL LANITRA. TELL HER WE'RE GOING AFTER BIG GAME.
PHEL WON'T KNOW WHAT HIT HIM.
HE HAD HIS REASONS. STAY HERE. I CAN'T HAVE YOU GETTING IN THE WAY.
I...I'M GLAD YOU'RE SAFE.
CHILD, YOU'RE A STARROS. YOU KNOW SENTIMENT DOESN'T PAY THE DEBT WHEN YOU'VE JUST ROBBED THE BANKER.
MOM? GRAMMY?
THANK GOODNESS YOU'RE SAFE.
NO PROBLEMS?
ONLY PHEL RUINING THINGS AS USUAL. I FOUND THE DATA CUBE. IT'S ON BOARD.
SO LET'S GRAB IT AND GET OUT OF HERE.
EASIER SAID THAN DONE, I THINK.
MORE THAN YOU KNOW. MY WATER JUST BROKE.

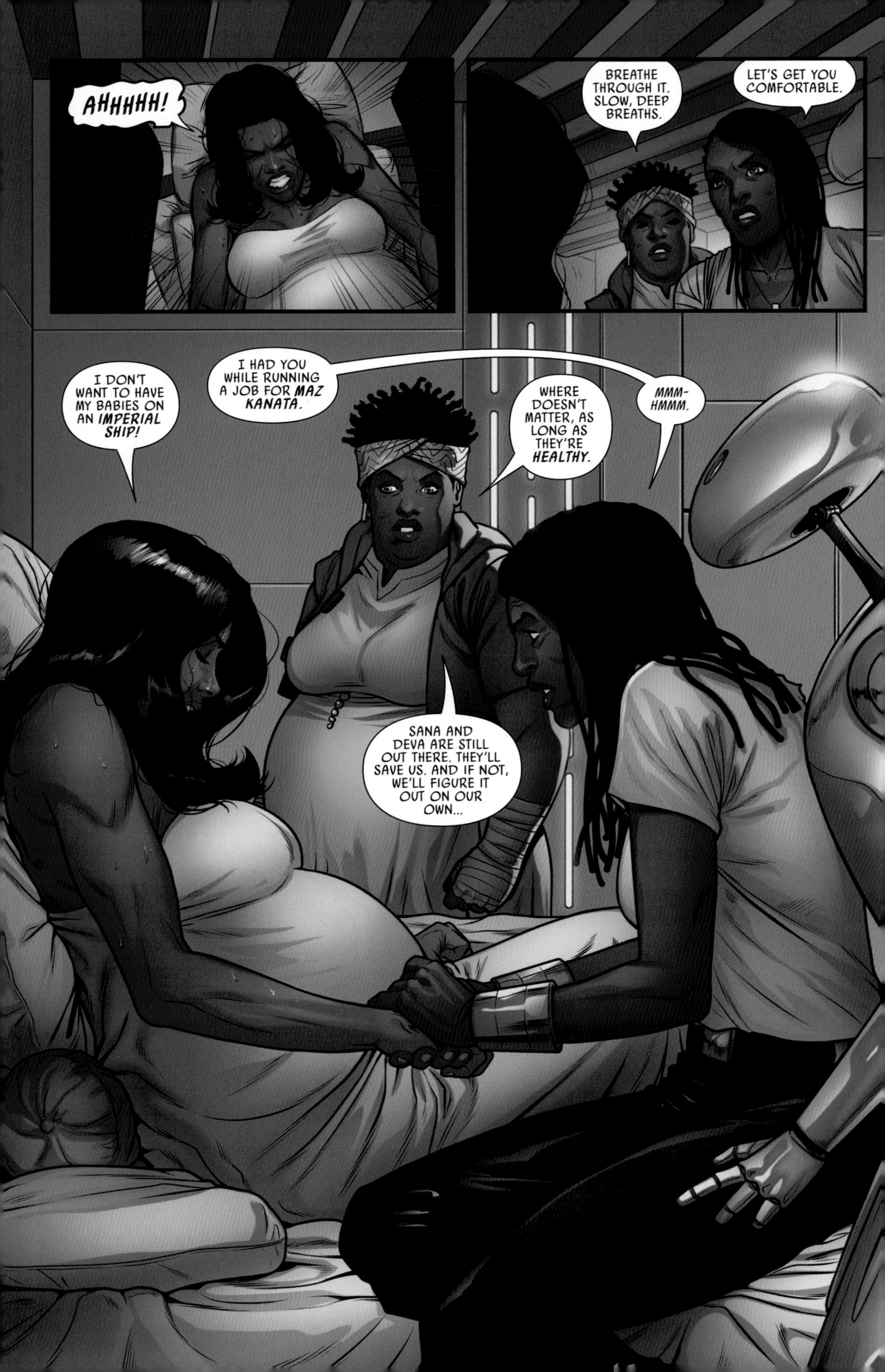
AHHHHH!
BREATHE THROUGH IT. SLOW, DEEP BREATHS.
LET'S GET YOU COMFORTABLE.
I DON'T WANT TO HAVE MY BABIES ON AN IMPERIAL SHIP!
I HAD YOU WHILE RUNNING A JOB FOR MAZ KANATA.
MMM-HMMM.
WHERE DOESN'T MATTER, AS LONG AS THEY'RE HEALTHY.
SANA AND DEVA ARE STILL OUT THERE. THEY'LL SAVE US. AND IF NOT, WE'LL FIGURE IT OUT ON OUR OWN...

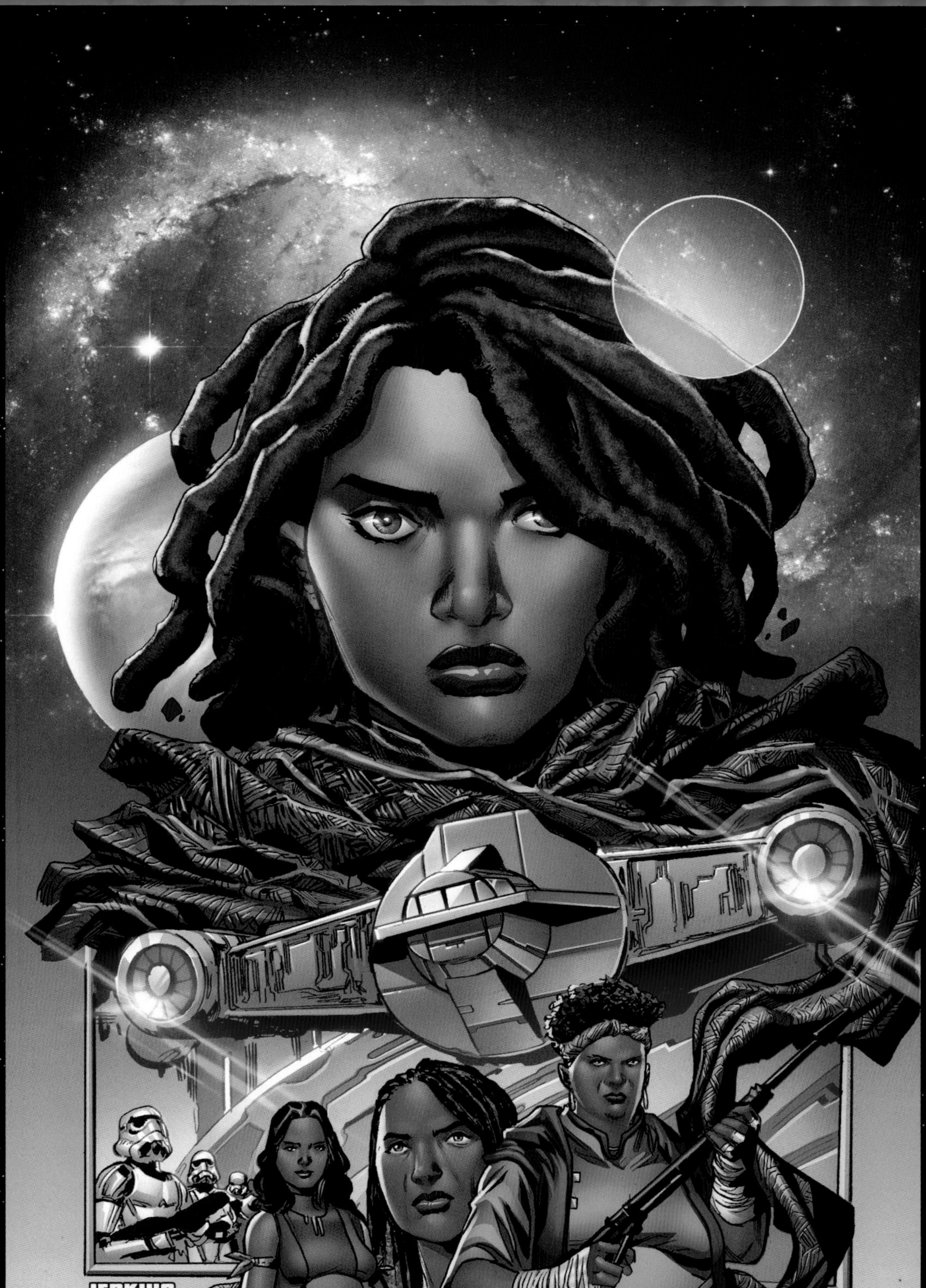
LEDKILLA

5 — FACTS OF LIFE

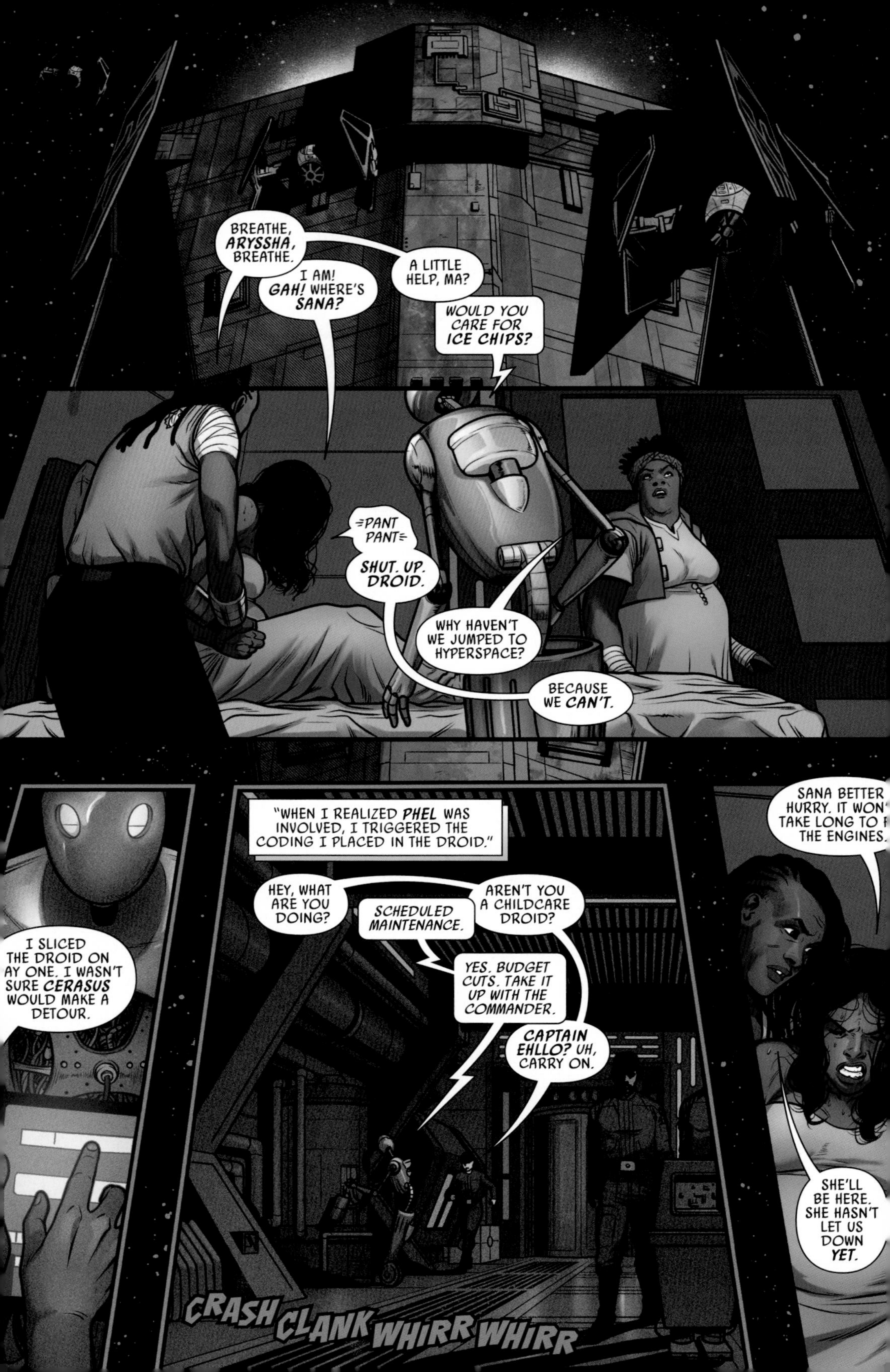
BREATHE, ARYSSHA, BREATHE.
I AM! GAH! WHERE'S SANA?
A LITTLE HELP, MA?
WOULD YOU CARE FOR ICE CHIPS?
PANT PANT
SHUT. UP. DROID.
WHY HAVEN'T WE JUMPED TO HYPERSPACE?
BECAUSE WE CAN'T.
I SLICED THE DROID ON AY ONE. I WASN'T SURE CERASUS WOULD MAKE A DETOUR.
"WHEN I REALIZED PHEL WAS INVOLVED, I TRIGGERED THE CODING I PLACED IN THE DROID."
HEY, WHAT ARE YOU DOING?
SCHEDULED MAINTENANCE.
AREN'T YOU A CHILDCARE DROID?
YES. BUDGET CUTS. TAKE IT UP WITH THE COMMANDER.
CAPTAIN EHLLO? UH, CARRY ON.
CRASH CLANK WHIRR WHIRR
SANA BETTER HURRY. IT WON' TAKE LONG TO THE ENGINES.
SHE'LL BE HERE. SHE HASN'T LET US DOWN YET.

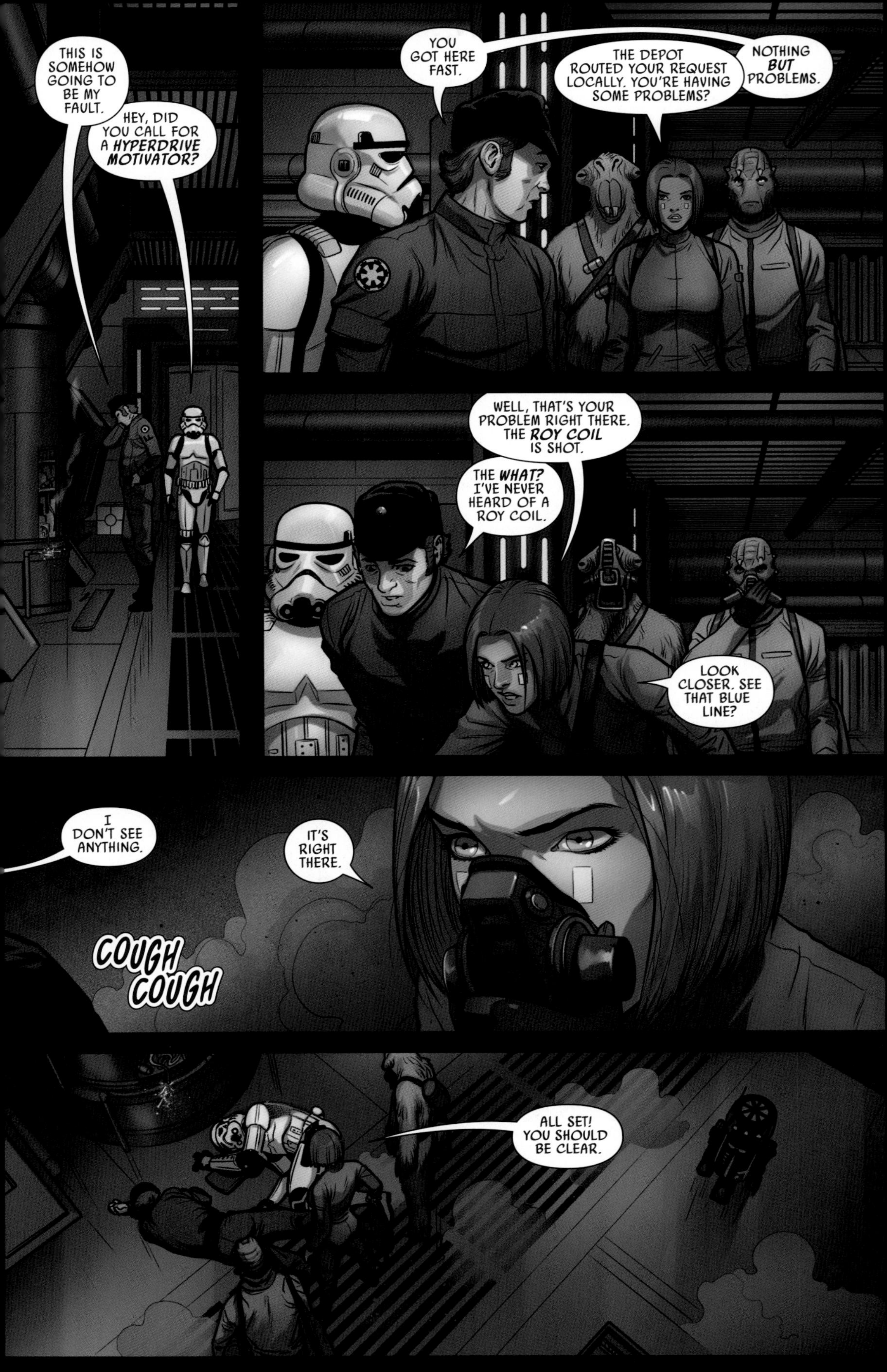
THIS IS SOMEHOW GOING TO BE MY FAULT.
HEY, DID YOU CALL FOR A HYPERDRIVE MOTIVATOR?
YOU GOT HERE FAST.
THE DEPOT ROUTED YOUR REQUEST LOCALLY. YOU'RE HAVING SOME PROBLEMS?
NOTHING BUT PROBLEMS.
WELL, THAT'S YOUR PROBLEM RIGHT THERE. THE ROY COIL IS SHOT.
THE WHAT? I'VE NEVER HEARD OF A ROY COIL.
LOOK CLOSER. SEE THAT BLUE LINE?
I DON'T SEE ANYTHING.
IT'S RIGHT THERE.
COUGH COUGH
ALL SET! YOU SHOULD BE CLEAR.

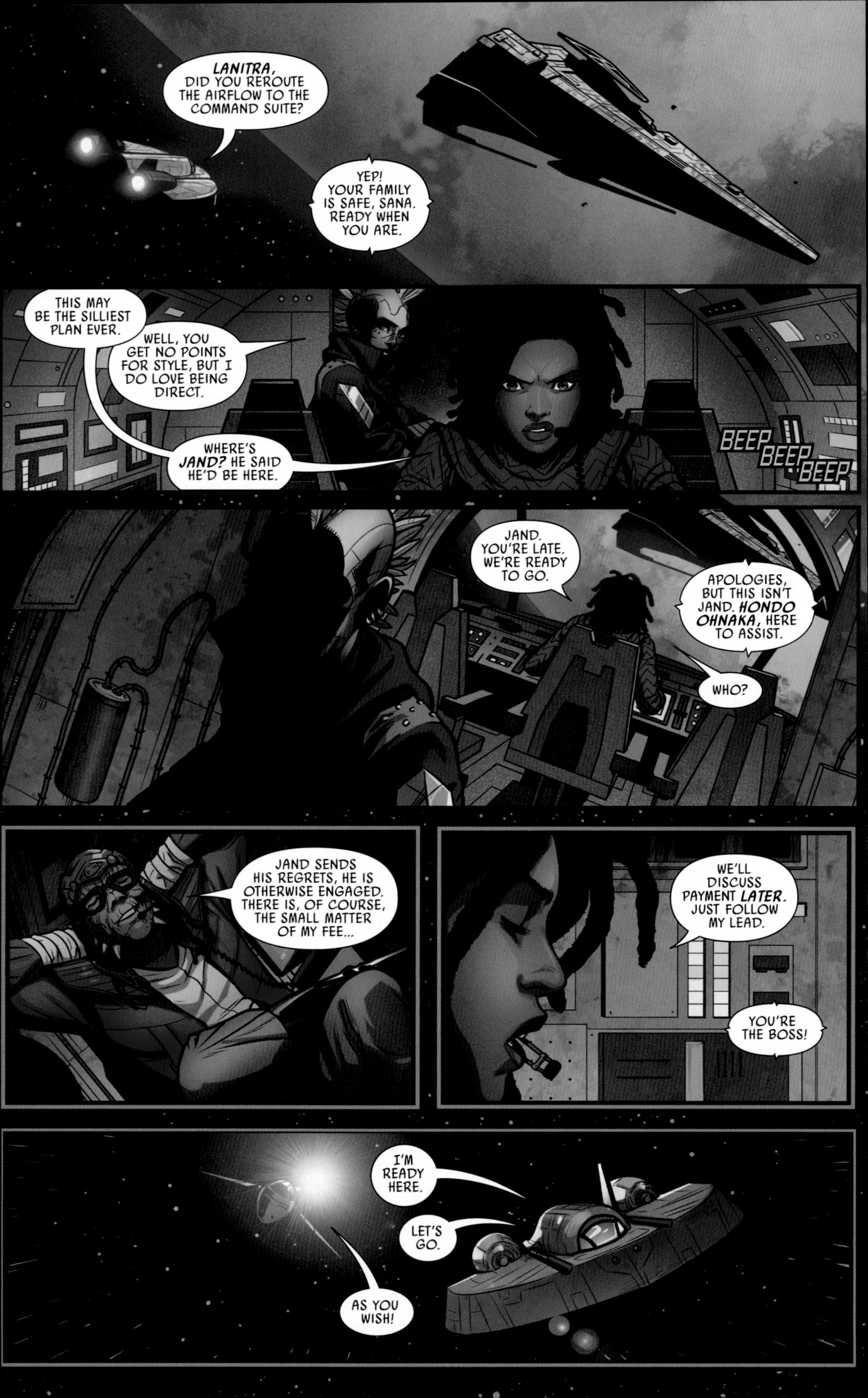
LANITRA, DID YOU REROUTE THE AIRFLOW TO THE COMMAND SUITE?
YEP! YOUR FAMILY IS SAFE, SANA. READY WHEN YOU ARE.
THIS MAY BE THE SILLIEST PLAN EVER.
WELL, YOU GET NO POINTS FOR STYLE, BUT I DO LOVE BEING DIRECT.
WHERE'S JAND? HE SAID HE'D BE HERE.
BEEP BEEP BEEP
JAND. YOU'RE LATE. WE'RE READY TO GO.
APOLOGIES, BUT THIS ISN'T JAND. HONDO OHNAKA, HERE TO ASSIST.
WHO?
JAND SENDS HIS REGRETS, HE IS OTHERWISE ENGAGED. THERE IS, OF COURSE, THE SMALL MATTER OF MY FEE...
WE'LL DISCUSS PAYMENT LATER. JUST FOLLOW MY LEAD.
YOU'RE THE BOSS!
I'M READY HERE.
LET'S GO.
AS YOU WISH!

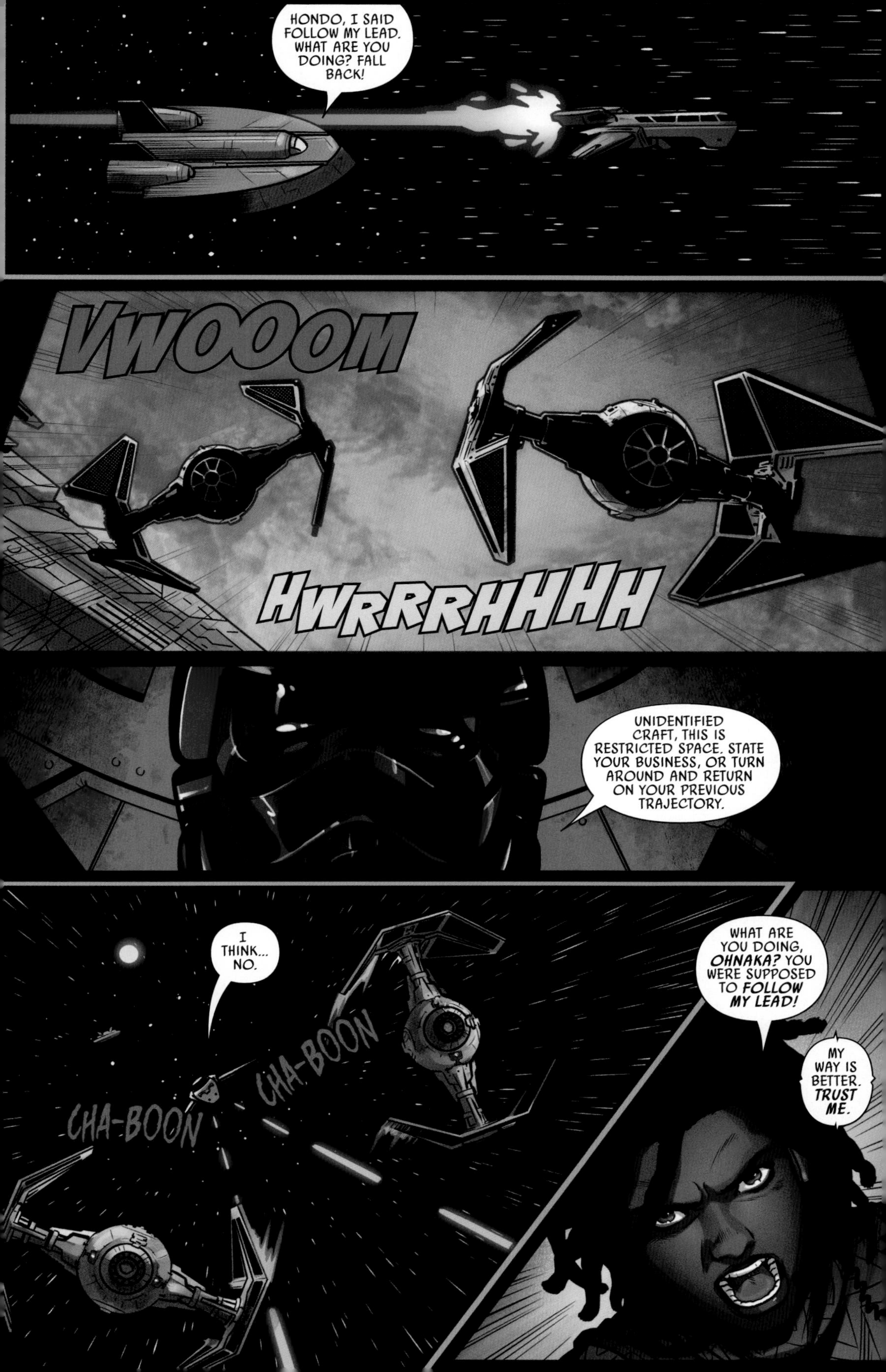
HONDO, I SAID FOLLOW MY LEAD. WHAT ARE YOU DOING? FALL BACK!
VWOOOM
HWRRRHHHH
UNIDENTIFIED CRAFT, THIS IS RESTRICTED SPACE. STATE YOUR BUSINESS, OR TURN AROUND AND RETURN ON YOUR PREVIOUS TRAJECTORY.
I THINK... NO.
CHA-BOON
CHA-BOON
WHAT ARE YOU DOING, OHNAKA? YOU WERE SUPPOSED TO FOLLOW MY LEAD!
MY WAY IS BETTER. TRUST ME.

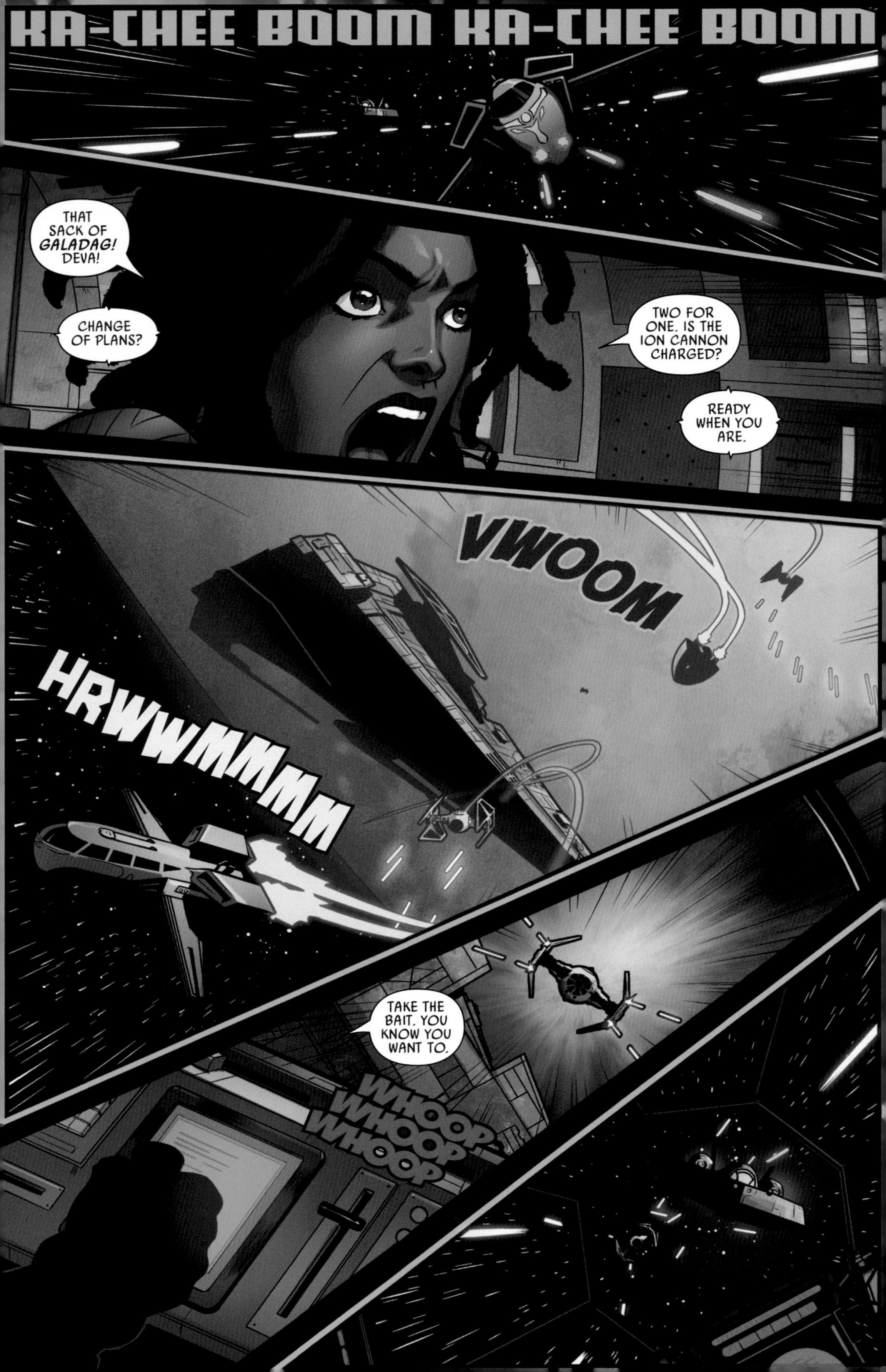
KA-CHEE BOOM KA-CHEE BOOM
THAT SACK OF GALADAG! DEVA!
CHANGE OF PLANS?
TWO FOR ONE. IS THE ION CANNON CHARGED?
READY WHEN YOU ARE.
VWOOM
HRWWMMMM
TAKE THE BAIT. YOU KNOW YOU WANT TO.
WHOOP WHOOP WHOOP

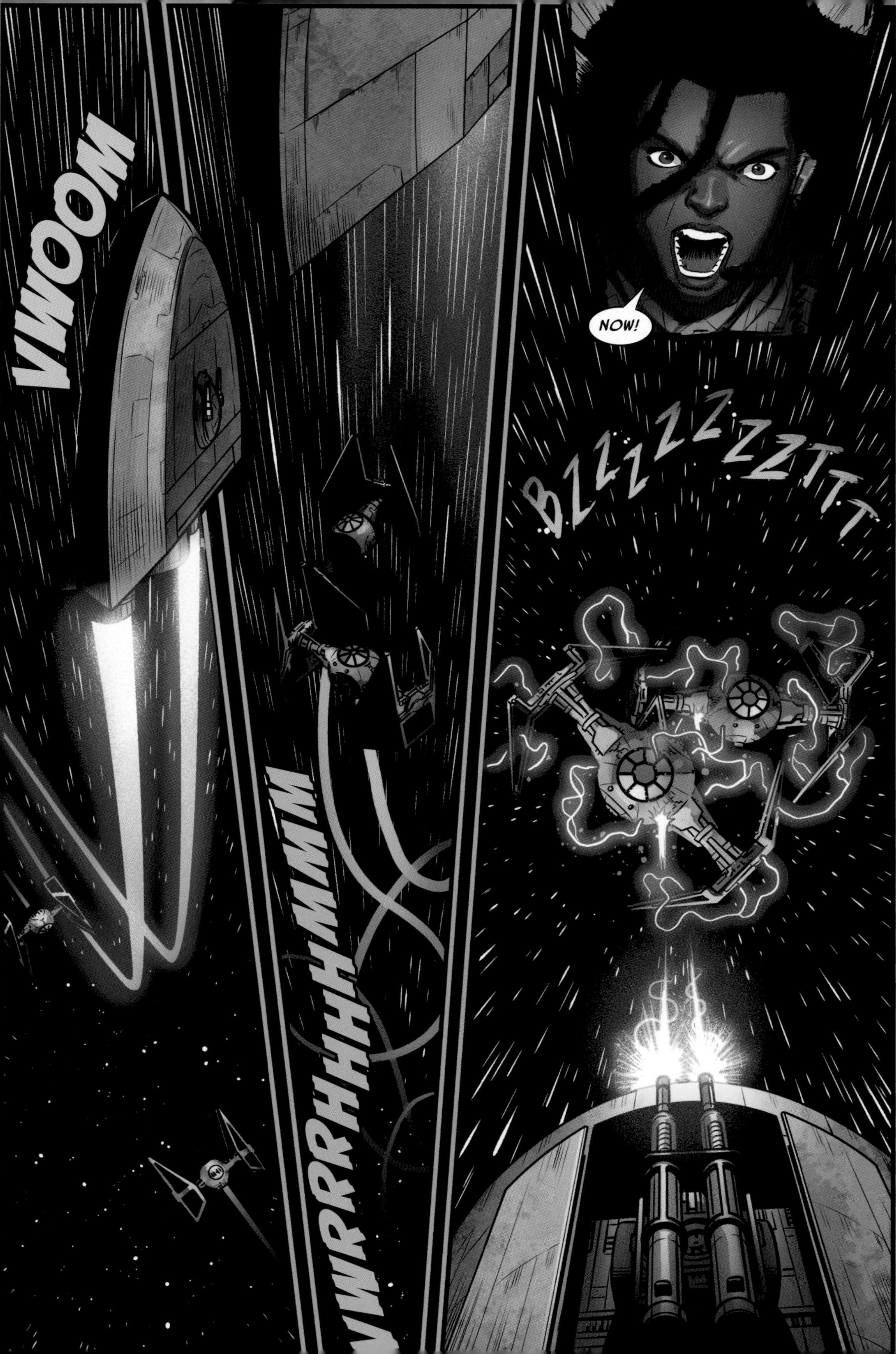

VWOOM
WWRRRRHHHHHMMMMM
NOW!
BZZZZZZZTTTT

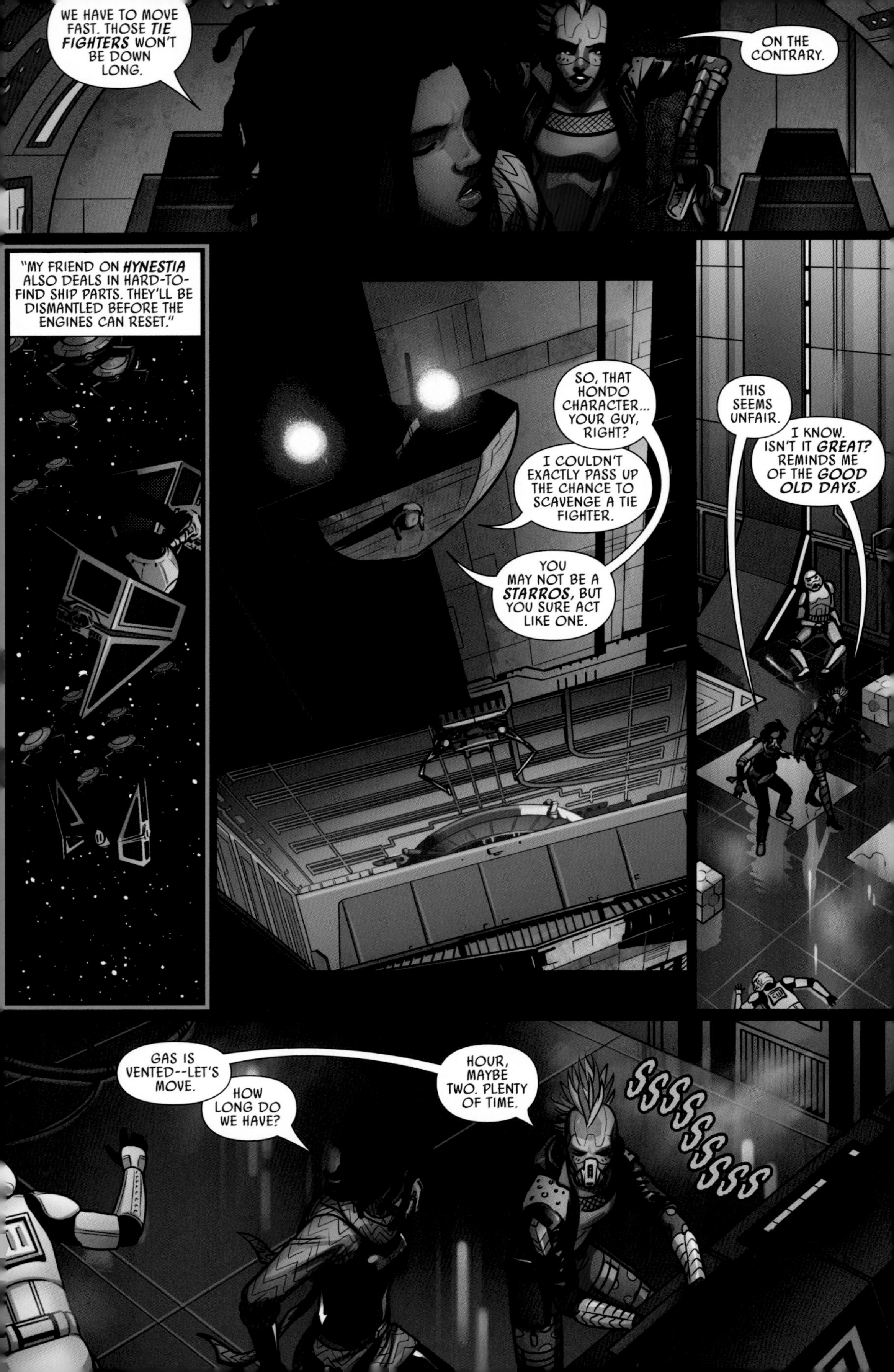
WE HAVE TO MOVE FAST. THOSE TIE FIGHTERS WON'T BE DOWN LONG.
ON THE CONTRARY.
"MY FRIEND ON HYNESTIA ALSO DEALS IN HARD-TO-FIND SHIP PARTS. THEY'LL BE DISMANTLED BEFORE THE ENGINES CAN RESET."
SO, THAT HONDO CHARACTER... YOUR GUY, RIGHT?
I COULDN'T EXACTLY PASS UP THE CHANCE TO SCAVENGE A TIE FIGHTER.
YOU MAY NOT BE A STARROS, BUT YOU SURE ACT LIKE ONE.
THIS SEEMS UNFAIR.
I KNOW. ISN'T IT GREAT? REMINDS ME OF THE GOOD OLD DAYS.
GAS IS VENTED--LET'S MOVE.
HOW LONG DO WE HAVE?
HOUR, MAYBE TWO. PLENTY OF TIME.
SSSSSSSSSS

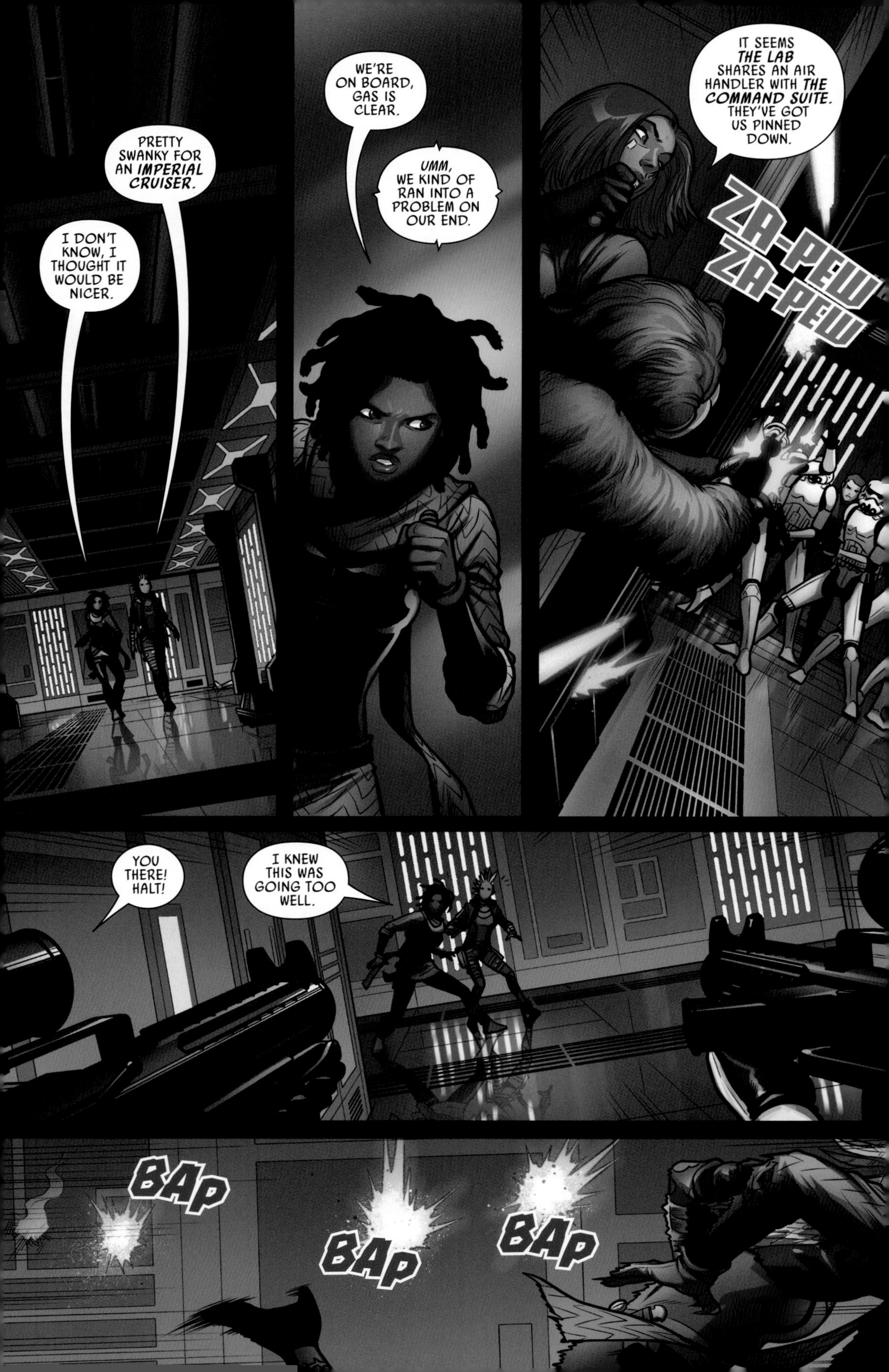
PRETTY SWANKY FOR AN *IMPERIAL CRUISER*.
I DON'T KNOW, I THOUGHT IT WOULD BE NICER.
WE'RE ON BOARD, GAS IS CLEAR.
UMM, WE KIND OF RAN INTO A PROBLEM ON OUR END.
IT SEEMS *THE LAB* SHARES AN AIR HANDLER WITH *THE COMMAND SUITE*. THEY'VE GOT US PINNED DOWN.
ZA-PEW
ZA-PEW
YOU THERE! HALT!
I KNEW THIS WAS GOING TOO WELL.
BAP
BAP
BAP

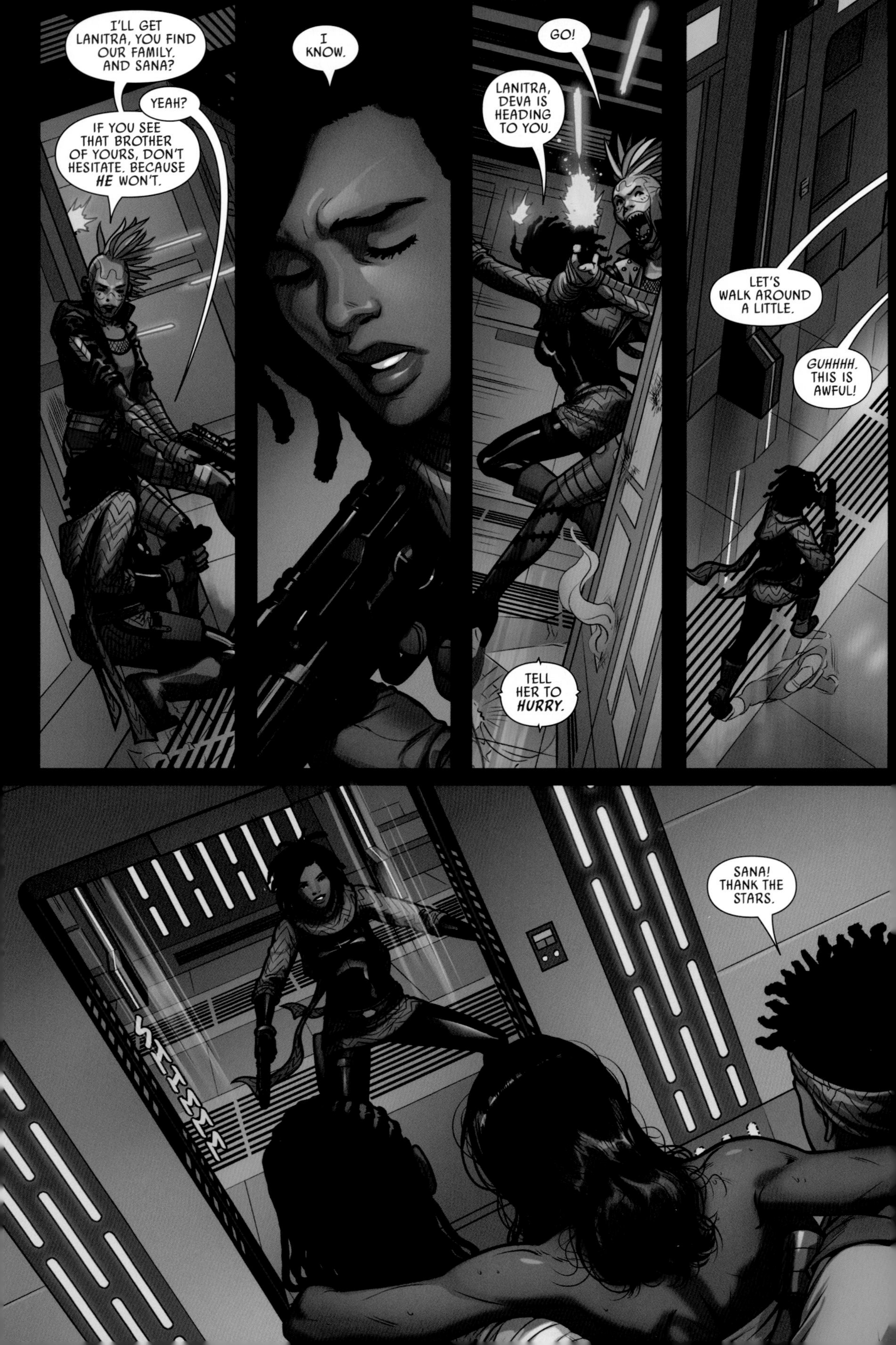
I'LL GET LANITRA, YOU FIND OUR FAMILY. AND SANA?
YEAH?
IF YOU SEE THAT BROTHER OF YOURS, DON'T HESITATE. BECAUSE *HE* WON'T.
I KNOW.
GO!
LANITRA, DEVA IS HEADING TO YOU.
TELL HER TO *HURRY.*
LET'S WALK AROUND A LITTLE.
GUHHHH. THIS IS AWFUL!
SANA! THANK THE STARS.

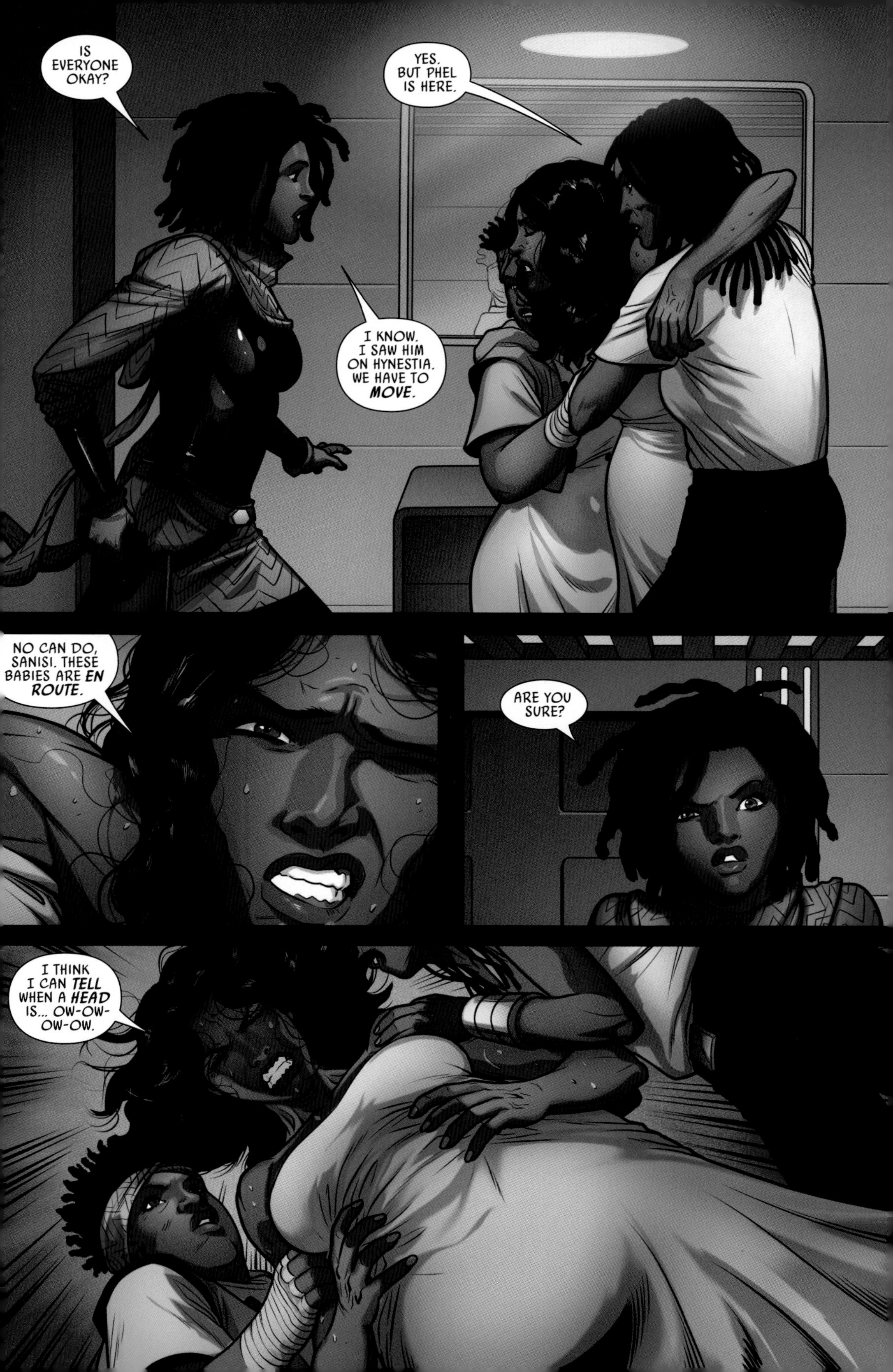
IS EVERYONE OKAY?
YES. BUT PHEL IS HERE.
I KNOW. I SAW HIM ON HYNESTIA. WE HAVE TO MOVE.
NO CAN DO, SANISI. THESE BABIES ARE EN ROUTE.
ARE YOU SURE?
I THINK I CAN TELL WHEN A HEAD IS... OW-OW-OW-OW.

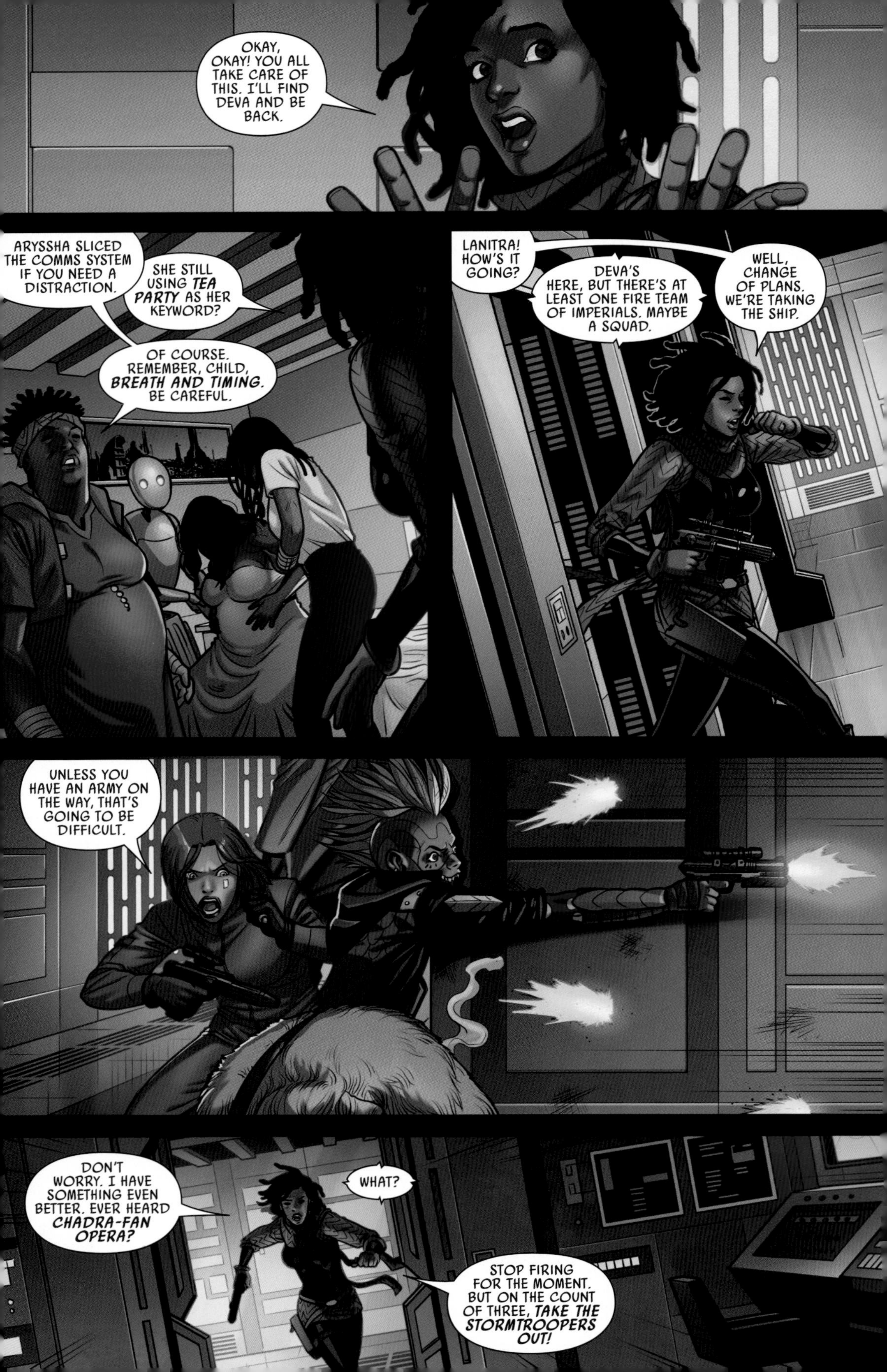
OKAY, OKAY! YOU ALL TAKE CARE OF THIS. I'LL FIND DEVA AND BE BACK.
ARYSSHA SLICED THE COMMS SYSTEM IF YOU NEED A DISTRACTION.
SHE STILL USING TEA PARTY AS HER KEYWORD?
OF COURSE. REMEMBER, CHILD, BREATH AND TIMING. BE CAREFUL.
LANITRA! HOW'S IT GOING?
DEVA'S HERE, BUT THERE'S AT LEAST ONE FIRE TEAM OF IMPERIALS. MAYBE A SQUAD.
WELL, CHANGE OF PLANS. WE'RE TAKING THE SHIP.
UNLESS YOU HAVE AN ARMY ON THE WAY, THAT'S GOING TO BE DIFFICULT.
DON'T WORRY. I HAVE SOMETHING EVEN BETTER. EVER HEARD CHADRA-FAN OPERA?
WHAT?
STOP FIRING FOR THE MOMENT. BUT ON THE COUNT OF THREE, TAKE THE STORMTROOPERS OUT!

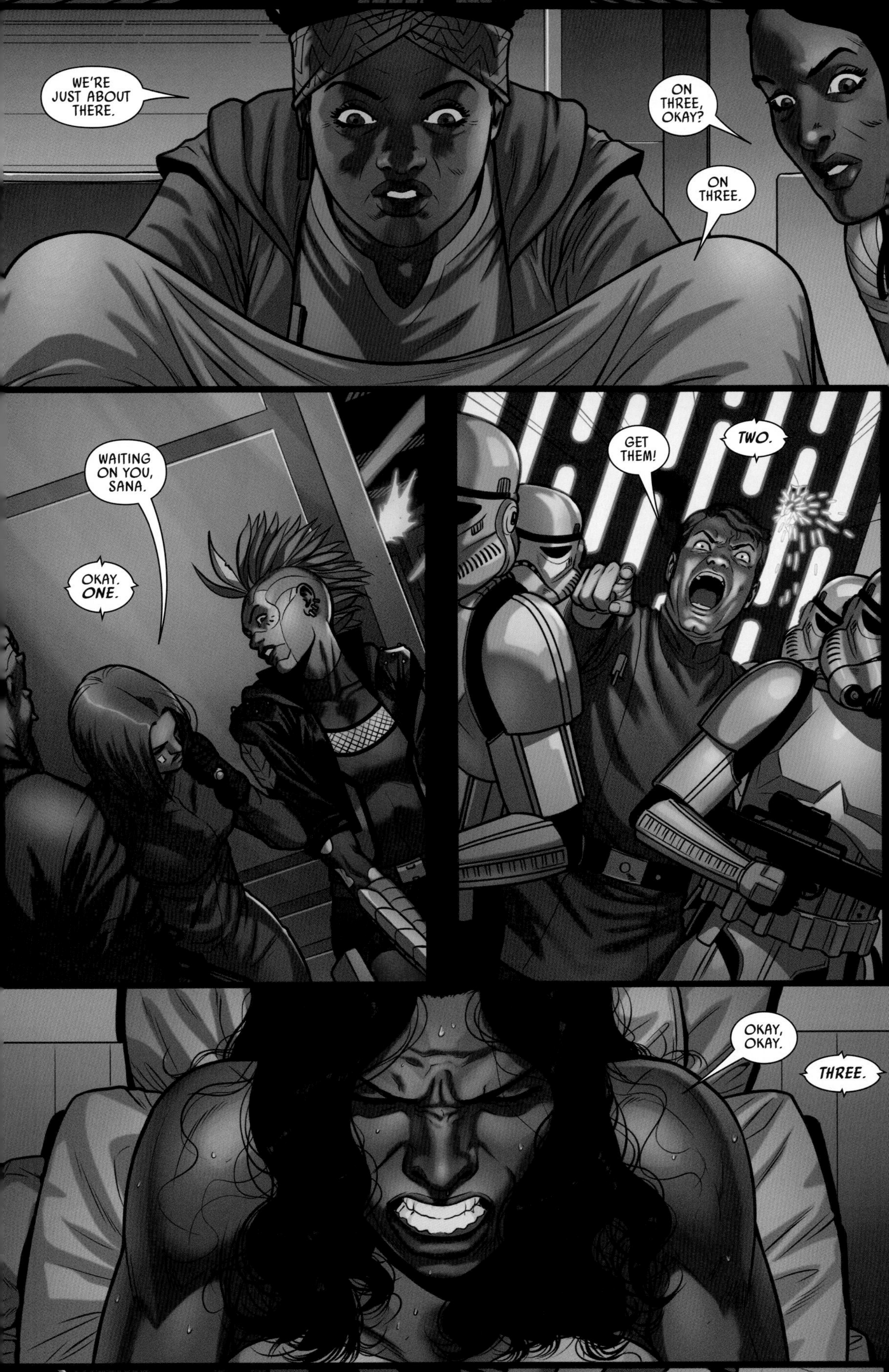
WE'RE JUST ABOUT THERE.
ON THREE, OKAY?
ON THREE.
WAITING ON YOU, SANA.
OKAY. ONE.
GET THEM!
TWO.
OKAY, OKAY.
THREE.

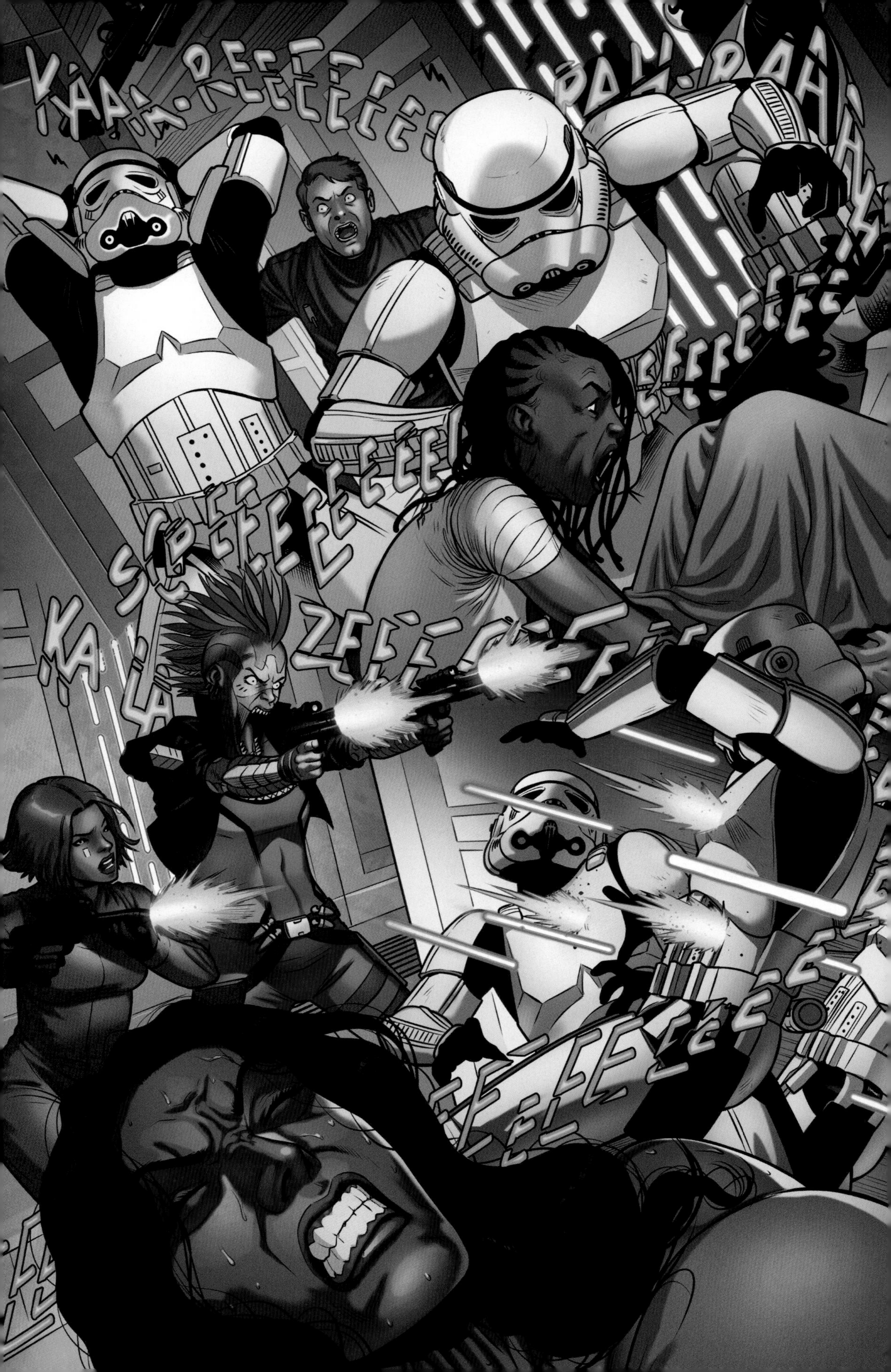

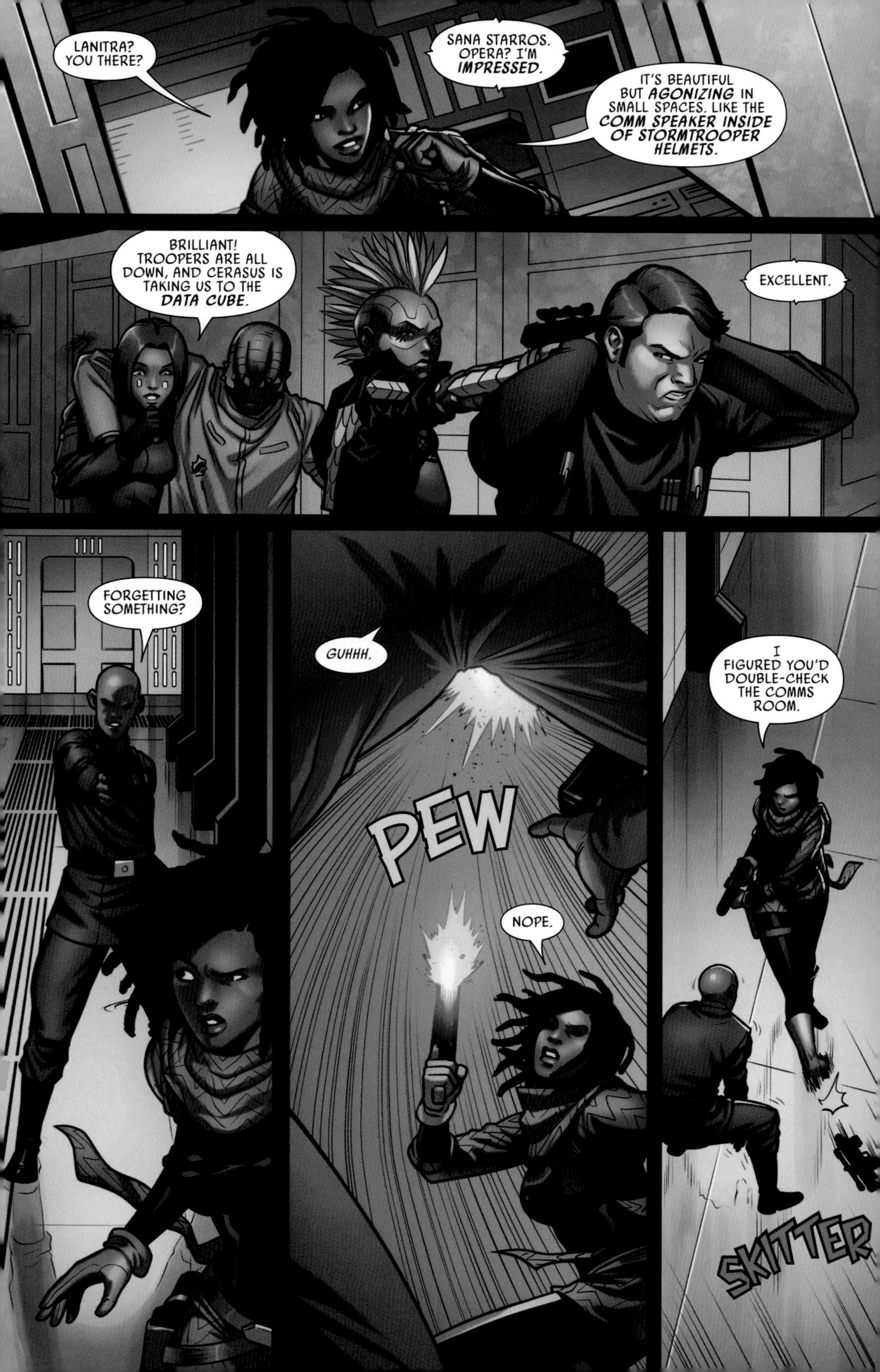
LANITRA? YOU THERE?
SANA STARROS. OPERA? I'M IMPRESSED.
IT'S BEAUTIFUL BUT AGONIZING IN SMALL SPACES. LIKE THE COMM SPEAKER INSIDE OF STORMTROOPER HELMETS.
BRILLIANT! TROOPERS ARE ALL DOWN, AND CERASUS IS TAKING US TO THE DATA CUBE.
EXCELLENT.
FORGETTING SOMETHING?
GUHHH.
PEW
NOPE.
I FIGURED YOU'D DOUBLE-CHECK THE COMMS ROOM.
SKITTER

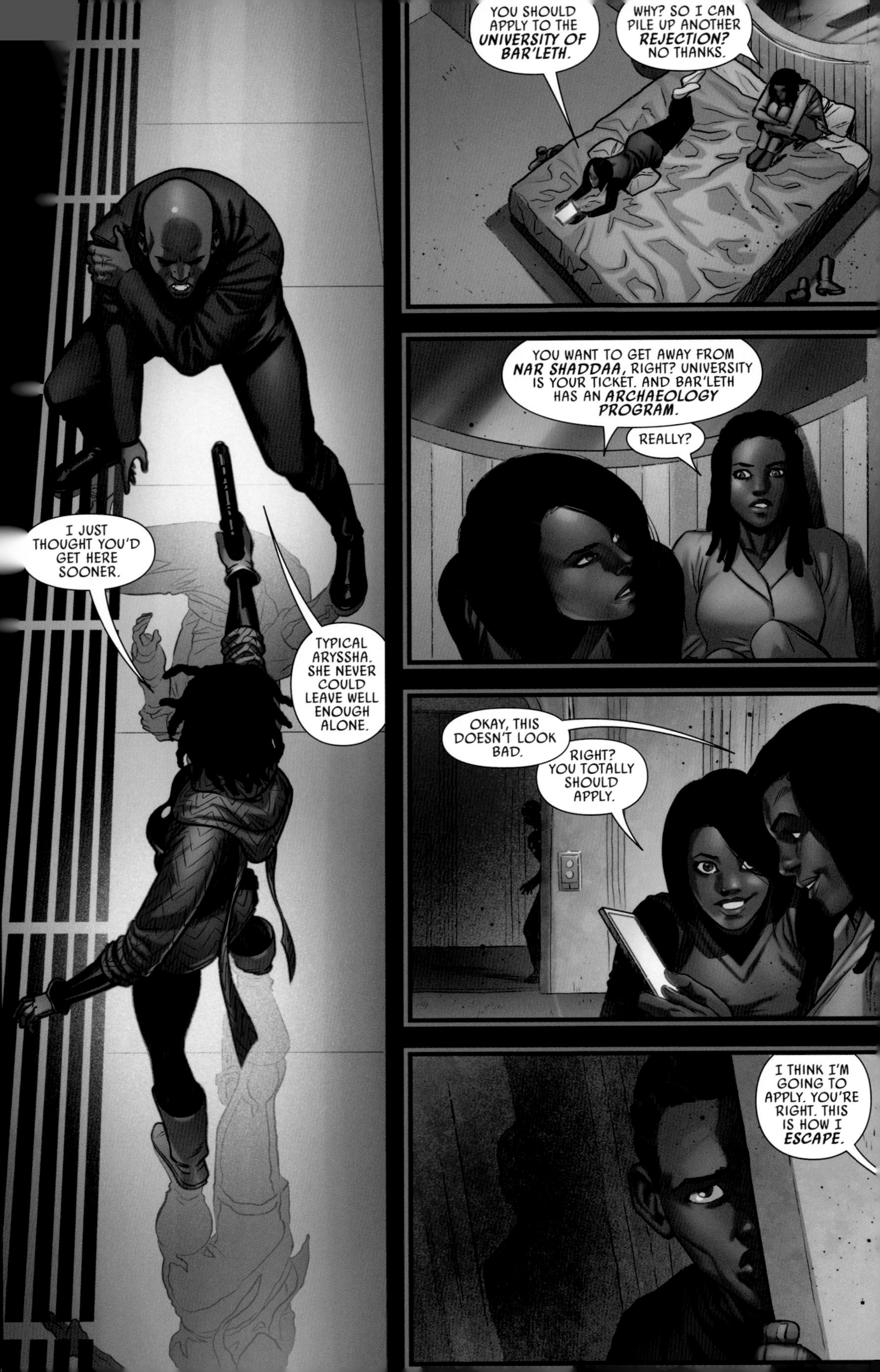
I JUST THOUGHT YOU'D GET HERE SOONER.
TYPICAL ARYSSHA. SHE NEVER COULD LEAVE WELL ENOUGH ALONE.
YOU SHOULD APPLY TO THE UNIVERSITY OF BAR'LETH.
WHY? SO I CAN PILE UP ANOTHER REJECTION? NO THANKS.
YOU WANT TO GET AWAY FROM NAR SHADDAA, RIGHT? UNIVERSITY IS YOUR TICKET. AND BAR'LETH HAS AN ARCHAEOLOGY PROGRAM.
REALLY?
OKAY, THIS DOESN'T LOOK BAD.
RIGHT? YOU TOTALLY SHOULD APPLY.
I THINK I'M GOING TO APPLY. YOU'RE RIGHT. THIS IS HOW I ESCAPE.

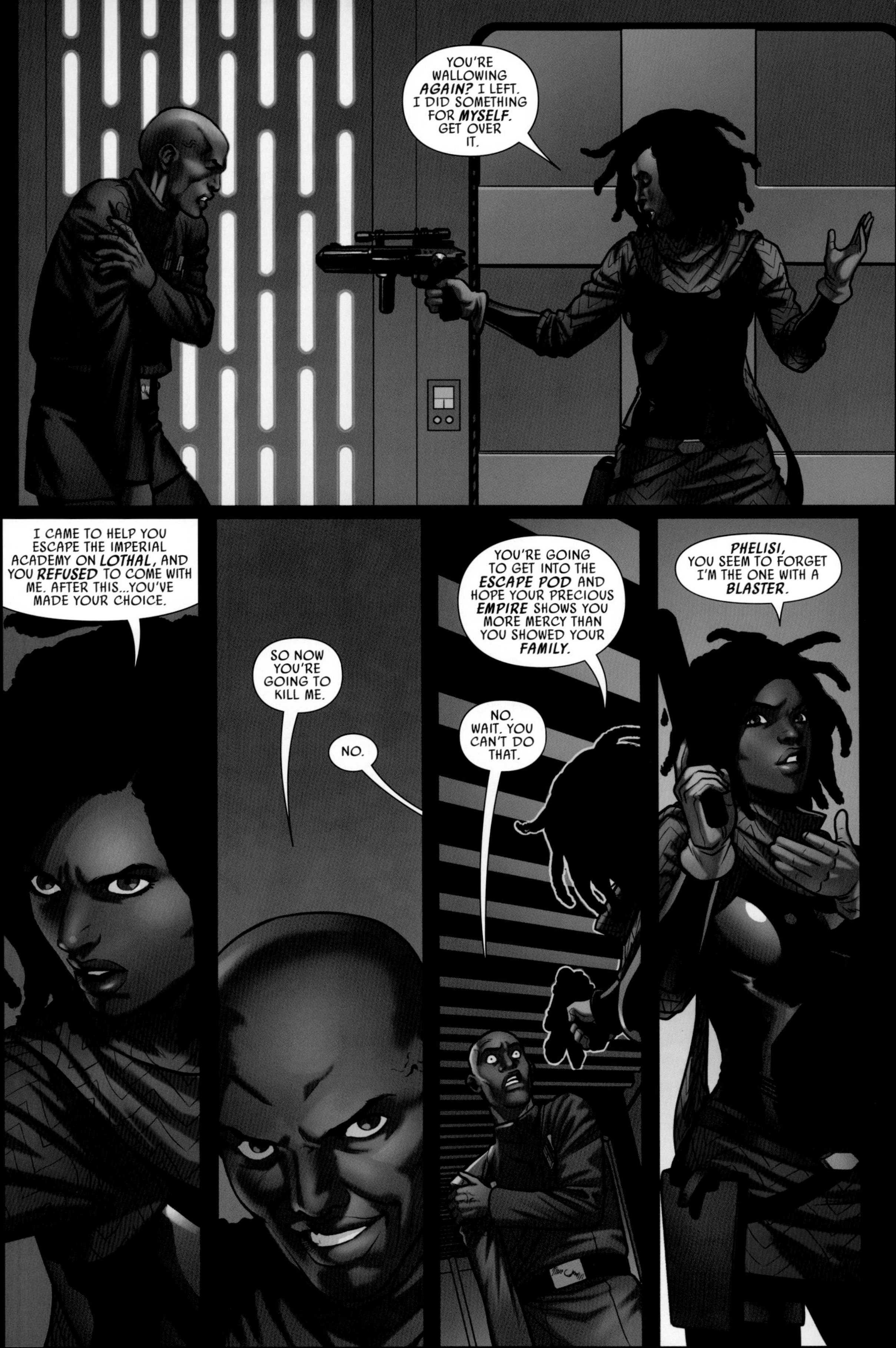
YOU'RE WALLOWING AGAIN? I LEFT. I DID SOMETHING FOR MYSELF. GET OVER IT.
I CAME TO HELP YOU ESCAPE THE IMPERIAL ACADEMY ON LOTHAL, AND YOU REFUSED TO COME WITH ME. AFTER THIS...YOU'VE MADE YOUR CHOICE.
SO NOW YOU'RE GOING TO KILL ME.
NO.
YOU'RE GOING TO GET INTO THE ESCAPE POD AND HOPE YOUR PRECIOUS EMPIRE SHOWS YOU MORE MERCY THAN YOU SHOWED YOUR FAMILY.
NO. WAIT. YOU CAN'T DO THAT.
PHELISI, YOU SEEM TO FORGET I'M THE ONE WITH A BLASTER.

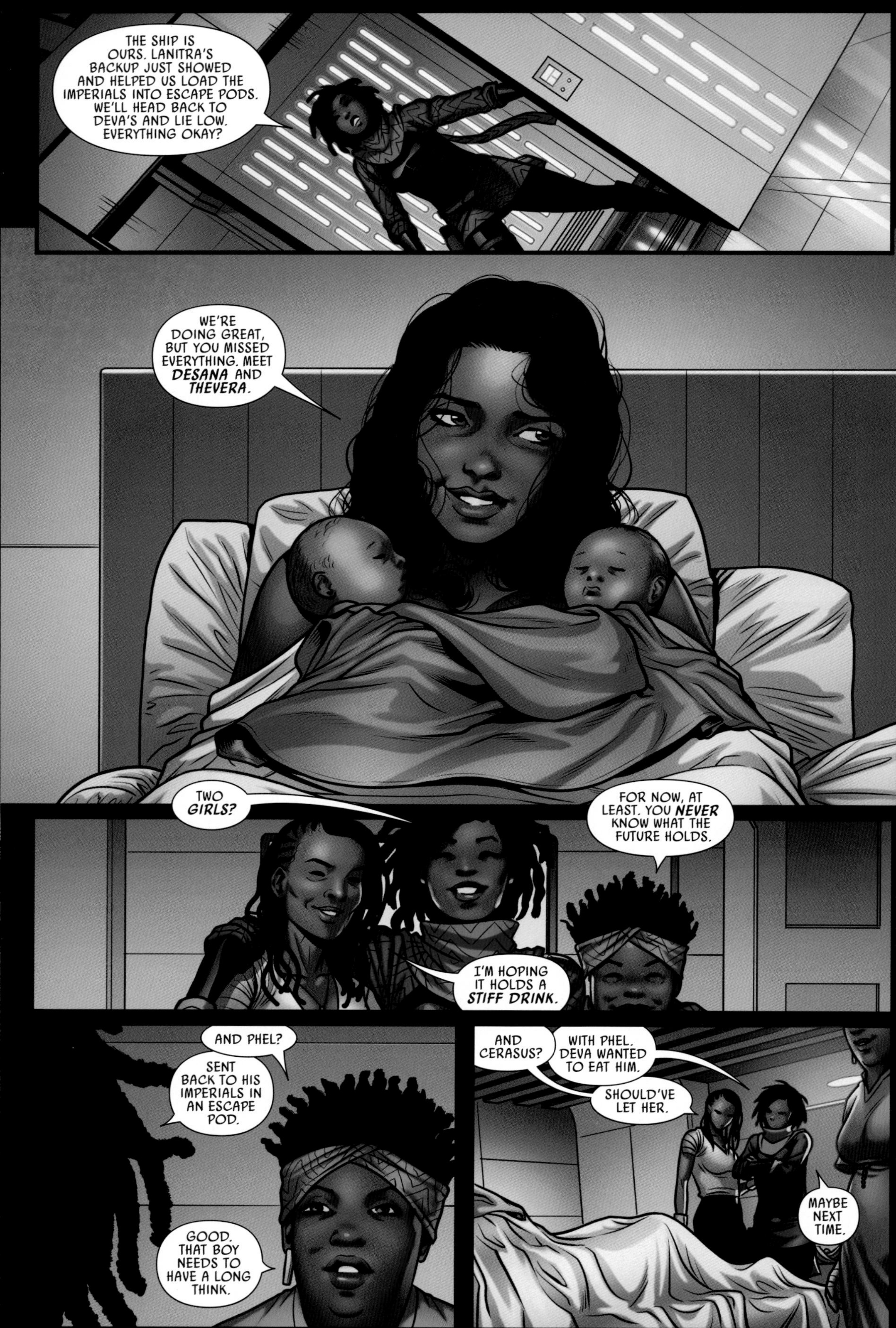
THE SHIP IS OURS. LANITRA'S BACKUP JUST SHOWED AND HELPED US LOAD THE IMPERIALS INTO ESCAPE PODS. WE'LL HEAD BACK TO DEVA'S AND LIE LOW. EVERYTHING OKAY?
WE'RE DOING GREAT, BUT YOU MISSED EVERYTHING. MEET DESANA AND THEVERA.
TWO GIRLS?
FOR NOW, AT LEAST. YOU NEVER KNOW WHAT THE FUTURE HOLDS.
I'M HOPING IT HOLDS A STIFF DRINK.
AND PHEL?
SENT BACK TO HIS IMPERIALS IN AN ESCAPE POD.
GOOD. THAT BOY NEEDS TO HAVE A LONG THINK.
AND CERASUS?
WITH PHEL. DEVA WANTED TO EAT HIM.
SHOULD'VE LET HER.
MAYBE NEXT TIME.

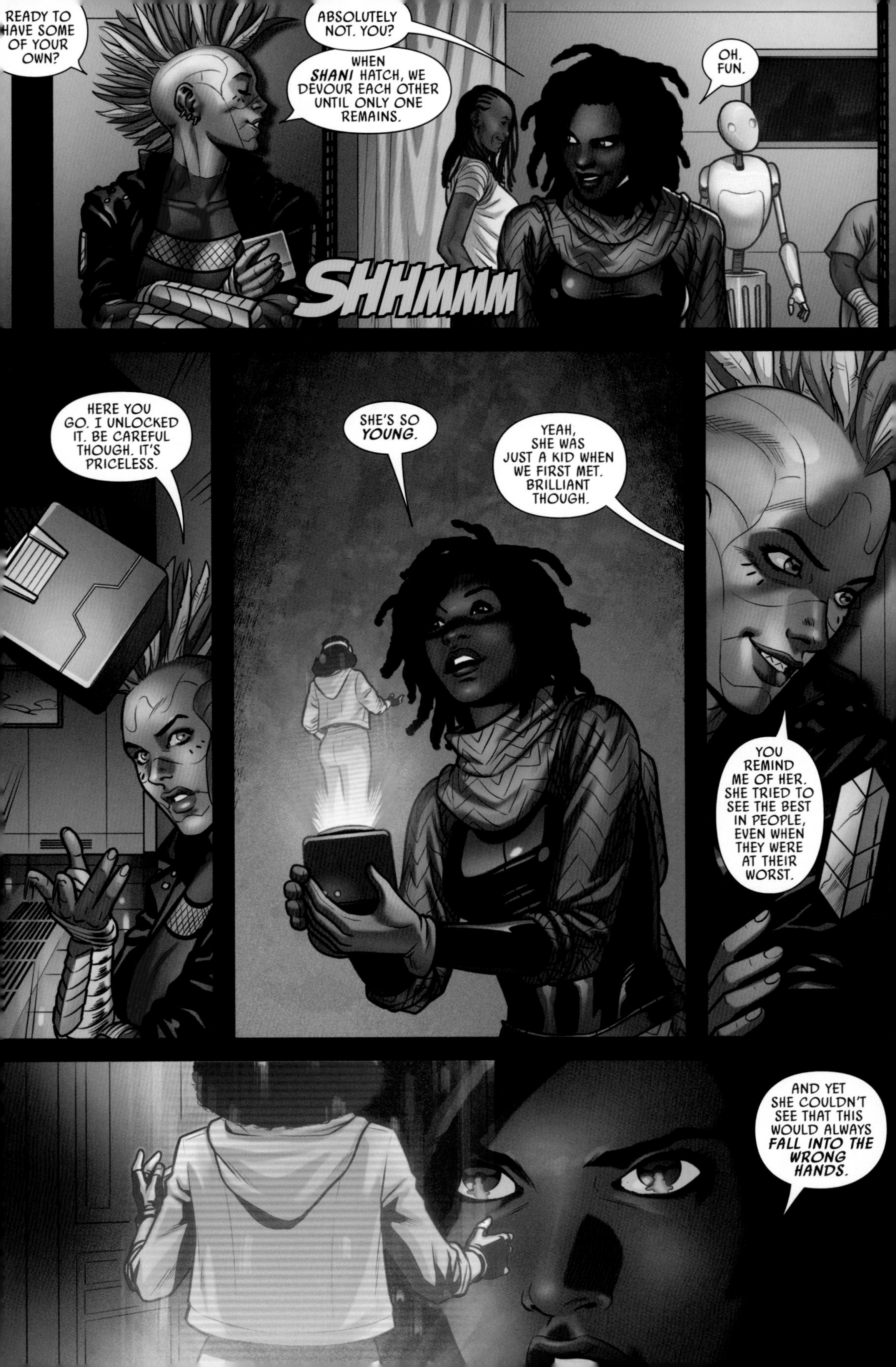
READY TO HAVE SOME OF YOUR OWN?
ABSOLUTELY NOT. YOU?
WHEN SHANI HATCH, WE DEVOUR EACH OTHER UNTIL ONLY ONE REMAINS.
OH. FUN.
SHHMMM
HERE YOU GO. I UNLOCKED IT. BE CAREFUL THOUGH. IT'S PRICELESS.
SHE'S SO YOUNG.
YEAH, SHE WAS JUST A KID WHEN WE FIRST MET. BRILLIANT THOUGH.
YOU REMIND ME OF HER. SHE TRIED TO SEE THE BEST IN PEOPLE, EVEN WHEN THEY WERE AT THEIR WORST.
AND YET SHE COULDN'T SEE THAT THIS WOULD ALWAYS FALL INTO THE WRONG HANDS.

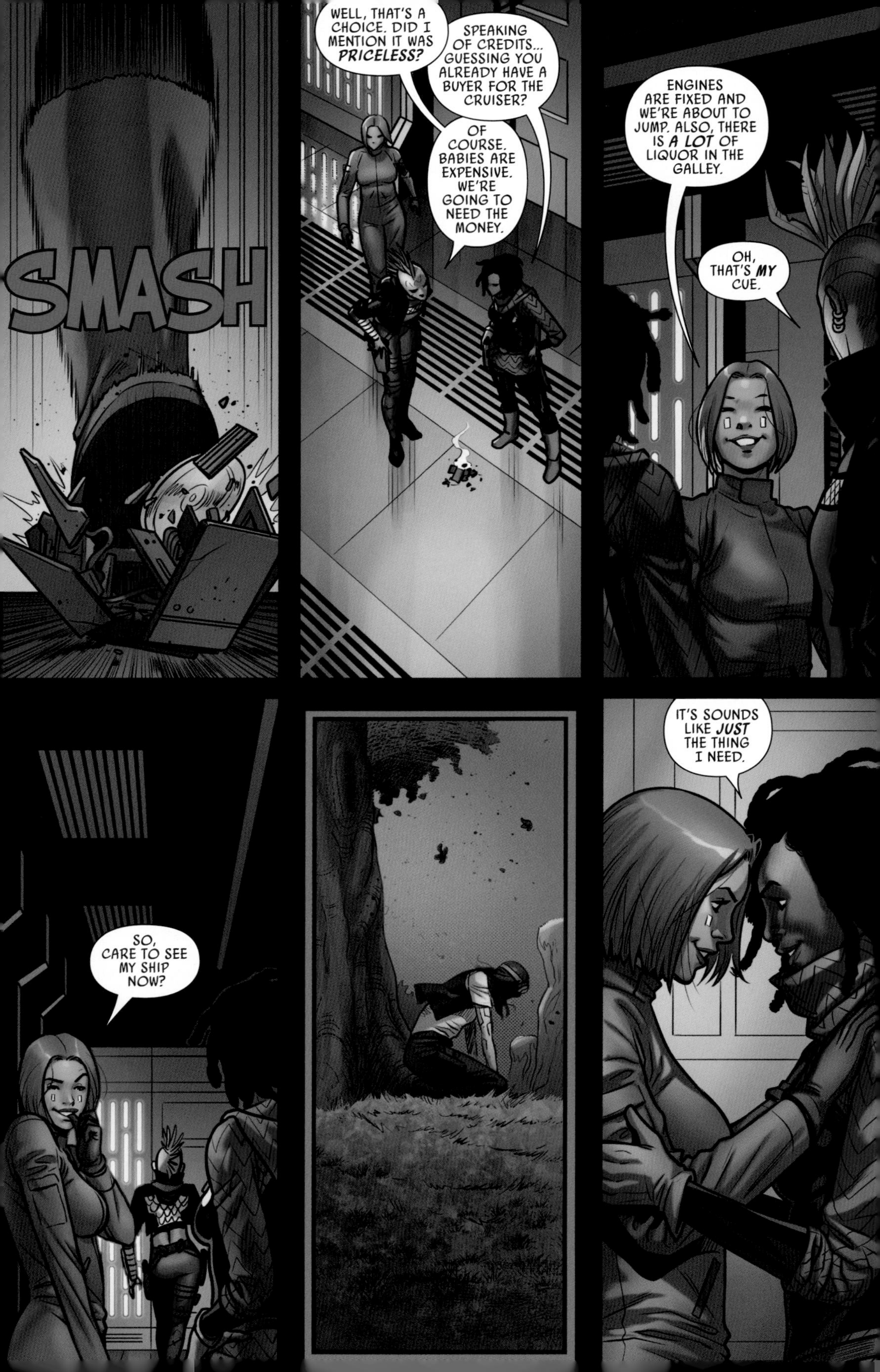
SMASH
WELL, THAT'S A CHOICE. DID I MENTION IT WAS PRICELESS?
SPEAKING OF CREDITS... GUESSING YOU ALREADY HAVE A BUYER FOR THE CRUISER?
OF COURSE. BABIES ARE EXPENSIVE. WE'RE GOING TO NEED THE MONEY.
ENGINES ARE FIXED AND WE'RE ABOUT TO JUMP. ALSO, THERE IS A LOT OF LIQUOR IN THE GALLEY.
OH, THAT'S MY CUE.
SO, CARE TO SEE MY SHIP NOW?
IT'S SOUNDS LIKE JUST THE THING I NEED.

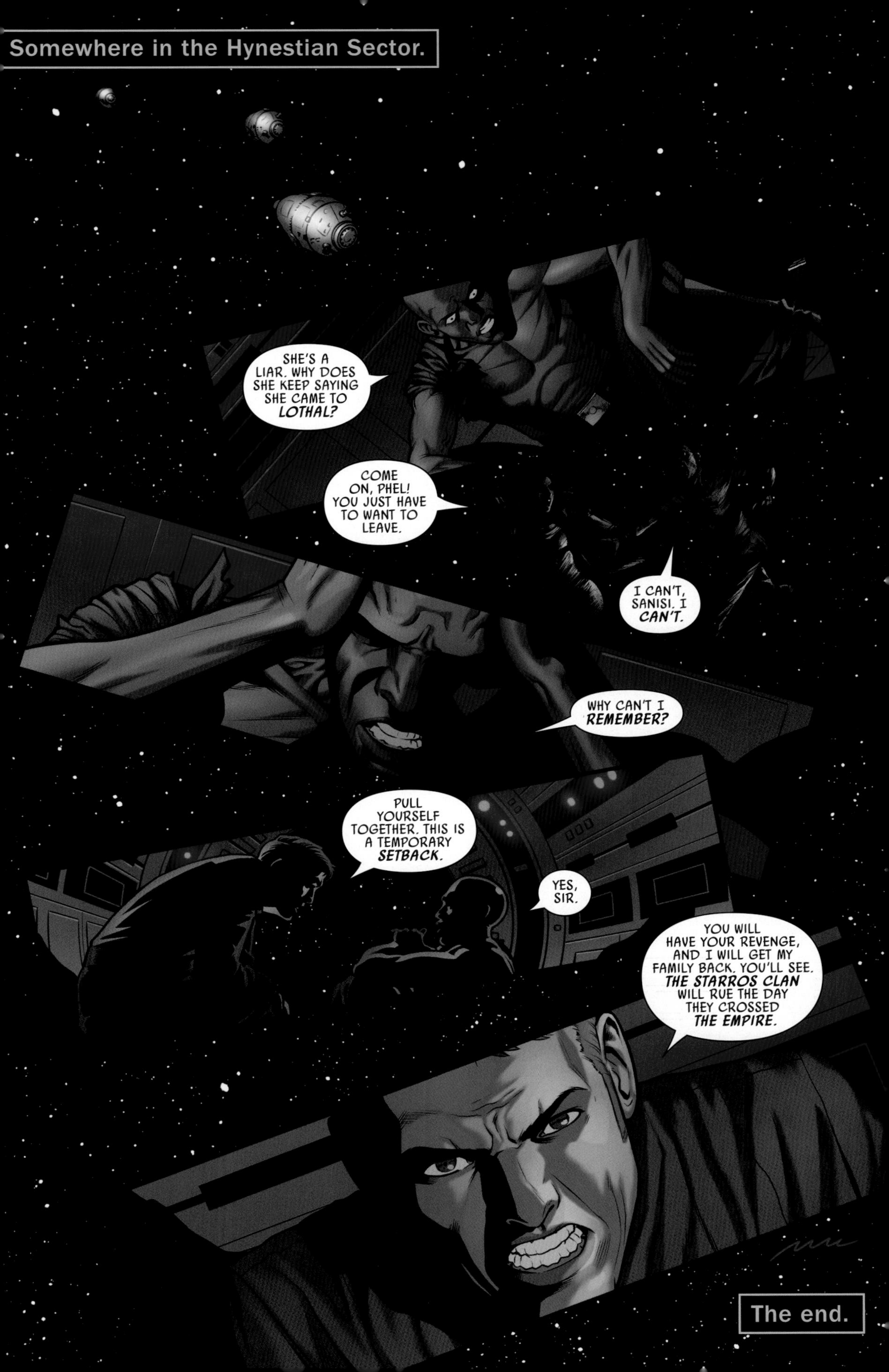

Somewhere in the Hynestian Sector.
SHE'S A LIAR. WHY DOES SHE KEEP SAYING SHE CAME TO LOTHAL?
COME ON, PHEL! YOU JUST HAVE TO WANT TO LEAVE.
I CAN'T, SANISI. I CAN'T.
WHY CAN'T I REMEMBER?
PULL YOURSELF TOGETHER. THIS IS A TEMPORARY SETBACK.
YES, SIR.
YOU WILL HAVE YOUR REVENGE, AND I WILL GET MY FAMILY BACK. YOU'LL SEE. THE STARROS CLAN WILL RUE THE DAY THEY CROSSED THE EMPIRE.
The end.

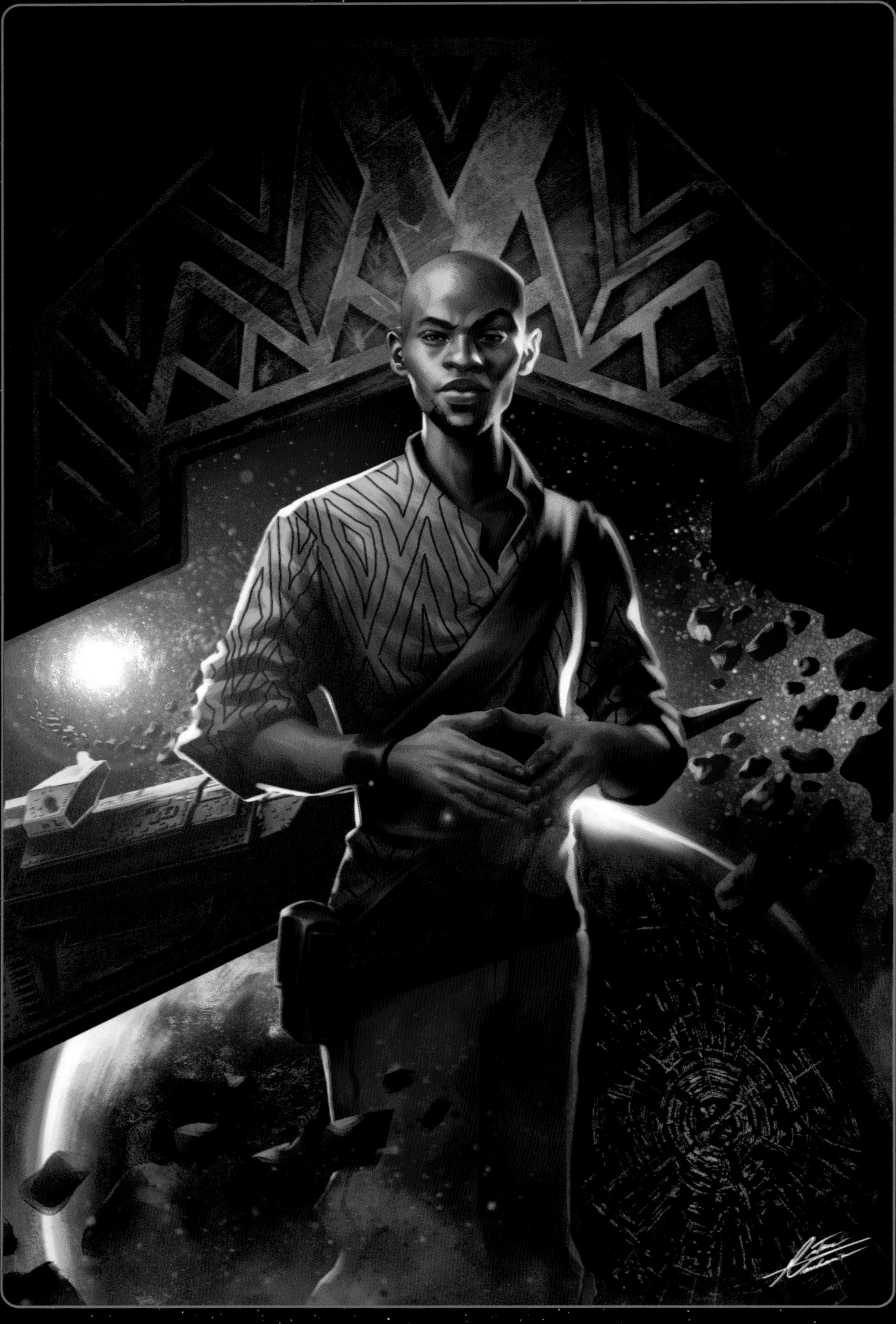

#1 Black History Month Variant by
MATEUS MANHANINI

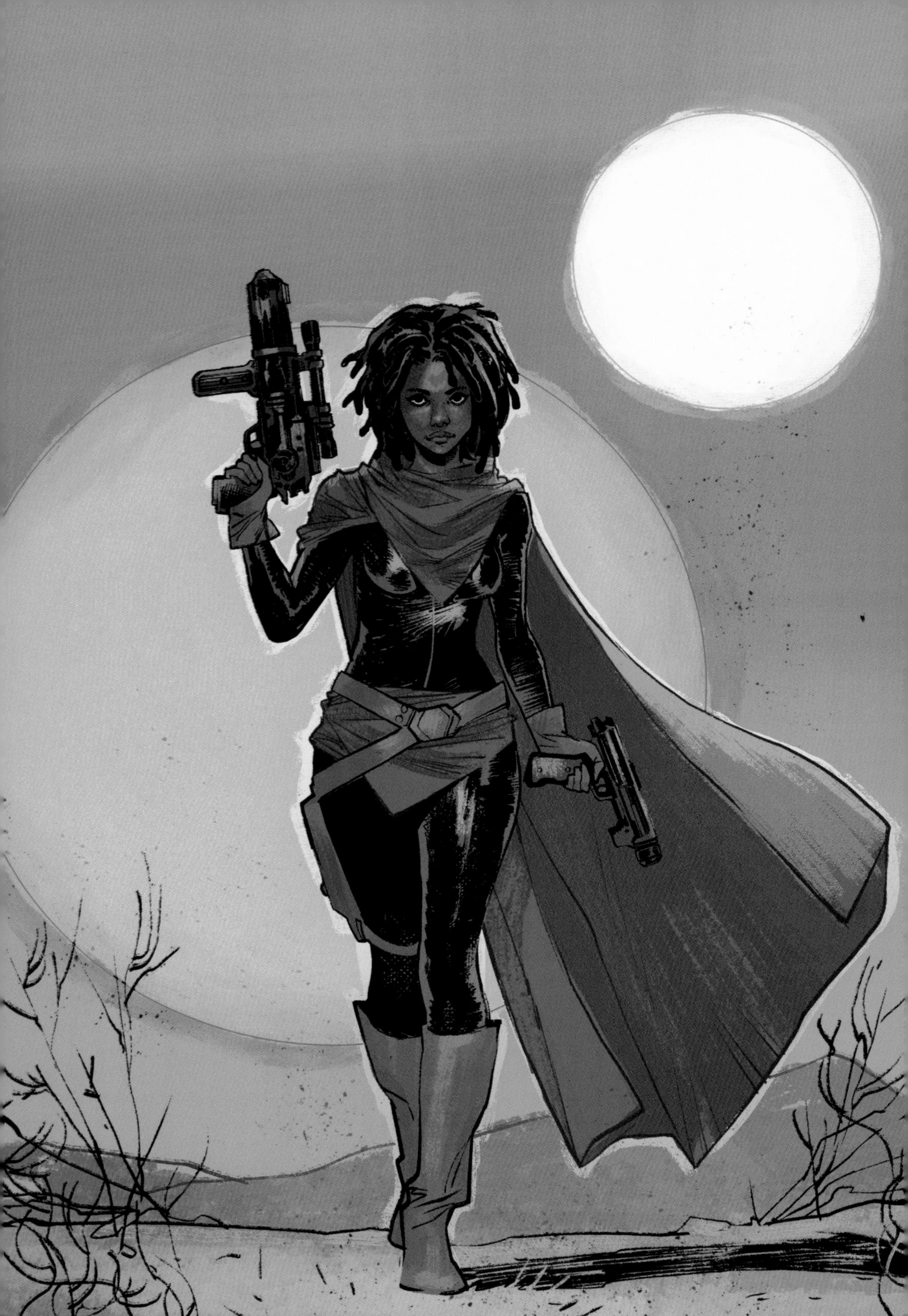

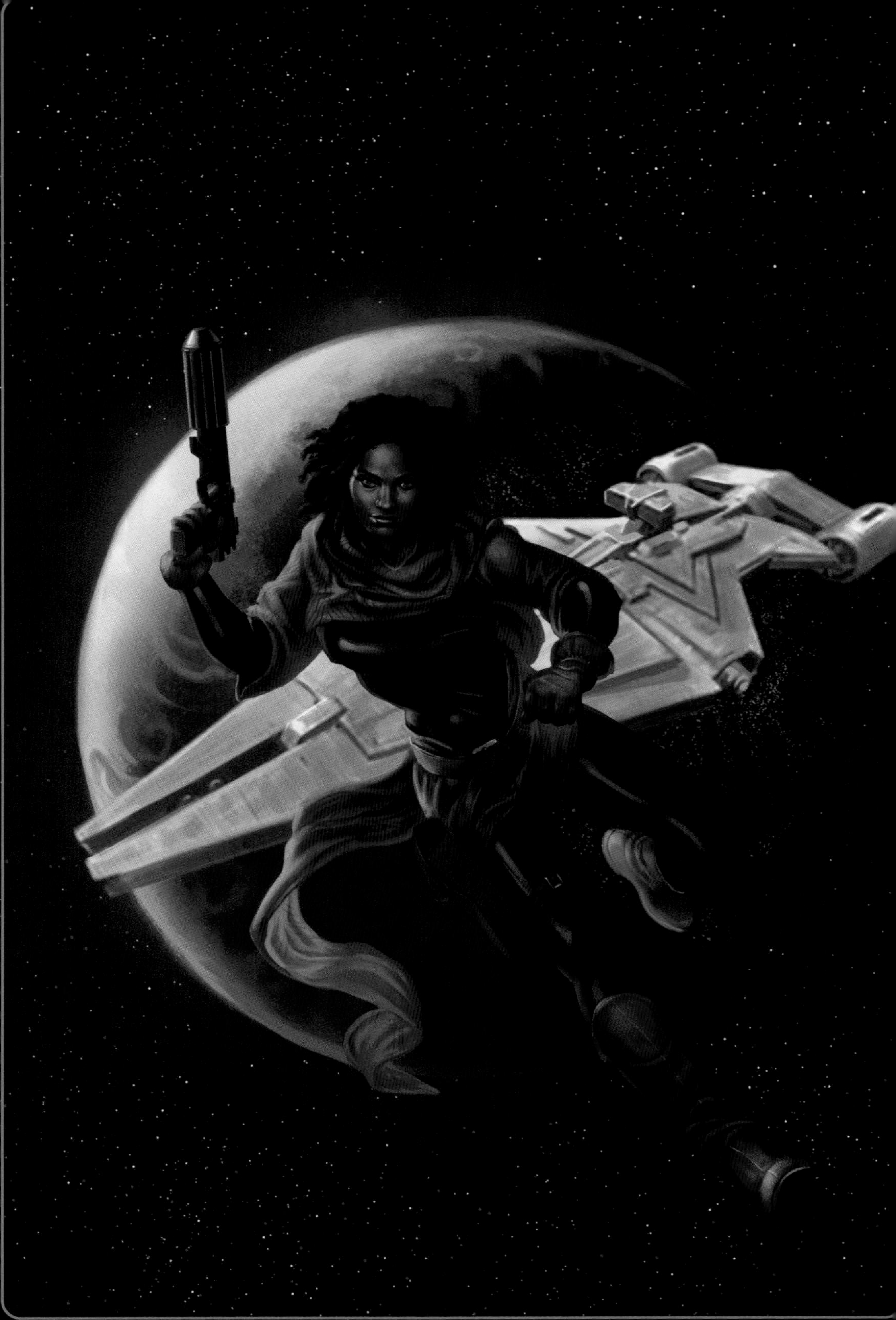

#1 Variant by
ERNANDA SOUZA

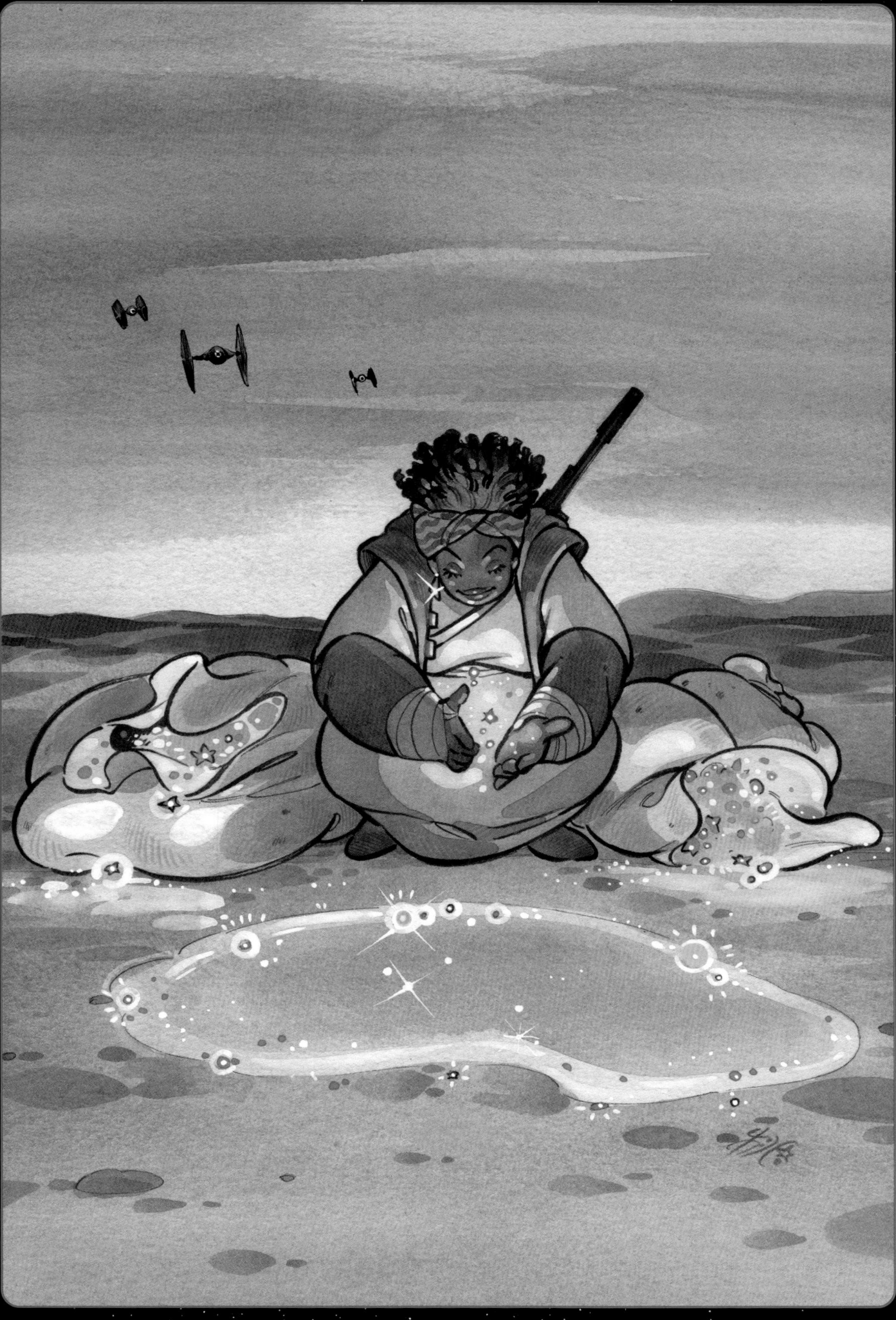

#2 Women's History Month Variant by
PEACH MOMOKO

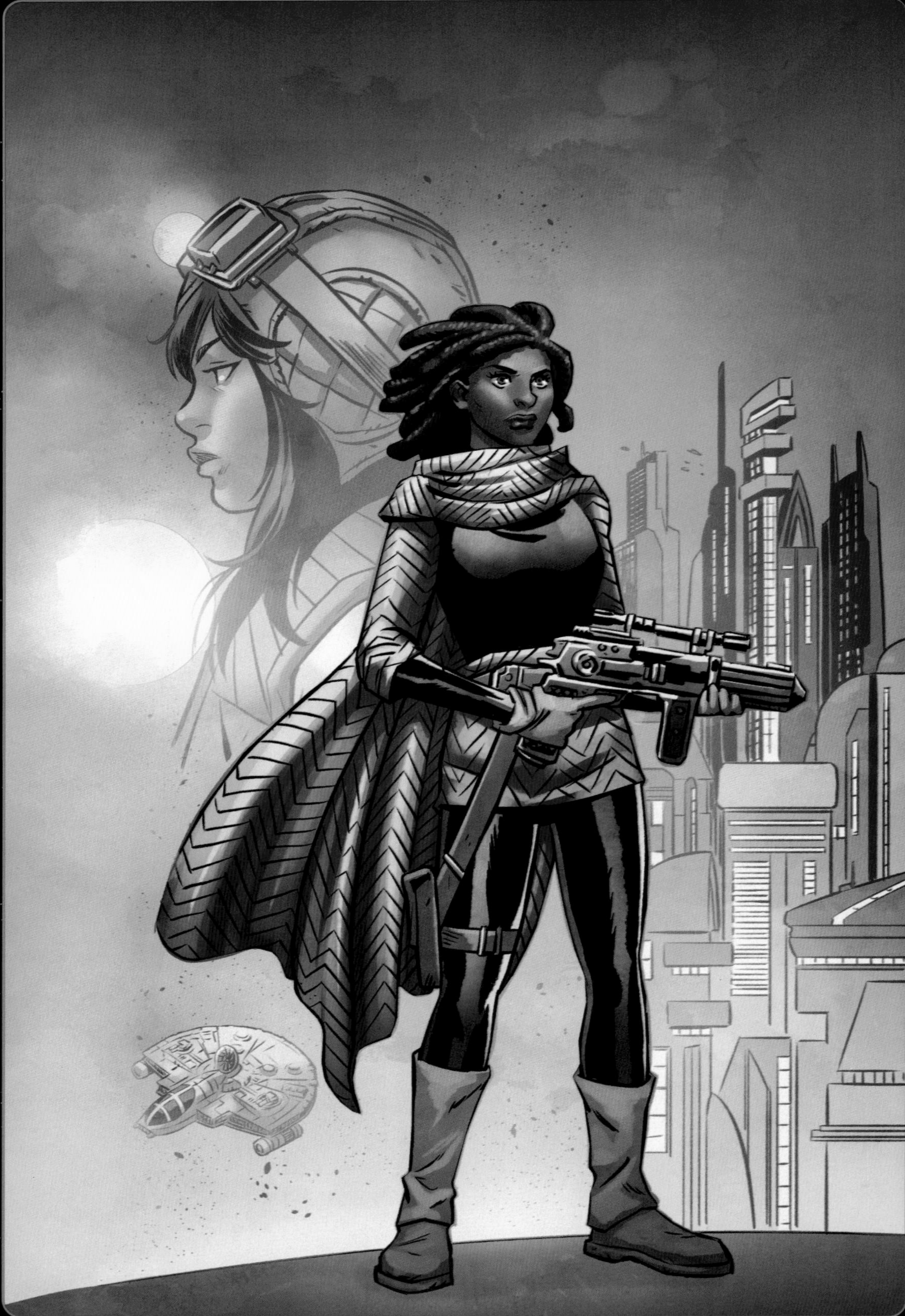

#2 Variant by
NATACHA BUSTOS & RACHELLE ROSENBERG

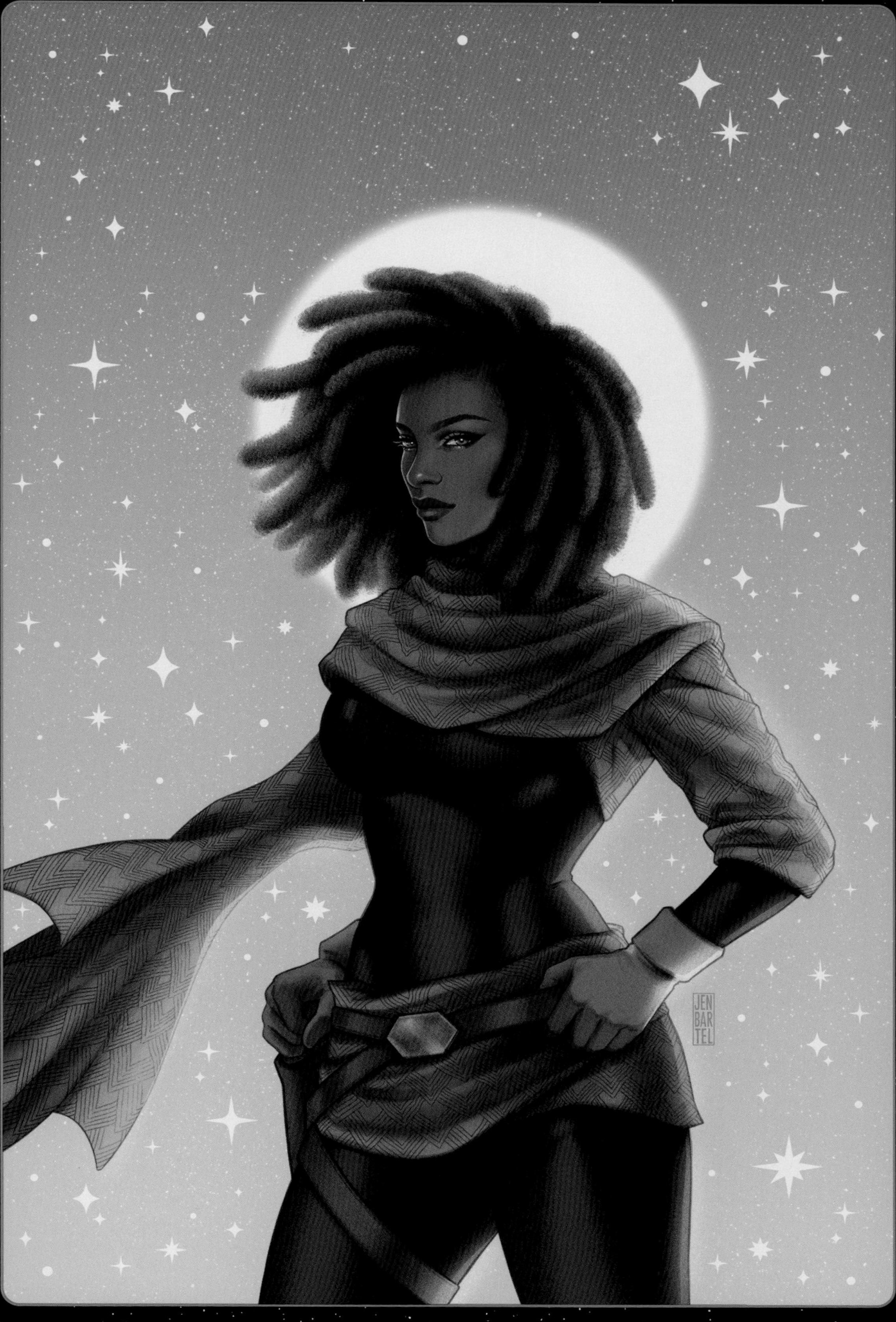
JEN
BAR
TEL

#3 Variant by
JEN BARTEL

#4 Variant by
EMA LUPACCHINO & JESUS ABURTOV

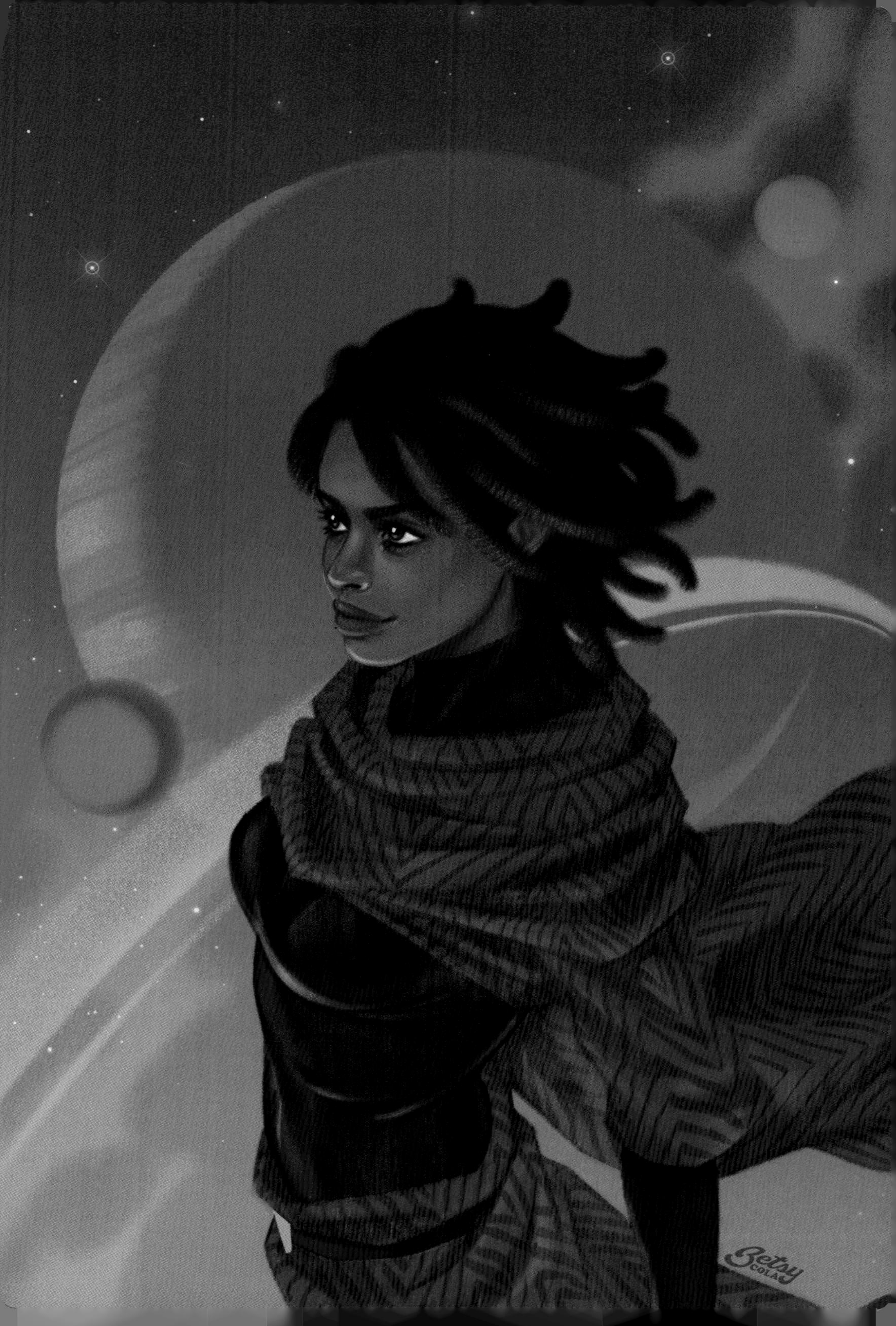
Betsy
COLA

VADER DEMONSTRATES WHAT HAPPENS TO THOSE WHO WOULD CHALLENGE THE EMPIRE!
ALSO AVAILABLE:
PAK • IENCO • MENON
MARVEL
STAR WARS
DARTH VADER
DARK HEART OF THE SITH
STAR WARS: DARTH VADER BY GREG PAK VOL. 1: DARK HEART OF THE SITH TPB
978-1302920814
PAK • IENCO • MENON
MARVEL
STAR WARS
DARTH VADER
INTO THE FIRE
STAR WARS: DARTH VADER BY GREG PAK VOL. 2: INTO THE FIRE TPB
978-1302920821
STAR WARS
WAR OF THE BOUNTY HUNTERS
DARTH VADER
PAK
VILANOVA
IENCO
MARVEL
STAR WARS: DARTH VADER BY GREG PAK VOL. 3: WAR OF THE BOUNTY HUNTERS TPB
978-1302926229
GREG PAK
WEAVES A DARK TALE OF VIOLENCE AND VENGEANCE IN THE WAKE OF *THE EMPIRE STRIKES BACK.*
PAK • KIRK • VILANOVA • IENCO
MARVEL
STAR WARS
DARTH VADER
CRIMSON REIGN
STAR WARS: DARTH VADER BY GREG PAK VOL. 4 - CRIMSON REIGN TPB
978-1302926236
ON SALE NOW
IN PRINT AND DIGITAL WHEREVER BOOKS ARE SOLD.
TO FIND A COMIC SHOP NEAR YOU, VISIT COMICSHOPLOCATOR.COM.
MARVEL
© 2022 MARVEL

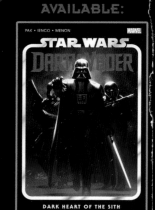

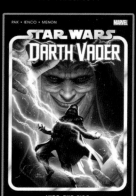

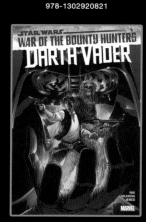

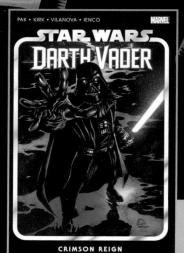

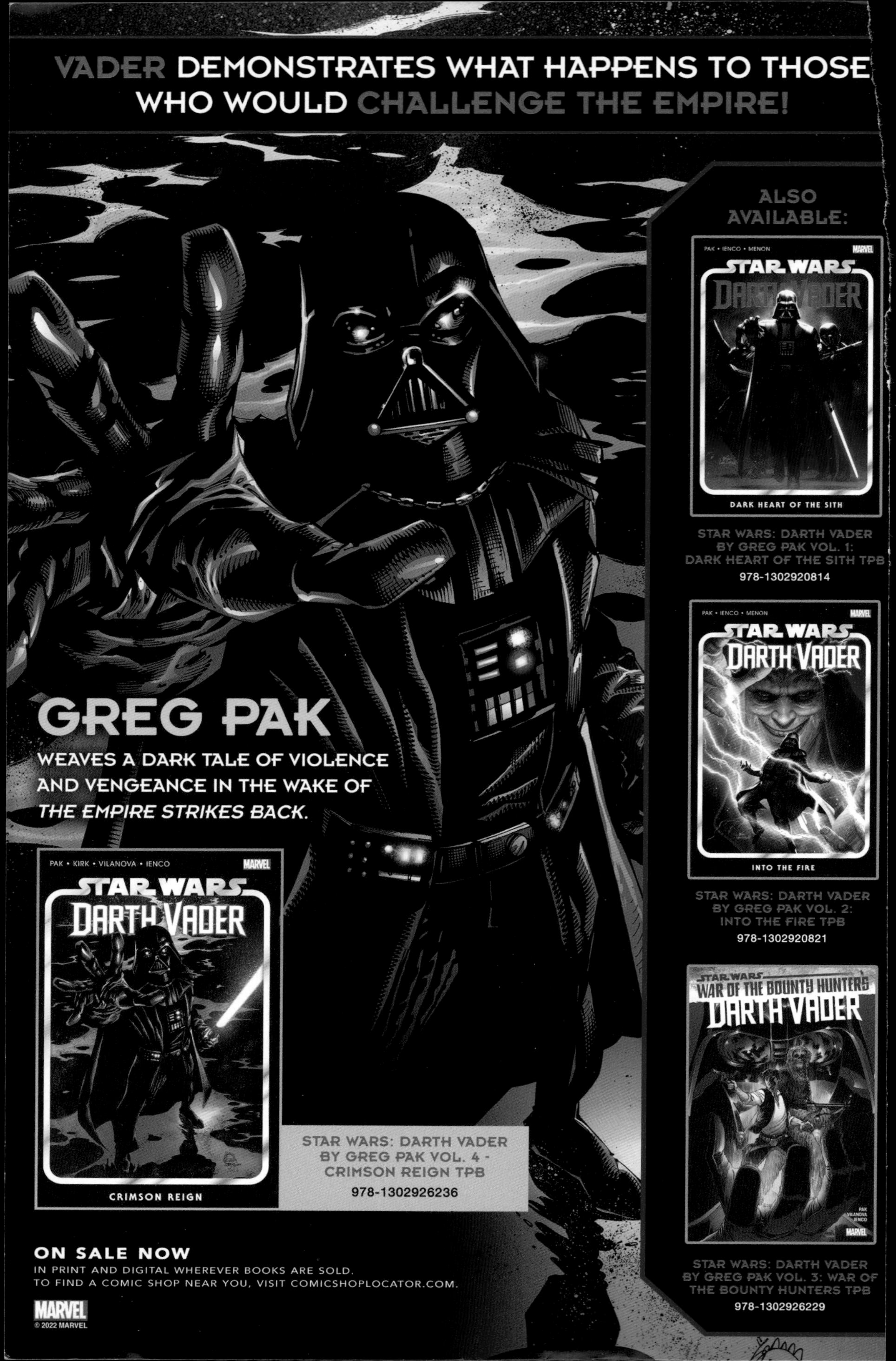